Challenges and Choices: Seeking Security in Troubled Times

Abiturschwerpunkt: Challenges and Choices in an Insecure World (Focus on USA)

Erarbeitet von

Christoph Deeg
Florian Nuxoll
Gerburg Rolvering

Fachliche Beratung

Professor Dr. Horst Tonn

Diesterweg

Challenges and Choices: Seeking Security in Troubled Times

Abiturschwerpunkt: Challenges and Choices in an Insecure World (Focus on USA)

Schüler-Arbeitsbuch

Druck A³ / Jahr 2015
Alle Drucke der Serie A sind im Unterricht parallel verwendbar.

Redaktion: Daniel Shatwell unter Mitarbeit von Charlotte Finn und Chleona Young
Layout und Herstellung: Harald Thumser, Frankfurt am Main
Gestaltung und Satz: KCS GmbH · Verlagsservice & Medienproduktion, Buchholz/Hamburg
Druck und Bindung: westermann druck GmbH, Braunschweig

ISBN 978-3-425-**04804**-8

Contents

A1 Look at the following challenges and place them in one of the three categories in the diagram below.

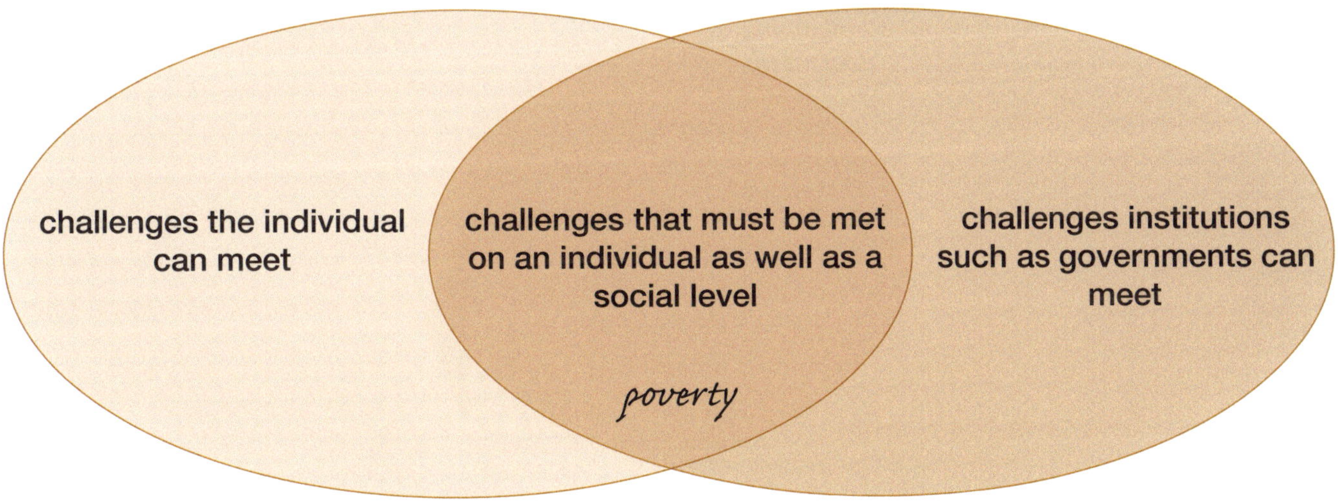

A2 Compare your results with one or two partners.

word bank

a considerable, enormous, huge, radical, serious, significant, tough challenge

to face a challenge = to have to deal with one

to meet a challenge = to deal with it successfully

to accept/to take up a challenge

to rise to a challenge = to show that you are able to deal with a challenge

to seek a challenge = to look for a challenge

to respond to a challenge = to react to a challenge

a challenge to sth. = a statement/action that shows that so. refuses to accept sth. / questions whether it is right

a challenging experience = an experience that tests your abilities

to overcome a problem = to succeed in dealing with or controlling it

to surmount a difficulty = to overcome it

an obstacle = a situation/event that makes it difficult for you to do or achieve sth. (syn: hindrance)

to put sth./so. to the test

to be faced with = to be confronted with

Speaking

A3 a) Work with a partner. Discuss which of the challenges you looked at in A1 are the most recent ones. Together put them into chronological order.

oldest	most recent
floods	

b) Search the internet for information about challenges like floods, terrorism, divorce, global warming, etc. and the improvements that have been achieved in these areas over the last 200 years. Use your findings to fill in the boxes below.

areas	from	to
education	*restricted to males* *access to education depended on social background*	*education for everyone*

self-evaluation: words and phrases that you don't know in English yet and that you need to look up

Steuern hinterziehen -

Writing

"We must look for the opportunity in every difficulty instead of being paralyzed at the thought of the difficulty in every opportunity." (Walter E. Cole)

A4 The following texts are two comments on the quote above.

a) Highlight the phrases in the comments that the authors have used to present their opinions.

b) Use the space on the right-hand side and write down the name and the function of each paragraph, if possible.

conclusion / body/ introduction / example 1 / example 2 / example 3 / argument 1 / argument 2 / argument 3

Comment 1

"We must look for the opportunity in every difficulty instead of being paralyzed at the thought of the difficulty in every opportunity". This quote by Walter E. Cole describes two different ways of dealing with a challenge, either giving up without having tried at all or concentrating on the chance in each problem and taking up the challenge. The quote reminds me of another one that says that you have to make the best out of every situation no matter how bad it is. In other words, you have to quit being a pessimist, a victim of circumstance, and have to start being an optimist.

introduction, author explains the meaning of the quote to the reader

From time to time every one of us is confronted with difficulties and challenges which have to be dealt with. Is Walter Cole right that people benefit from challenges if they try to surmount them even though effort is needed and success not guaranteed? In the following I intend to deal with this question.

introduction, part 2, the author ...

Many students complain that the weeks before the holidays are difficult for them since they have to cope with a great number of class tests. They deal with this situation in different ways. Some students try to be optimistic and carry on working continuously, even though the amount of work is immense. They look at each class test as an opportunity to prove to themselves that they can do it. This is the right way of dealing with class tests. It is my conviction that most students would achieve much better results if they looked at class tests this way.

There are sceptics who say: each opportunity bears a high risk of failing. And if you focus on the difficulties and – as a consequence – don't take up the challenge in the first place, you won't fail. I have to admit that I am sometimes tempted to look at things this way, simply because this is easier, this doesn't involve much effort. But whenever I have given in, I ended up being unhappy. Let me give you an example: two years ago a friend of mine asked me if I wanted to run a marathon with him. To cut a long story short, I said no, thinking of all the hardships I would have to endure and thinking of the risk of failing. My friend, however, was so determined that he trained for months and finally ran a marathon and succeeded. I'm still disappointed with myself when I think of the story.

And even if you fail – and of course there is no denying that you sometimes fail when you tackle a difficult problem – there are positive ways of dealing with failure. My experience is that it's best to simply try again. A failure can teach you to be better prepared next time. In some areas it is very common that people don't succeed at the first attempt. Just take a look at sports such as ice-skating or juggling. I don't know anyone who can juggle three balls and hasn't trained for some time. And during this time, the balls have fallen to the ground hundreds of times. A sceptic might say: hundreds of failures. And yes, he's right. But failures belong to success. If you look at the difficulties in every opportunity and – as a consequence – don't seize the opportunity, you will not fail – but you won't succeed either.

The world has always been full of difficulties and always will be. And I'm convinced the human race has only survived because many people have looked at the opportunities in those difficulties and seized these opportunities – in times of war and in times of peace. I think Walter E. Cole is perfectly right and we should all write this quote on a piece of paper and stick it on the bathroom mirror.

Comment 2

Walter E. Cole must be a brave man. What he said really impresses me and I truly hope that you hold the same opinion as I do because if everybody was as brave as Walter E. Cole, the world would be a better place. I can only encourage you to seize all the opportunities that you are offered. Just think of all the people who won the lottery. They only won millions because they seized the opportunity and played in the lottery. Maybe this example is a little far-fetched. I have an even better example: take all the American pioneers and explorers and settlers. They all considered their journeys to be great opportunities, even though the difficulties were sometimes almost insurmountable. I don't want to deny that in the course of American history, some of these pioneers and settlers failed. I'm writing about those people who explored and conquered the West in the 18th and 19th centuries, just in case you didn't realise. Seizing opportunities always includes the possibility of failure and not everyone succeeds. If they hadn't been as brave and optimistic as they were – I mean, the settlers –, the American continent would never have been conquered and civilized. As a society we definitely need people who don't shy away from difficulties. The only thing I don't like about this quote is that Walter E. Cole says "every difficulty".

Using words such as "every" and "always" and "everywhere" is always dangerous. I think the quote would be much better, if he had said "most difficulties". I'm truly convinced that there are difficulties that people can't overcome and regarding these difficulties as opportunities would be utterly stupid. Cole generalizes in a way that I don't really like. I think one should be very careful with words such as "every" and "always" and "everywhere".

Something that I almost forgot to mention is this quote starts with the pronoun "we". He tries to convince people by including himself. He doesn't say "You must look", but he says "We must look" and thereby he tells people that he himself must also regard difficulties as opportunities. I'm not sure if this is important but I have the feeling that it might be a good point and that's why I've mentioned it.

A5 Summarize (key words only) the arguments in the boxes below and rate them from very strong (++) to very weak (- -).

Comment 1	**Comment 2**
+ *Argument 1: Exam results better if students focused on opportunities*	

A6 Compare and assess the structure of the two comments.

Writing

A7 "Mankind will be extinct in 100 years." Comment on this quote.

Before you start writing your comment, use the boxes below to collect arguments and examples and make notes on any aspects you want to use in your introduction and conclusion. Look back at your notes for A4 for help. ⇨ skills: how to write a comment, p. 109

Introduction

Argument 1

Example

Argument 2

Example

Argument 3

Example

Conclusion

B1 Look at the photos and speculate about the choices of the people shown.Think of areas such as education, family life, professional life and mobility. The phrases in the word bank below might be helpful. Make notes in the boxes below.

notes	notes	notes

word bank

education:
to go to elementary school
to have a secondary education
to go to university
to earn a degree at university
to have no formal education
to be sent to a school

family life:
to be married
to choose a spouse
to raise children / to be raised in a family
the burden of choice
to meet your parents' expectations

professional life / job:
to have a well-paid job
to choose the profession you like
to make a living with your job
to work hard and be promoted
to stand in a tradition / to be part of a tradition
to choose from multiple job offers

social and geographical mobility:
migrant worker
to move from one job to another
to go on holiday
to climb the social ladder
to hope for betterment
to have no influence on your social position

Mediation

B2 a) Überlege Dir Fragen an Deine Großmutter/Deinen Großvater für die Kategorien Familie, Bildung, Beruf, geographische und soziale Mobilität sowie politische Gestaltungsmöglichkeiten.

b) Führe das Interview und nimm es auf.

c) Höre Dir das Interview anschließend an und übertrage die im Hinblick auf das Thema „choices“ relevanten Informationen in Stichpunkten auf das Arbeitsblatt (auf Englisch). ⇨ skills: how to mediate p. 110

categories	language support
family:	to be engaged to propose to someone to start a family to talk about family planning household chores to be in charge of
education/job:	to discuss opportunities to apply for a job/position to have limited access to education to be promoted to be unemployed to be employed with a company
geographical/social mobility:	to move house to move into a middle class neighborhood lower class/middle class/upper class to succeed in to strive for a higher social status to maintain your status to climb the social ladder
political participation:	the right to vote/to cast your vote to be influenced by to be a member of a political party/ an action group such as Stuttgart 21 to take an active part in to take part in demonstrations

C1 Look at the photo and discuss the advantages and disadvantages of choices.

Reading

C2 **Partner 1**:
Read the text below and take notes on the challenges and choices that Ragged Dick is confronted with. Look back at what you found out about challenges in the A-section. Make up your mind whether Ragged Dick's world is insecure. Then present your results to your partner.

The following extract is taken from the novel Ragged Dick; or, Street Life in New York with the Boot Blacks by Horatio Alger, an author who is best known for novels characterized by rags-to-riches narratives, which focus on the rise of impoverished boys from difficult backgrounds to middle-class respectability and wealth. Published in 1867, Ragged Dick is the story of a fourteen-year-old boot black called Ragged Dick, who, although circumstances are not favorable, is determined to grow up in a respectable way and to succeed in life. Focusing on virtues such as honesty, hard work, determination and courage, Ragged Dick finally escapes poverty.

"WAKE up there, youngster," said a rough voice. Ragged Dick opened his eyes slowly, and stared stupidly in the face of the speaker, but did not offer to get up. "Wake up, you young vagabond!" said the man a little impatiently; "I suppose you'd lay there all day, if I hadn't called you." "What time is it?" asked Dick. "Seven o'clock." "Seven o'clock! I oughter've been up an hour ago. I know what 'twas made me so precious sleepy. I went to the Old Bowery last night, and didn't turn in till past twelve." "You went to the Old Bowery? Where'd you get your money?" asked the man, who was a porter in the employ of a firm doing business on Spruce Street. "Made it by shines[1], in course. My guardian don't allow me no money for theatres, so I have to earn it." "Some boys get it easier than that," said the porter significantly. "You don't catch me stealin', if that's what you mean," said Dick. "Don't you ever steal, then?" "No, and I wouldn't. Lots of boys does it, but I wouldn't." "Well, I'm glad to hear you say that. I believe there's some good in you, Dick, after all." "Oh, I'm a rough customer!" said Dick. "But I wouldn't steal. It's mean." "I'm glad you think so, Dick," and the rough voice sounded gentler than at first. "Have you got any money to buy your breakfast?" "No, but I'll soon get some." While this conversation had been going on, Dick had got up. His bedchamber had been a wooden box half full of straw, on which the young bootblack had reposed his weary limbs, and slept as soundly as if it had been a bed of down. (...) He jumped out of the box, shook himself, picked out one or two straws that had found their way into rents in his clothes, and, drawing a well-worn cap over his uncombed locks, he was all ready for the business of the day.(...)

Dick's business hours had commenced[2]. He had no office to open. His little blacking-box was ready for use, and he looked sharply in the faces of all who passed, addressing each with, "Shine yer boots, sir?" "How much?" asked a gentleman on his way to his office."Ten cents," said Dick, dropping his box, and sinking upon his knees on the sidewalk, flourishing his brush with the air of one skilled in his profession. "Ten cents! Isn't that a little steep?" "Well, you know 'taint all clear profit," said Dick, who had already set to work. "There's the blacking costs something, and I have to get a new brush pretty often." "And you have a large rent too," said the gentleman quizzically, with a glance at a large hole in Dick's coat.
"Yes, sir," said Dick, always ready to joke; "I have to pay

such a big rent for my mansion[3] up on Fifth Avenoo, that I can't afford to take less than ten cents a shine. I'll give you a bully shine, sir." "Be quick about it, for I am in a hurry. So your house is on Fifth Avenue, is it?" "It isn't anywhere else, said Dick, and Dick spoke the truth there. "What tailor[4] do you patronize?" asked the gentleman, surveying Dick's attire. "Would you like to go to the same one?" asked Dick, shrewdly. "Well, no; it strikes me that he didn't give you a very good fit." "This coat once belonged to General Washington," said Dick, comically. "He wore it all through the Revolution, and it got torn some, 'cause he fit so hard. When he died he told his widder to give it to some smart young feller that hadn't got none of his own; so she gave it to me. But if you'd like it, sir, to remember General Washington by, I'll let you have it reasonable." "Thank you, but I wouldn't want to deprive you of it. And did your pants come from General Washington too?" "No, they was a gift from Lewis Napoleon. Lewis had outgrown 'em and sent 'em to me, – he's bigger than me, and that's why they don't fit." "It seems you have distinguished friends. Now, my lad, I suppose you would like your money." "I shouldn't have any objection," said Dick. "I believe," said the gentleman, examining his pocket-book, "I haven't got anything short of twenty-five cents. Have you got any change?" "Not a cent," said Dick. "All my money's invested in the Erie Railroad[5]." "That's unfortunate." "Shall I get the money changed, sir?" "I can't wait; I've got to meet an appointment immediately. I'll hand you twenty-five cents, and you can leave the change at my office any time during the day." "All right, sir. Where is it?" "No. 125 Fulton Street. Shall you remember?" "Yes, sir. What name?" "Greyson, – office on second floor." "All right, sir; I'll bring it." "I wonder whether the little scamp will prove honest," said Mr Greyson to himself, as he walked away. "If he does, I'll give him my custom regularly. If he don't as is most likely, I shan't mind the loss of fifteen cents." (...)

annotations

[1] *shine* = here: shoe shine / Schuhe putzen

[2] *to commence* = to start

[3] *mansion* = big, luxurious house

[4] *tailor* = Schneider

[5] *Erie Railroad* = Erie Railroad Corporation, a major railroad corporation

challenges	line(s)	choices	line(s)

Partner 2:
Read the article below from *Newsweek* by Jhumpa Lahiri, a successful American author and daughter of Indian immigrants. Take notes on the challenges and choices she faced when she grew up as well as the things that made her feel insecure. Then present your results to your partner.

I have lived in the United States for almost 37 years and anticipate growing old in this country. Therefore, with the exception of my first two years in London, "Indian-American" has been a constant way to describe me. Less constant is my relationship to the term. When I was growing up in Rhode Island in the 1970s I felt neither Indian nor American. Like many immigrant offspring[1] I felt intense pressure to be two things, loyal to the old world and fluent in the new, approved of on either side of the hyphen. Looking back, I see that this was generally the case. But my perception as a young girl was that I fell short[2] at both ends, shuttling between two dimensions that had nothing to do with one another.
At home I followed the customs of my parents, speaking

Bengali[3] and eating rice and dal with my fingers. These ordinary facts seemed part of a secret, utterly alien way of life, and I took pains[4] to hide them from my American friends. For my parents, home was not our house in Rhode Island but Calcutta, where they were raised. I was aware that the things they lived for – the Nazrul[5] songs they listened to on the reel-to-reel, the family they missed, the clothes my mother wore that were not available in any store in any mall – were at once as precious and as worthless as an outmoded currency.
I also entered a world my parents had little knowledge or control of: school, books, music, television, things that seeped in and became a fundamental aspect of who I am. I spoke English without an accent, comprehending the language in a way my parents still do not. And yet there was evidence that I was not entirely American. In addition to my distinguishing name and looks, I did not attend Sunday school[6], did not know how to ice-skate, and disappeared to India for months at a time. Many of these friends proudly called themselves Irish-American or Italian-American. But they were several generations removed from the frequently humiliating[7] process of immigration, so that the ethnic roots they claimed had descended underground whereas mine were still tangled and green. According to my parents I was not American, nor would I ever be no matter how hard I tried. I felt doomed[8] by their pronouncement, misunderstood and gradually defiant. In spite of the first lessons of arithmetic, one plus one did not equal two but zero, my conflicting selves always canceling each other out. (...)
As I approach middle-age, one plus one equals two, both in my work and in my daily existence. The traditions on either side of the hyphen[9] dwell[10] in me like siblings, still occasionally sparring[11], one outshining the other depending on the day. But like siblings, they are intimately familiar with one another, forgiving and intertwined. When my husband and I were married five years ago in Calcutta, we invited friends who had never been to India, and they came full of enthusiasm, for a place I avoided talking about in my childhood, fearful of what people might say. Around non-Indian friends, I no longer feel compelled[12] to hide the fact that I speak another language. I speak Bengali to my children, even though I lack the proficiency to teach them to read or write the language. As a child I sought perfection and so denied myself the claim to any identity. As an adult I accept that a bicultural upbringing is a rich but imperfect thing.

annotations

1 *offspring* = children
2 *to fall short* = not succeed
3 *Bengali* = language in parts of India and in Bangladesh
4 *to take pains* = to try hard
5 *Nazrul* = Bengali musician
6 *Sunday school* = lessons offered by Christian churches on Sundays
7 *humiliating* = demütigend
8 *doomed* = verurteilt
9 *hyphen* = Bindestrich, here it refers to the term "Indian-American"
10 *to dwell* = to live
11 *to spar with so.* = to fight
12 *to feel compelled* = to feel forced

challenges	line(s)	choices	line(s)

C3 Discuss whether it is always good to have choices. Use examples from both texts to support your opinion.

D1 Decide if definition a), b) or c) is correct. Sometimes two definitions are correct. Cross out the wrong definitions.

	a)	b)	c)
insecure job	~~a safe job~~	a job from which removal or expulsion is always possible	~~a job that doesn't provide any satisfaction~~
safe job	a job that you're likely to keep for a long time	a well-paid job	a job with a company that is not likely to go bankrupt
She is insecure about her looks.	She doesn't like her looks.	She is unsure whether she likes her looks and whether others find her attractive.	She is extremely good-looking, but doesn't know how to deal with it.
The company's computer system was insecure.	The company's computer system wasn't up-to-date.	The company's computer system broke down regularly.	The company's computer system could easily be broken into.
He is confident about his future.	He is convinced that he will be promoted.	He is certain that his plans will work.	He is hoping to have a bright future.
He feels safe in his house.	He doesn't expect any surprises.	He doesn't expect anyone to break into his house.	He is convinced that keeping all his money in his house is better than taking it to a bank.
He is anxious about his daughter's future.	He is confident that his daughter will be successful.	He is worried about his daughter's future.	He is afraid his daughter might be threatened in the future.
Talking about her exams next month makes her feel uneasy.	She feels troubled when she talks about her exams.	She is confident that she will pass her exams next month.	She feels uncomfortable when talking about next month's exams.

D2 Translate the following phrases.

English	German
insecure job	*unsicherer Arbeitsplatz*
safe job	
insecure about her looks	
an insecure computer system	
he is confident about his future	
he feels safe in his house	
he is anxious about his future	
she feels uneasy	
she is unsure if she likes her looks	
she feels troubled when thinking her future	
to break into a computer system	
he is worried about his future	
the terrorists threatened to take action against American soldiers	

Reading

D3 a) Have a look at the following statistics. In a few sentences summarize what they tell you about the job market and how Americans feel about it.

Figure 1: Unemployment rate, United States of America

source: http://www.deptofnumbers.com/unemployment/us/

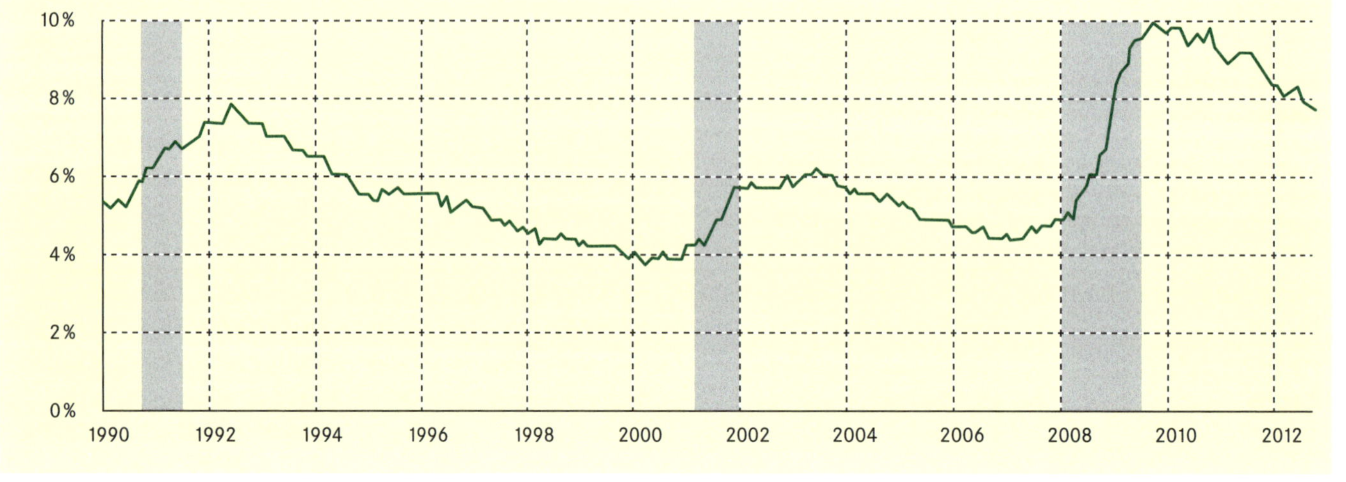

Figure 2: Number of people unemployed, United States of America

source: http://www.deptofnumbers.com/unemployment/us/

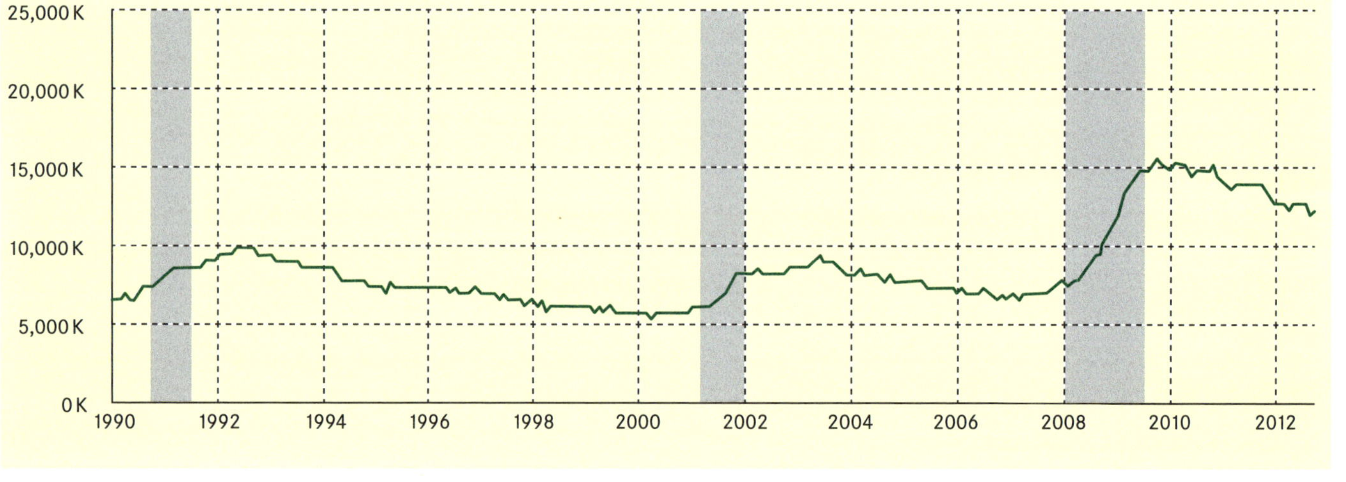

Figure 3: Americans' assessment of current job situation

http://www.gallup.com/poll/147170/americans-views-job-market-improve-mostly-negative.aspx

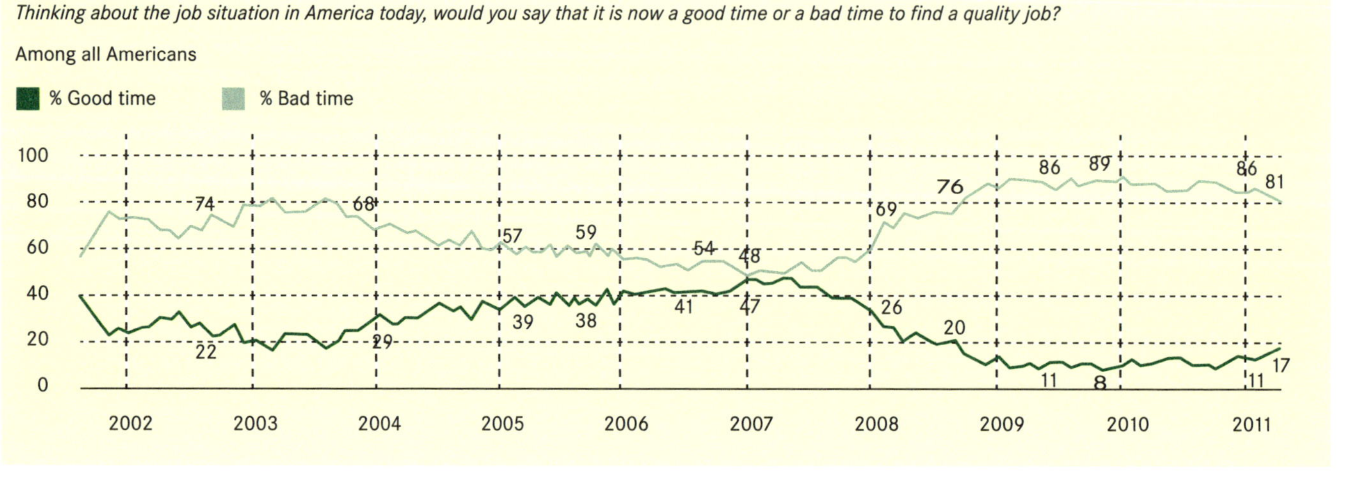

Figure 4: Americans' fear of losing their jobs

http://www.gallup.com/poll/154052/know-laid-off-worker-don't-fear-job-loss.aspx

Thinking about the next twelve months, how likely do you think it is that you will lose your job or be laid off – is it very likely, fairly likely, not too likely, or not at all likely?

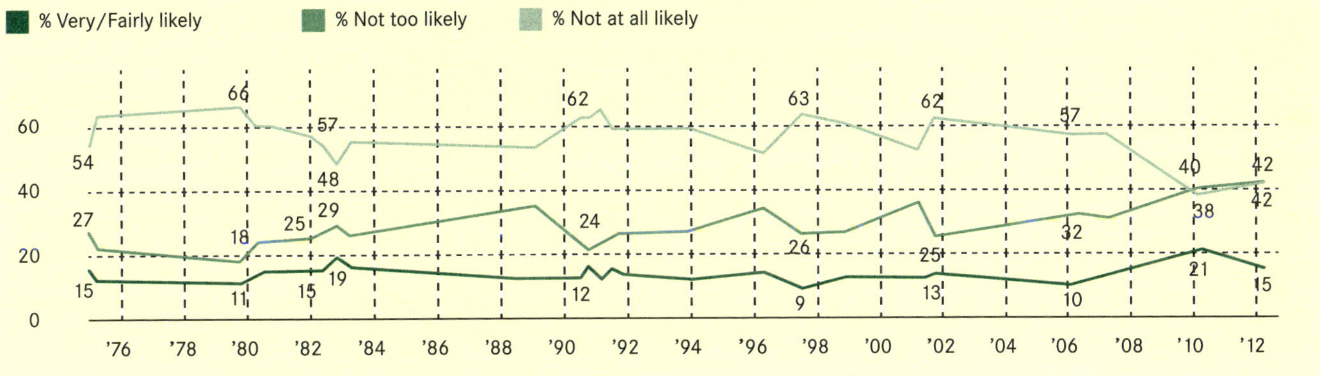

b) Read the texts and highlight words and phrases that are useful for the analysis of statistics.

The line graph in figure 1 shows the development of the unemployment rate in the US from 1990 onwards. The grey areas indicate economic recessions. We can clearly see that the unemployment rate increases in times of recession. The unemployment rate reached a peak in 2010 and has – since then – fallen steadily. However, it's still very high, compared to the other two recessions shown in the graph. Currently the unemployment rate is at 7.7 percent with around 12 million Americans unemployed, as the second line graph (figure 2) shows.

The line graph in figure 3 provides information on what Americans have thought about the job market since 2002. It is not surprising that between 2009 and 2010 – in the middle of the last recession – the vast majority of Americans held the opinion that this was a bad time to find a job. It shows that Americans have been realistic in their assessment of the job market.

What's interesting about the line graph in figure 4 is that before and during the recessions of 1991 and 2001 a large majority of Americans were confident of keeping their jobs over the following year and only a small number of Americans considered it fairly likely that they would lose their jobs. Apparently Americans had a realistic grasp of the situation on the job market in 1991 and 2001, but were quite unrealistic when it came to assessing their own situation. This pattern even holds true for the 2009 crisis. In such a crisis you would expect a majority of people to say they were likely to lose their jobs. But the graphs show that this was not the case. It shows that the percentage of people who thought this way was only a little higher than in 2001.

Speaking

D4 **Partner 1:** Prepare a short presentation about the following statistics for a classmate. Use the words and phrases that you highlighted on page 17. ⇒ skills: how to analyze and interpret statistics, pp. 111 – 112

Figure 1: Perceptions of trends in crime: is there more crime in the U.S. than there was a year ago, or less?
http://www.gallup.com/poll/150464/americans-believe-crime-worsening.aspx

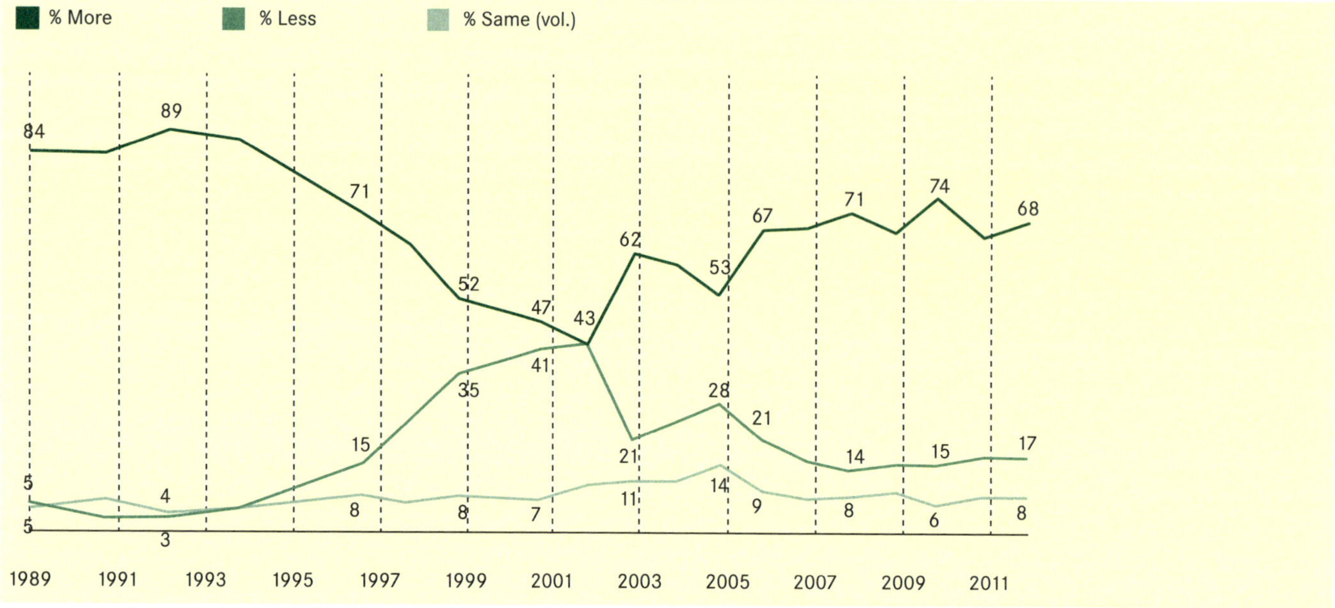

Table 1: U.S. crime rates: 1980 to 2009

Year	Violent crime rate per 100,000 population				
	Total	**Murder**	**Rape**	**Robbery**	**Assault**
1980	597	10	37	251	299
1985	558	8	37	209	304
1990	729	9	41	256	423
1995	684	8	37	221	418
1996	637	7	36	202	391
1997	611	7	36	186	382
1998	568	6	35	166	361
1999	523	6	33	150	334
2000	507	6	32	145	324
2001	506	6	32	149	319
2002	495	6	33	146	310
2003	476	6	32	143	295
2004	464	6	32	137	289
2005	470	6	32	141	291
2006	482	6	32	151	293
2007	472	6	31	148	287
2008	457	4	30	146	277
2009	430	5	29	133	263

Data from http://www.census.gov

Table 2: Americans' satisfaction with the opportunity for the next generation of Americans to live better than their parents

http://www.gallup.com/poll/155021/majority-dissatisfied-next-generation-prospects.aspx

	National adults	18 to 34 years	35 to 54 years	55 and older
	%	%	%	%
Satisfied	40	45	40	34
Dissatisfied	58	53	58	62
No opinion	2	1	2	3

Partner 2: Prepare a short presentation about the following statistics for a classmate. Use the words and phrases that you highlighted on page 17. ⇨ skills: how to analyze and interpret statistics, pp. 111 – 112

Figure 1: Americans' perception of the U.S. job market. Question: Would you say that it is a good time or a bad time now to find a quality job?

http://www.gallup.com/poll/158972/americans-best-job-climate-financial-crisis.aspx

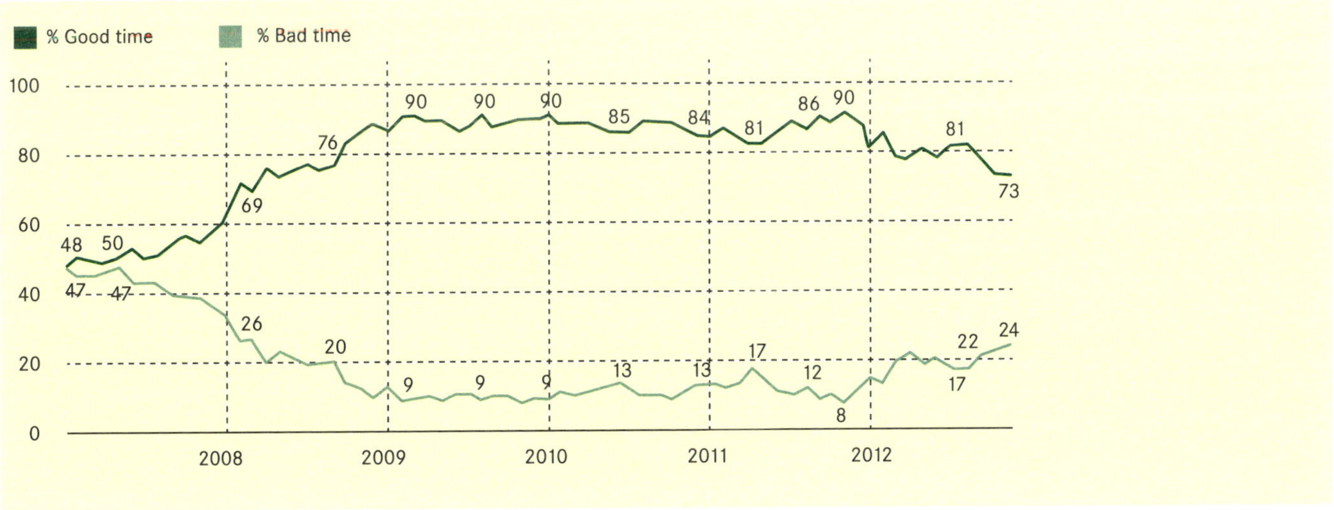

Figure 2: Confidence in the public school system

(Am E: public schools = Br E: state schools)

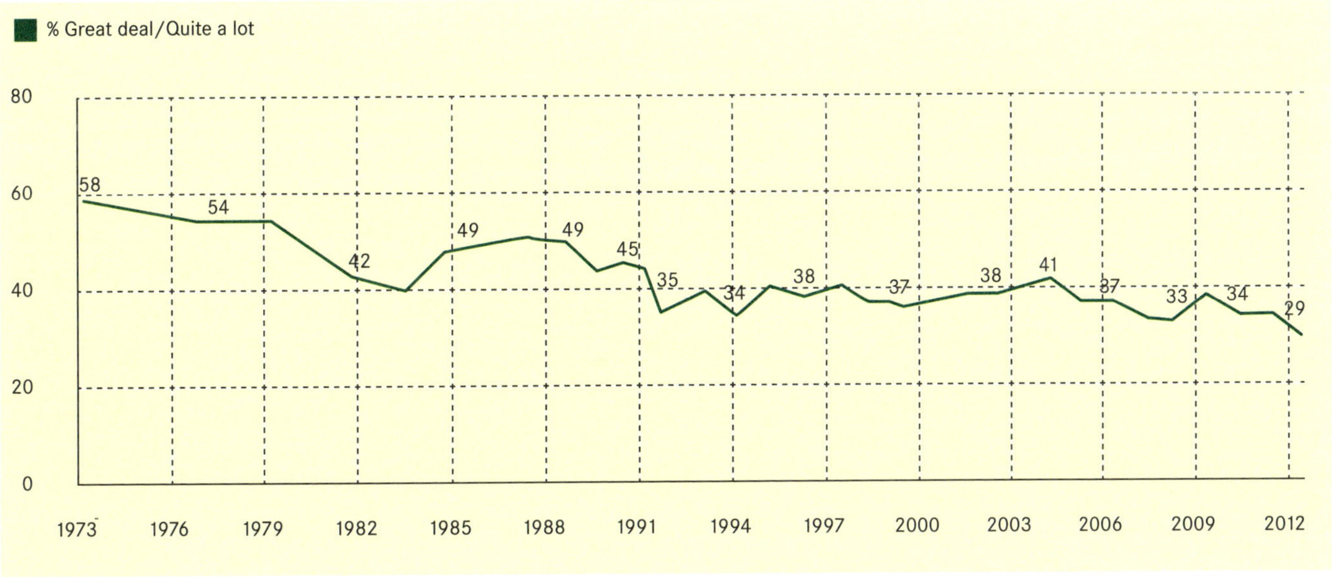

Figure 3: Confidence in U.S. Medical System

http://www.gallup.com/poll/155381/confidence-medical-system-health-law-passed.aspx

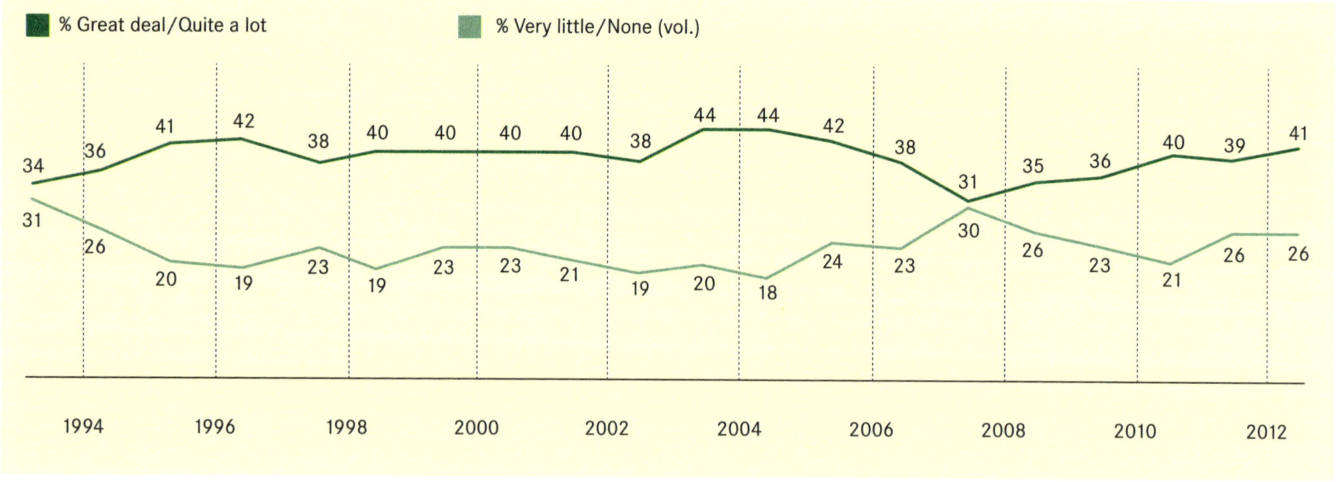

Writing

D5 "Americans currently live in an insecure country." Comment on this quote.

Before you start writing your comment, collect arguments and examples and take notes on the aspects you want to use in your introduction and conclusion. ➩ skills: how to write a comment, p. 109

Introduction

Argument 1
Example

Argument 2
Example

Argument 2
Example

Conclusion

A1 a) Think about when the following pictures were taken and give reasons for your answer.

b) Write down what each picture tells you about relations between white and black people in the United States.

①

time:

1950s, Civil Rights Movement / desegregation of schools and universities

What this picture tells me about race relations:

②

time:

What this picture tells me about race relations:

③

time:

What this picture tells me about race relations:

④

time:

What this picture tells me about race relations:

⑤

time:

What this picture tells me about race relations:

⑥ 

time:

What this picture tells me about race relations:

⑦ 

time:

What this picture tells me about race relations:

⑧ 

time:

What this picture tells me about race relations:

⑨ 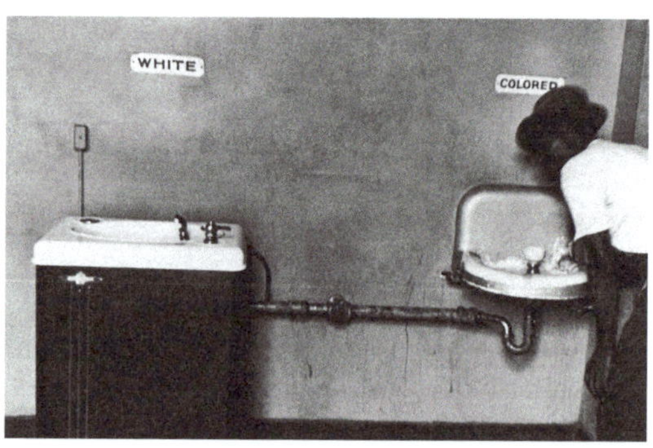

time:

What this picture tells me about race relations:

⑩ 

time:

What this picture tells me about race relations:

A2 a) The following text is an example of an analysis of picture 10. Read the text and highlight phrases and words that you might want to use in your interpretation.

introduction

The photograph was taken in the United States in the 1950s. It shows two African-American students attending an American high school, surrounded by white students walking beside and behind them. It appears to be a snapshot taken on their way into school. While the African-Americans are looking ahead, some white students are staring at them. The photograph suggests that this was probably the first time that black students had enrolled at this high school, which had most likely only been previously attended by white students.

description

The group of white students to the left of the African-American pair that are staring at them largely shows arrogance and contempt towards them. Their attitude is presumably a result of racism, and so demonstrates the relationship between whites and blacks in the American South at the time. These young students didn't even know the pair, and had probably never seen them before, yet the students are looking at the African-Americans with disgust. This gives the viewer the impression that the white students loathe the idea of going to school with them. Additionally, the male in the middle's facial expression shows curiosity, which supports the impression that this is the first time that black students have attended the school.
The African-Americans are looking straight ahead and appear calm and determined in what must have been difficult and uncomfortable circumstances for them. I imagine they had had enough of being regarded as second-best to white people and were determined to gain equality. They wanted the same education and opportunities available to white people.

interpretation

The photograph wants to point out the consequences of slavery and racism in the American South. Whites and blacks may have been living in the same country, the same states and even the same communities, but the two groups were living in completely different worlds. People at the time grew up in a racist and segregated society. All in all, white people claimed superiority and were taught to regard African-Americans as inferior and became used to treating them with disrespect as reflected by the white students' contempt towards the African-American students.

evaluation

What makes the photo so striking is that the viewers' attention is drawn to the facial expressions of the white students and the African-American pair. The students are ordinary teenagers caught on camera carrying out their every day routine of attending school. By taking a snapshot of the everyday life of American teenagers, the viewer gains the impression that the white students' negative attitude was normal and the African-Americans were used to being treated as such. In my opinion, the photographer has successfully shown that such racism was an ordinary and accepted part of life in the South.

b) Analyze one of the pictures on pages 21 – 22 with regard to the relationship between African-Americans and whites. Before you start writing your analysis, collect ideas in the following table.
➩ skills: how to analyze and interpret pictures, pp. 113 – 114

Introduction	
Description	
Interpretation	
Evaluation	

B1 Identify the stereotypes in the two cartoons and discuss if they are true.

B2 Look at the following quotes and fill out the table on page 25.

Stop in middle of street! Mexicans! No know how to drive! She blake too fast! … Crazy Mexican! I call immigration on you. Look you do on my car.

Asian woman

Ria

I blake when I see long line cars stop in front of me. You see over steering wheel, maybe you blake, too.

Dirk

Yo, Osama, plan the jihad on your own time. … Yeah, I'm ignorant. You're liberating my country and I'm flying 747s into your mud huts and incinerating your friends. Get the fuck out of my store.

Farhad

You try and cheat me, right? You have friend who fix door?

	Stereotyped group	Stereotype
Ria		
Asian woman	*Hispanics*	*1. All Hispanics are Mexican.* *2. All Hispanics are bad drivers.* *3. All Hispanics are in the country illegally.*
Dirk		
Farhad		

Info **stereotype, prejudice and discrimination**

Stereotypes are generalizations. They are oversimplified ideas or images of people or things that emphasize certain traits or aspects in a way that distorts reality, for example, "All Hispanics are in the country illegally".
A **prejudice** is a preconceived opinion or attitude that is not based on reason or actual experience, for example, "Hispanics are undesirable".
Discrimination refers to any positive or negative kind of behaviour towards an object of prejudice. Common forms of discrimination are racial discrimination, discrimination based on gender or discrimination based on age, for example, "I won't let my kids play with Hispanics".
Stereotypes, **prejudice** and **discrimination** are not necessarily negative but can be positive, as well. For example a positive stereotype might be: "All Asians are good at math". A prejudice might then be: "Asians are better suited to working in the financial sector than Europeans." Bank managers with this prejudice might then discriminate in favor of Asians when looking for new employees. If a stereotype is reasonably accurate, then it can be helpful. Stereotypes only become a problem when they are inaccurate. This is particularly the case when the inaccuracies are negative and hostile.

B3 Read the transcript and find examples of stereotypes/stereotyping and discrimination. Then fill out the table below. The timing for the film excerpt is 07:47 – 09:15.

Anthony: You see any white people in there waiting an hour and thirty two minutes for a plate of spaghetti? Huh? And how many cups of coffee did we get?
Peter: You don't drink coffee and I didn't want any.
Anthony: That person poured cup after cup to any white person around us. Did she even ask you if you wanted any?
Peter: We didn't get any coffee that you didn't want and I didn't order, and that's evidence of racial discrimination? Did you notice our waitress was black?
Anthony: And black women don't think in stereotypes? When's the last time you met one who didn't think she knew everything about your little lazy ass before you even opened your mouth? That waitress sized us up in two seconds. We're black and "black people don't tip" so she wasn't gonna waste her time. Somebody like that, nothing you can do to change their mind.
Peter: So how much did you leave her?
Anthony: You expect me to pay for that kind of service?
...
Anthony: You see what that woman just did?
Peter: She's cold, man.
Anthony: She got colder soon as she saw us.
Peter: Here it comes.
Anthony: Look around. You couldn't find a whiter, safer or better-lit part of the city right now. But this white woman sees two black guys who could be UCLA students, strolling down the sidewalk and her reaction is blind fear.

Anthony	Peter	Jean
– *has to wait for his meal for an hour and thirty two minutes -> thinks that he is being discriminated against because he is African-American* –		

Writing

B4 Write an answer to the following blog entry: *In* Crash *everything that happens is triggered by negative stereotypes.*

Speaking

C1 a) Look at the picture on the right. What do you think it shows?

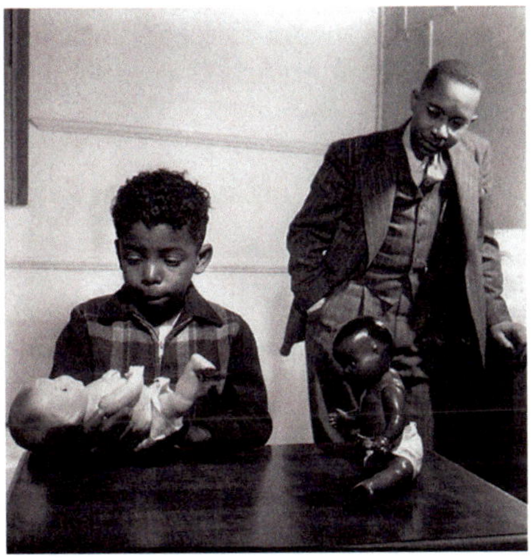

Partner 1:
1. Read the text about Mamie and Kenneth Clark's *doll experiment*.
2. Analyze graph 1 *The Racial Wealth Gap is Not Improving* and prepare to present it to your partner.

Partner 2:
1. Read the text about Mamie and Kenneth Clark's *doll experiment*.
2. Analyze graph 2 *Life expectancy at birth, by race and sex* and prepare to present it to your partner.

b) Present your graphs to each other.
c) Discuss possible causes of the inequalities.

The doll experiment

In the early 1940s, American psychologists Mamie Clark and Kenneth Clark conducted an experiment with 253 Afro-American children to determine their attitude towards race. The children were aged between three and seven and came from different regions of the United States. The doll experiment involved a child being presented with two dolls. Both of these dolls were completely identical except for the skin and hair color. One doll was white with yellow hair, while the other doll was brown with black hair. The child was then given eight different instructions. The following table shows the results for requests 1 – 4.

choice	request 1 *(Give me the doll that you like to play with)*	request 2 *(Give me the doll that is a nice doll)*	request 3 *(Give me the doll that looks bad)*	request 4 *(Give me the doll that is a nice color)*
Colored doll	32 %	38 %	59 %	38 %
White doll	67 %	59 %	17 %	60 %
Don't know or no response	1 %	3 %	24 %	2 %

This experiment has often been repeated up to this day. The results were always similar showing deeply rooted prejudices.

Graph 1: The Racial Wealth Gap is Not Improving

Average family wealth by race and ethnicity, 1983 – 2010

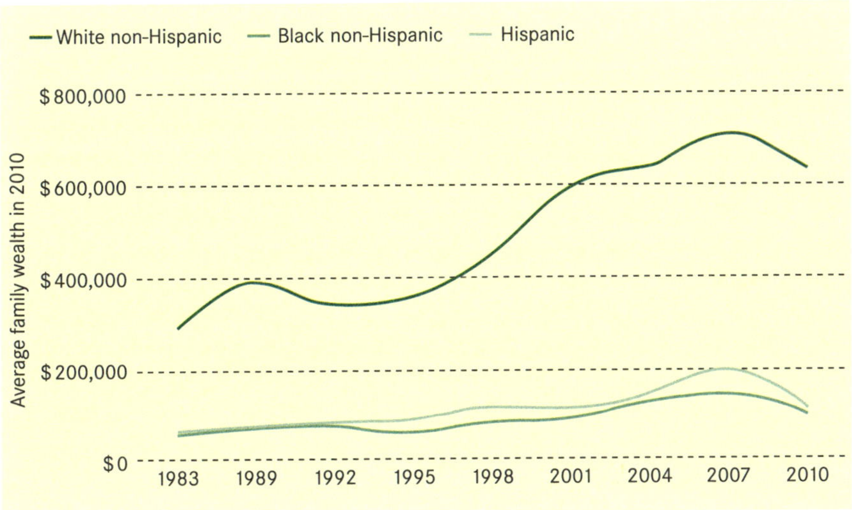

Graph 2: Life expectancy at birth, by race and sex

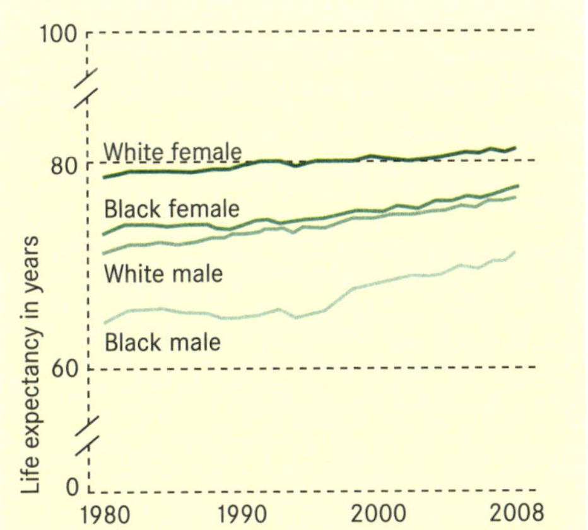

Source: CDC/NCHS, Health, United States, 2011, Table 22. Data from the National Statistics System (NVSS).

Reading

C2 Read the text about stereotypes and note down the adjectives for each stereotype in the boxes below. Add the German translations that go with them.

Stereotypes of African Americans in the United States

by Laura Green, Virginia Commonwealth University

The racial stereotypes of early American history had a significant role in shaping attitudes toward African-Americans during that time. Images of the Sambo, Jim Crow, the Savage and the Mammy may not be as powerful today, yet they are still alive.

Sambo

One of the most enduring stereotypes in American history is that of the Sambo (Boskin, 1986). This pervasive image of a simple-minded, docile black man dates back at least as far as the colonization of America. The Sambo stereotype flourished during the reign of slavery in the United States. In fact, the notion of the "happy slave" is the core of the Sambo caricature. White slave owners molded African-American males, as a whole, into this image of a jolly, overgrown child who was happy to serve his master. However, the Sambo was seen as naturally lazy and therefore reliant upon his master for direction. In this way, the institution of slavery was justified. (...) Although Sambo was born out of a defense for slavery, it extended far beyond these bounds. It is essential to realize the vast scope of this stereotype. It was transmitted through music titles and lyrics, folk sayings, literature, children's stories and games, postcards, restaurant names and menus, and thousands of artifacts (Goings, 1994). (...)

simple-minded – einfältig
docile – unterwürfig
lazy
happy to serve his master
reliant upon his master

The Savage

(...) Beliefs that blacks were "mentally inferior, physically and culturally unevolved, and apelike in appearance" (Plous & Williams, 1995, p. 795) were supported by prominent white figures like Abraham Lincoln, Andrew Johnson, and Thomas Jefferson. Theodore Roosevelt publicly stated that "As a race and in the mass [the Negroes] are altogether inferior to whites" (Plous & Williams, 1995, p. 796). (...) This idea of African-Americans as apelike savages was exceptionally pervasive. For example, in 1906, the New York Zoological Park featured an exhibit with an African-American man and a chimpanzee. Several years later, the Ringling Brothers Circus exhibited "the monkey man," a black man was caged with a female chimpanzee that had been trained to wash clothes and hang them on a line (Plous & Williams, 1995).

inferior (to the whites)
apelike savages
physically & culturally unevolved

The Mammy

The Mammy was a large, independent woman with pitch-black skin and shining white teeth (Jewell, 1993). (...) The Mammy understood the value of the white lifestyle. The stereotype suggests that she raised the "massa's" children and loved them dearly, even more than her own. Her tendency to give advice to her mistress was seen as harmless and humorous. (...) Possibly the most outstanding example is the Mammy role played by Hattie McDaniel in "Gone with the Wind" (Goings, 1994). The book, published in 1936 by Margaret Mitchell, helped to keep the mythical past of African-Americans in the old South alive. The large number of people whose attitudes were shaped by this portrayal is demonstrated through its phenomenal sales record. The Bible is the only book that rivals "Gone with the Wind" in total sales. (...)

independent
harmless
humorous
tendency to give advice

Conclusion and Implications

(...) (It) seems that many people are unaware of the remaining stereotypes, negative attitudes, and oppression of African-Americans. Because stereotypes are so often accepted as the truth, defining the problem is a crucial step of intervention.

(Many) individuals look for information that supports stereotypes. Therefore, encouraging people to recognize information that is inconsistent with stereotypes may be helpful in dispelling damaging stereotypes within society.

It is, then, essential to provide people with information that challenges stereotypes. Because the media's portrayal of African-Americans has been and still is conducive to the formation of stereotypes, interventions in this area are a good place to start. Currently, African-Americans are over-represented as sports figures (Peffley et al, 1997). Reevaluation of the content of television commercials, magazine advertisements, movies, plays, cultural events, museum exhibits, and other media reveals where African-American representation needs to be increased.

C3 Look at the pictures below and write down how the African-Americans are portrayed. Use adjectives. Then name the stereotypes that are portrayed here.

The Afro-American is portrayed as ...

creepy
obtrusive
scary

"Say, don't you think this piece of watermelon is rather large?"
"Golly, boss! Dat ain't half big nuff!"

submissive ?? (dumb ??)
not as educated as whites

Caring?
helpful
selfless

C4 Analyze the different African-American characters in *Crash* and explain whether in *Crash* stereotypes of African Americans are perpetuated or not.

Character	**profession and social status**	**is portrayed in a positive way / in a negative way – explain how**
Detective Waters 	police officer, is successful, has a career, is widely respected	detectives represent the law and are usually likeable, he is a typical detective; he is good-looking, intelligent and witty
Cameron Thayer 		
Shaniqua 		
Anthony 		
Peter Waters 		
Mrs. Waters 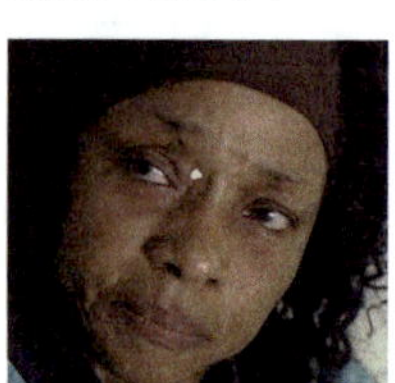		

Reading

D1 Read the following text and fill in the box below.

Affirmative Action

The term was first used by President John F. Kennedy in Executive Order 10925 which was issued in 1961. This order requires ***government contractors*** "to take affirmative action to ensure that ***applicants*** are employed and that ***employees*** are treated during employment without regard to their race, creed, color or national origin". Executive Order 10925 was aimed at ending racial discrimination and discrimination based on other factors.
Executive Order 11246, the latest order concerning affirmative action, mentions "race, color, religion, sex, or national origin" as factors that must be considered by government contractors. The executive orders, however, have not specified what exactly affirmative means. Affirmative action policies have been implemented in public institutions such as universities, schools, hospitals and among the police forces, but also in companies that produce goods or services for the government. Two of the major ***policies*** are campaigns among ***minority groups*** encouraging them to apply at public institutions and quotas that determine the percentage of people from ***minority groups*** that are admitted to or hired by institutions such as universities or hospitals. Some institutions also established point systems in which applicants were given points for certain qualities. A famous example of this system is the University of Michigan. The admissions policy for undergraduate students was based on 150 points, and it awarded points based on items such as race (20 points), athletic ability (20 points), depth of essay (up to 3 points), and personal achievement (up to 5 points).The point system automatically awarded admission points to ***underrepresented*** minorities.
The quota system and the points system particularly have attracted controversy and provoked serious opposition. In 2003, the US Supreme Court ruled that the University of Michigan was allowed to consider race as a factor when admitting students, but declared the strict point system at the university to be unconstitutional.

A government contractor is a private company that provides goods or services under contract for the government. The US government has contracts with hundreds of companies.

Applicants (Bewerber) are people who apply for (sich bewerben) jobs or places at universities or who apply for scholarships.

Employers (Arbeitgeber) are people or institutions that offer jobs. The people who are employed with a certain company or institution are called employees.

Minority groups: African Americans, Hispanics, Asians, etc.

A policy (Methode, Strategie) is a course of action adopted or proposed by a government, institution or private person.

Underrepresented in this context means, the proportion of students at a certain institution is lower than the proportion of people from this group in society. E.g. about 14 % of Americans are black and if at a certain university, only 9 % of all students are black, then they are underrepresented.

- to guarantee (sicherstellen) – *... action to ensure that applicants are -> to guarantee that applicants are ...*
- with regard to (bezüglich) – ____________
- to take into account (berücksichtigen) – ____________
- to put into effect (verwirklichen, in Kraft setzen) – ____________
- to set up (einrichten, aufbauen) – ____________
- features / characteristics (Eigenschaften) – ____________
- not in accordance with the constitution (nicht verfassungskonform) – ____________

D2 Read the transcript from *Crash* and summarize below Officer Ryan's attitude towards affirmative action in exactly 50 words. ⇨ self-assessment: how to write a summary, p. 128

Shaniqua: Mr. Ryan, my name is Shaniqua Johnson. I believe we spoke last night.
Ryan: Yeah, I wanted to apologize for that crack. I haven't been sleeping a lot. My father is in a lot of pain.
Shaniqua: I'm sorry to hear that.
Ryan: This doctor he's been going to tells him he has this urinary tract infection, and he's been taking this medicine for a month now, and he's just getting worse.
Shaniqua: And he's been back to see Dr. Robinson?
Ryan: Yeah, between me and you, the man is an idiot.
Shaniqua: Really?
Ryan: No offense, but the guy sees a hundred patients an hour. I think his nurses do most of the work.
Shaniqua: If you're unhappy, your father is welcome to see a doctor outside the network.
Ryan: And if this new doctor says it isn't an infection, says it's his prostate and it needs to be operated on, is that covered?
Shaniqua: Not unless Dr. Robinson –
Ryan: So, what good would that do?
Shaniqua: I'm sorry, but there is nothing else I can do.
Ryan: Do you know what I can't do? I can't look at you without thinking of the five or six better qualified white men who didn't get your job.
Shaniqua: Time for you to be going.
Ryan: I'm saying this because I'm really hoping I'm wrong about you. I'm hoping that someone like yourself, who may have been given a helping hand, might have a little compassion for someone in a similar situation.
Shaniqua: Carol, I need security in my office.
Ryan: You don't like me? Fine, I'm a prick. But my father doesn't deserve to suffer like this. He was a janitor, struggled his whole life, saved enough to start his own company. Twenty-three employees, all black. Paid them equal wages, when no one else was doing that. Forty years he worked side by side with those men, sweeping, carrying garbage. Then the city council decides to give minority-owned companies preference in city contracts. And overnight, my father loses everything. His business, his home, his wife, everything; and not once did he blame you people. I'm not asking you to help me. I'm asking that you do this small thing for a man who lost everything so that people like you could reap the benefits. And do you know what it's gonna cost you? Nothing, just the flick of your pen.
Shaniqua: Your father sounds like a good man. And if he'd come in here today, I probably would have approved this request. But he didn't come in, you did. And for his sake, that's a real shame.

... see a doctor outside the network ...
The term network refers to the health insurance that pays for the medical treatment of Officer Ryan's father. The insurance doesn't pay if you change to another doctor because you're not satisfied with his or her work.

... six better qualified white men who didn't ...
If you're qualified for a job, it means you are competent enough to do the job. People can be sufficiently qualified (ausreichend qualifiziert), well qualified and perfectly qualified.

Paid them equal wages ...
Today there is still a wage gap between men and women (for the same work, women are paid less than men) and between whites and African-Americans. Wages are paid to employees by their employers.

... to give minority-owned companies preference in city contracts.
This is an affirmative action policy aimed at righting the wrongs of the past. Minority-owned companies are companies owned by African-Americans, Hispanics, Asians or other minorities.

Officer Ryan believes ______________________________

____

____

____

____

____

____

Speaking

D3 **Partner 1:**

Affirmative action

a) Explain the cartoon to your partner and inform him about the opinions of the two bloggers on affirmative action

b) Discuss if affirmative action is an adequate way of righting the wrongs of the past, of meeting the challenge of racial inequality. You can refer to Shaniqua Johnson and Officer Ryan's father.

Affirmative action reduces the wealth gap

posted on June 18th, 2013 by AlbertA

Just look at the latest report on the wealth gap by the Urban Institute (http://www.urban.org/UploadedPDF/412802-Less-Than-Equal-Racial-Disparities-in-Wealth-Accumulation.pdf), it clearly shows that whites have passed on their wealth from generation to generation while most black families have never been wealthy and their children have never had the chance to go a prestigious university or start a business. We definitely need affirmative action, it is one way how we can close the wealth gap and give African-Americans a fair chance.
And on top of that, it's the only way to guarantee ethnic diversity at universities, something that a nation as diverse as the USA definitely needs. If we don't learn how we can peacefully live together with people of Hispanic or Asian or African origin at a young age, we'll keep our stereotypes and prejudices.

An African-American view on affirmative action

posted on June 19th, 2013 by WashingtonS

I have many white friends who show great interest in the debate over affirmative action and who look at affirmative action as a political issue. Yet for me as an African-American the significance is a different one: my family comes from Alabama and my ancestors have been discriminated against in many ways. My father was a gifted and hardworking student at school and he went to Alabama State University on a scholarship. Yet when my father had earned his degree (an MBA, master's of business administration) and tried to apply for a job, he was rejected in spite of his academic brilliance. He simply didn't have the same choices as white Americans. He finally found a badly-paid job in a small company run by an African-American in Montgomery. Affirmative action, for me, is a way to make up for the injustices of the past, that's why I support it.

word bank

to reach a goal / to achieve an aim = ein Ziel erreichen

disadvantage = Nachteil

to suffer from discrimination = unter Diskriminierung leiden

to make up for the injustices of the past = die Ungerechtigkeiten der Vergangenheit wiedergutmachen

Partner 2:

Affirmative action

a) Explain the cartoon to your partner and inform him about the opinions of the two bloggers on affirmative action
b) Discuss if affirmative action is an adequate way of righting the wrongs of the past, of meeting the challenge of racial inequality. You can refer to Shaniqua Johnson and Officer Ryan's father.

Affirmative action leads to injustice

posted on June 2nd by admin

Some people say affirmative action has the potential to right the wrongs of the past. This might be true. What's ironic about these policies is that they are aimed at ending discrimination, and at the same time they discriminate against white males. Affirmative action is reverse discrimination. Don't get me wrong. I'm not saying we shouldn't think about ways to end racism. But affirmative action is unfair, because the racial or ethnic background of a person is not a qualification, it's simply a fact. And this fact shouldn't be taken into account when a person applies at a university or for a job.

Affirmative action leads to stereotyping

posted on June 22nd by RonaldM

In the Declaration of Independence it says "We hold these truths to be self-evident that all men are created equal" and Martin Luther King has mentioned this phrase in his famous "I have a dream" speech. Equality also means equal treatment and affirmative action is unequal treatment. Affirmative action puts a label on African Americans: "you're a victim, you can't make it on your own". Let's stop victimizing blacks and let's get rid of affirmative action.

word bank

victim = Opfer

policy/measure = Methode, Strategie

to apply for a job = sich bewerben um eine Stelle

to take somebody's skin color into account = die Hautfarbe eines Menschen berücksichtigen

to be qualified = qualifiziert sein

A1 In the map below the countries of the world have been re-sized according to the number of people who have migrated to them from their countries of birth. Describe the map and explain what it tells you about international migration.

International migration

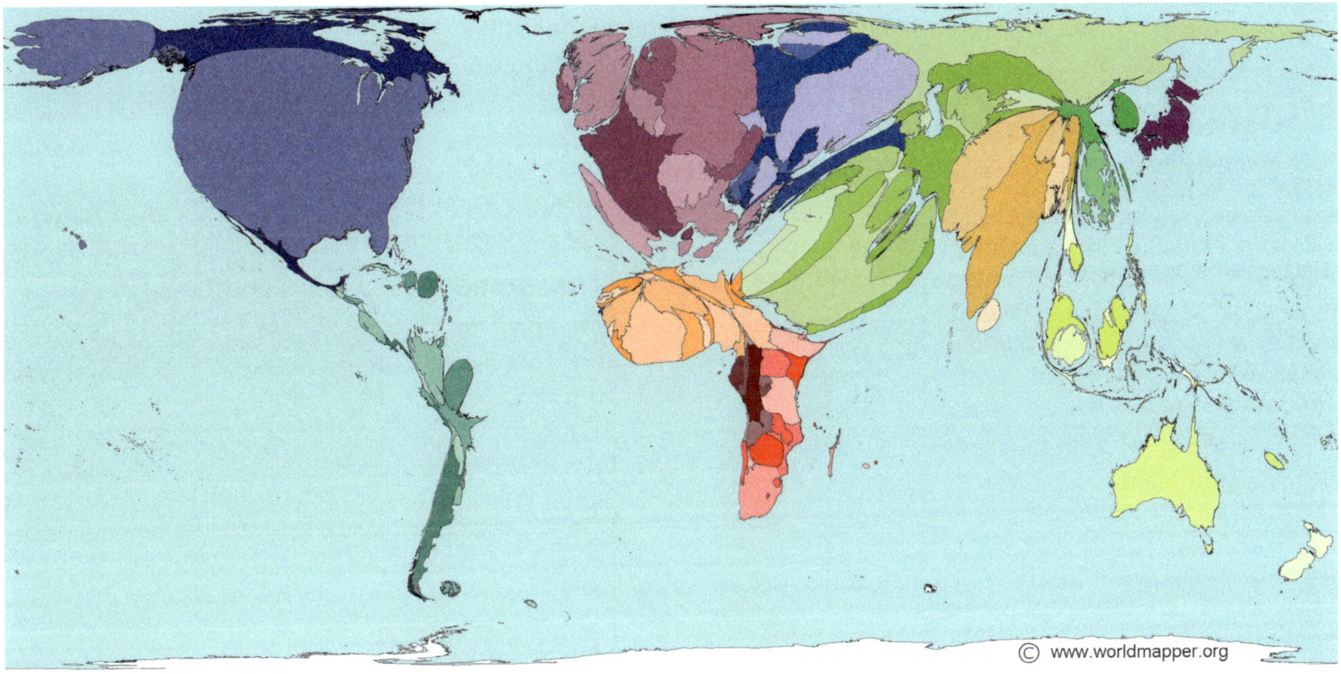

source: World mapper

Three percent of the world population in 2000 were born in a country different to where they now live: one hundred and seventy-four million people have moved to a new country. The United States receives the highest number of international immigrants.

A2 Read the following quote and think about the following questions:

Have you ever lost any of the roots mentioned by Rushdie?
Or do you know anyone else who has?

"The roots of self are the place that you know, the community that you come from, the language that you speak and the cultural assumptions within which you grow up. Those are the four great roots of the self and very, very often what happens to migrants is that they lose all four – they're in a different place, speaking an alien language, amongst people who don't know them and the cultural assumptions are very different. You can see that's something traumatic."

Salman Rushdie

Historical Push and Pull Theory:

The Push and Pull theory uses two kinds of factors to explain migration factors. On the one hand there are push factors that drive people away from a place and on the other pull factors that draw people into a country.

A3 a) Decide whether the factors in the grid on the left are push or pull factors and tick the boxes accordingly.
b) Note down additional push and pull factors in the grid on the right.

	Push	Pull
Not enough jobs		
Better living conditions		
Enjoyment		
Famine or drought		
Natural disasters		
Family links		
Discrimination		
Poor medical care		
Political fear or persecution		
Political and/or religious freedom		
Better chances of finding a partner		

	Push	Pull

c) Think of examples of people you know who have either moved away to live somewhere else or who have come to live in Germany or moved from another part of Germany. Identify factors why these people decided to uproot themselves like this.

A4 Read the passages from *Half Broke Horses* below and look at the film stills from *Crash*. Talk to a partner about:
- the push and pull factors that made Lily and the Asians migrate.
- which challenges Lily and which challenges the Asians in the van face in the situations below.

Life had been hard in west Texas, but that low yellow land was all I knew, and I loved it. Mom was saying, as she always did, that it was God's will, and this time I accepted it. God had saved us, but he had also taken our house from us. Whether as payment for saving us or as punishment because we didn't deserve it, I couldn't say. Maybe he was just giving us a kick in the behind to say: time to move on. (Jeannette Walls: Half Broke Horses, Diesterweg Verlag, p. 46)	Patches and I left at first light one morning in early August. (...) Mom, Dad, Buster, and Helen were all up, and we sat down at the long wooden table in the kitchen, passing the platter of johnnycakes and the tin teapot back and forth. "Will we ever see you again?" Helen asked. "Sure," I said. "When?" I hadn't thought about that, and I realized I didn't want to think about it. (Jeannette Walls: Half Broke Horses, Diesterweg Verlag, p. 74)	"We received a complaint, ma'am, alleging you took a potshot at one of the townspeople." "There was a menacing intruder, and I was defending myself and my children. I'll be happy to stand up in court and explain exactly what happened." The sheriff sighed. "Around here, we like people to work out their differences amongst themselves. But if you can't get along with these folks, and there's many that can't, you probably don't belong here." After that, I knew it was only a matter of time. I continued to teach in Main Street, telling those girls what I thought they needed to know about the world, but I stopped getting dinner invitations, and a bunch of the parents took their kids out of the school. In the spring I got a letter from the Mohave County superintendent saying that he didn't think it would be a good idea for me to continue teaching in Main Street come next fall. (Jeannette Walls: Half Broke Horses, Diesterweg Verlag, p. 213-4)

word bank

- to feel at home somewhere
- to be part of a community
- to have a sense of belonging
- to be familiar with a place, with people
- to have a feeling of security
- to face an uncertain future
- to be confident about your future

Extra task: find further examples of migration in *Half Broke Horses*.

A5 Imagine you are one of the Asians in the van. Describe your thoughts in the moments before you arrive in your new home. Write an interior monologue.

Writing

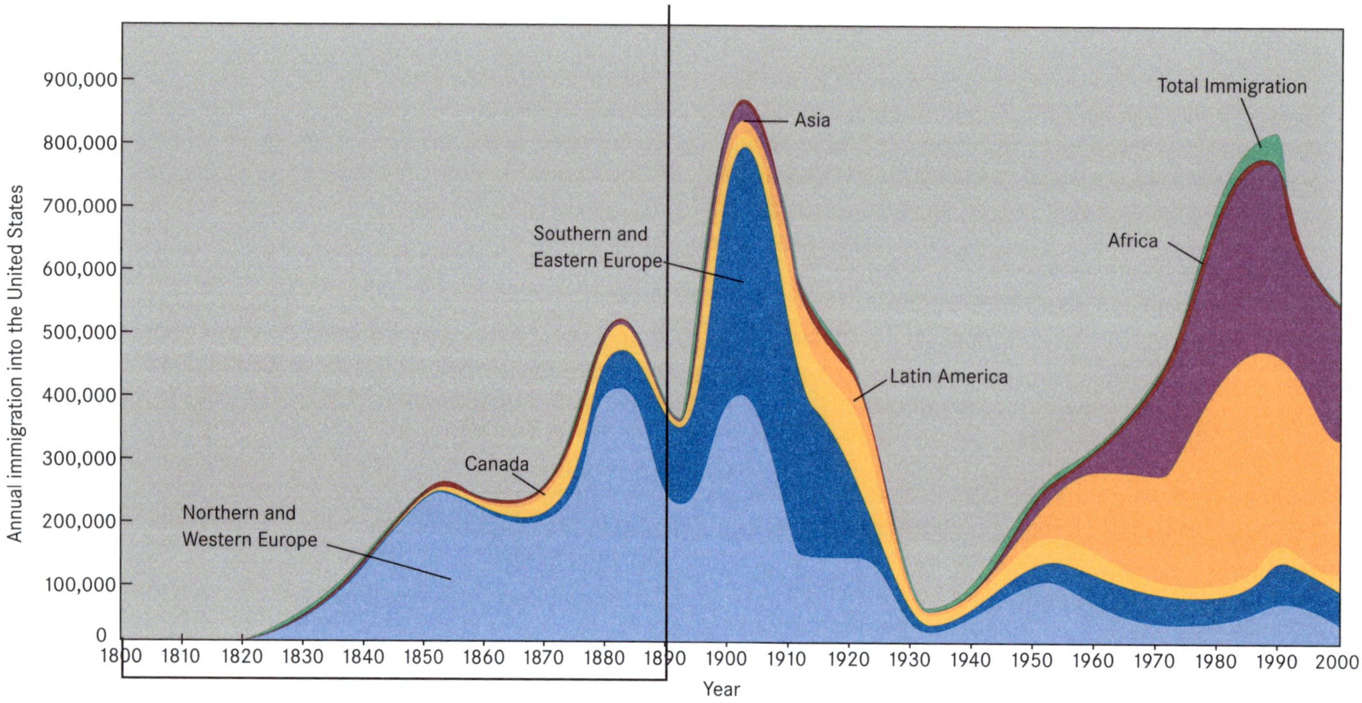

A6 You are often required to analyze statistics. The following text was written by a student whose task it was to analyze the statistics above up to the year 1890.
Read the analysis and highlight those words and phrases that you find helpful for analyzing statistics.
Then underline descriptions of the graph in green and explanations in red.

The line graph at hand provides information on immigration into the United States from 1800 to 2000. It clearly shows that until 1820 only few people immigrated into the United States. In the 1820s the number of immigrants continued to rise until the late 1840s and early 1850s. By this time, more than 200,000 immigrants were arriving in the United States each year, mostly from Northern and Central Europe. Many of them were lured into the country by the prospect of cheap land and jobs in prospering industries. The significant increase in the 1840s is also a result of the potato famine in Ireland with thousands of people arriving to escape poverty and death. The failure of the German revolution of 1848 is another event that accounts for the peak in 1850. In this context it is important to note that – besides cheap land and jobs in factories – family relations were a main pull factor. In the 1850s the number of immigrants continued to drop slowly throughout the decade.

The territorial expansion of the United States in the 19th century was a project that depended on hundreds of thousands of settlers from Europe. Mainly railroad companies and young states such as Nebraska sent advertisements and reports to Europe promising people cheap land in the west. These advertisements were highly successful luring thousands of settlers into the Western states. The number of immigrants rose sharply again in 1870, due largely to the introduction of steam-powered ships which operated between Europe and the United States and were faster and cheaper than sailboats.

The second peak in the mid 1880s, when over 500,000 immigrants arrived annually, marks a major change in the history of immigration. Until the late 1870s almost all immigrants came from Northern and Western Europe, predominantly from Britain, Ireland, Germany and Scandinavia. In the late 1870s – for the first time in American history – a considerable number of immigrants came from Southern and Eastern Europe. The line graph reveals that, after 1885, the total number of immigrants decreased whereas the number of immigrants from Southern and Eastern Europe rose.

A7 Analyze the statistics for the period 1890 – 2000. Use the additional information on page 144 to help you with your explanations. ⇨ skills: how to analyze and interpret statistics, pp. 111 – 112

B1 The following text was written by a student whose task it was to write a cartoon analysis.

a) Read the analysis below and identify the four different parts: introduction, description, interpretation, evaluation.

Introduction: lines __________ Interpretation: lines __________

Description: lines __________ Evaluation: lines __________

b) Highlight expressions in the text that are essential for cartoon analysis. ➩ skills: how to analyze and interpret cartoons, pp. 115 – 116

Info **Joseph Keppler** (1838 – 1894) was originally born in Vienna, Austria. As a cartoonist and caricaturist, he was very influential in the development of satirical cartooning in the United States.

The cartoon was drawn by Joseph Keppler and published in Puck magazine in 1880 under the title "Welcome to All". It deals with the question of immigrants to the United States at the end of the 19th century. In the foreground the picture shows a long line of people waiting to get on board a wooden ship, which is called the "US Ark of Refuge". Next to the boat there is the American flag. The people are lined up as couples of husbands and wives. They are wearing the traditional clothes of their time. Some of them appear to be rather simple folk carrying linen sacks and wearing shabby clothes. Others are very well dressed carrying leather bags as luggage. The most prominent figure is Uncle Sam – the typical symbol for America: an elderly man with a long white beard, a striped top hat, red-and-white striped pants and a blue jacket. He is standing at the entrance of the ship with his hands stretched out to express his welcome to all the passengers. There are two signs to be seen in the picture. One is posted on a pole next to the plank leading on to the ship. The sign shows the people what they can expect from the New World they are heading to: "No oppressive taxes, No expensive kings, No compulsory military service, …". At the entrance of the ship, in the upper left-hand corner there is another sign. It informs the passengers about other advantages like free speech, free land and free education. In the background of the cartoon you can see the sea stretching to the horizon. The upper part of the picture is divided into an area of black sky in the upper right-hand corner which includes a demon-like figure in it and bright blue sky to the left of the picture.

The significant change in the colors of the sky symbolizes the dark side of the Old World in the east and the bright future in the New World to the west. The people are walking towards the ship with happy smiles on their faces. They seem to have very positive expectations about the trip and their new life ahead. This impression seems to be warranted when one takes into account the two signs illustrating all the promises that await them as well as nice, welcoming Uncle Sam as the embodiment of a kind American person. The fact that they belong to different social classes underlines the message of the caption that everybody was welcome to immigrate to the United States. The cartoonist has succeeded in including many symbolic aspects in this cartoon and thus portrays the hopes and the promises which lured 19th century immigrants away from Europe to America.

Writing

B2 Study the cartoon "Looking backward" (1893) by Joseph Keppler. Use the boxes to describe and interpret the circled elements.

Man with non-matching shadow
↓
The shadow alludes to his immigration background

Different hats
↓
Immigrants come from different countries.

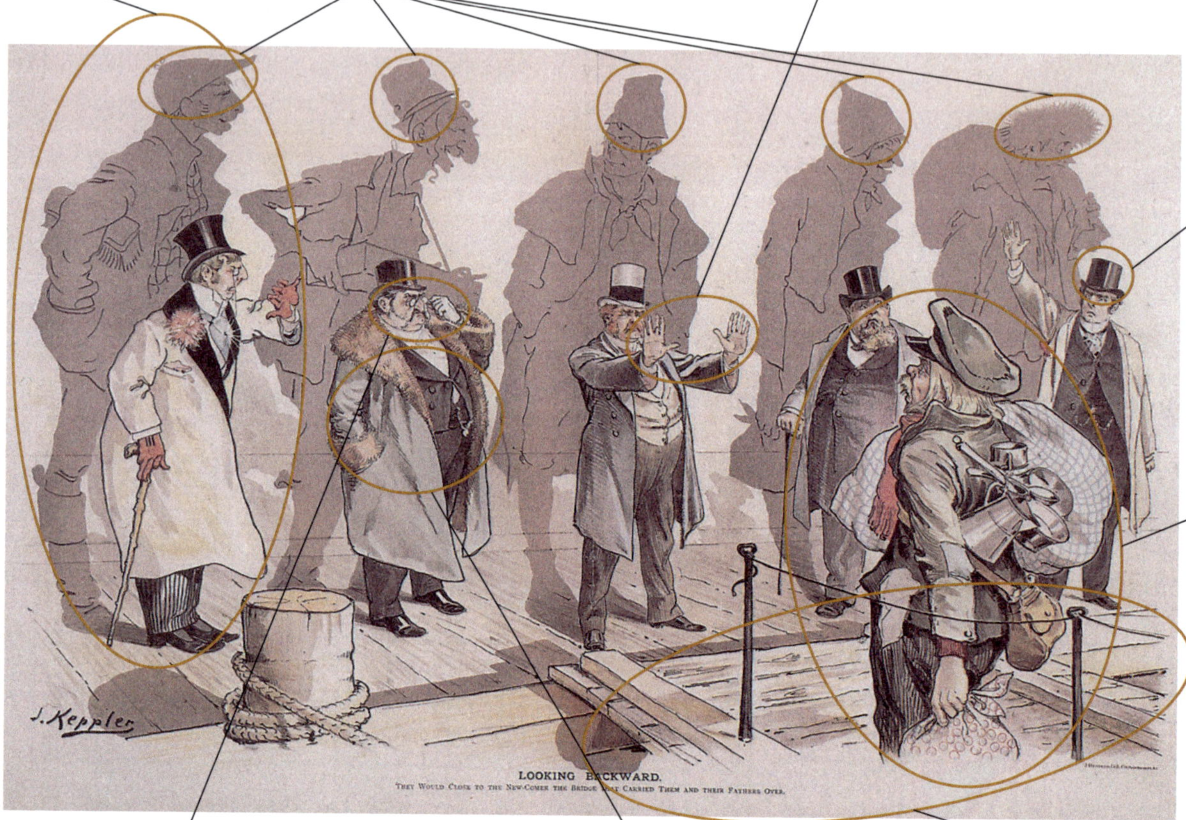

word bank

to symbolize sth.

to represent sth.

to indicate sth. = auf etwas hinweisen

to allude to sth. = auf etwas anspielen

The men are portrayed / depicted as ...

B3 Fill in the boxes below as preparation for your analysis of the cartoon. Look at the text on page 39 for help with expressions.

Introduction
Important aspects (notes only):
Helpful phrases

Description
Important aspects (notes only):
Helpful phrases

Interpretation
Important aspects (notes only):
Helpful phrases

Evaluation
Important aspects (notes only):
Helpful phrases

B4 Use your notes from B3 to write an analysis of the cartoon. ⇨ skills: how to analyze and interpret cartoons, pp. 115 – 116

C1 Look at the characters from *Crash*. They or their ancestors arrived in the United States at different points in history. Use your knowledge about the history of US immigration and speculate about when the characters (or their ancestors) first arrived in the United States. Rank them according to how long ago their ancestors arrived.

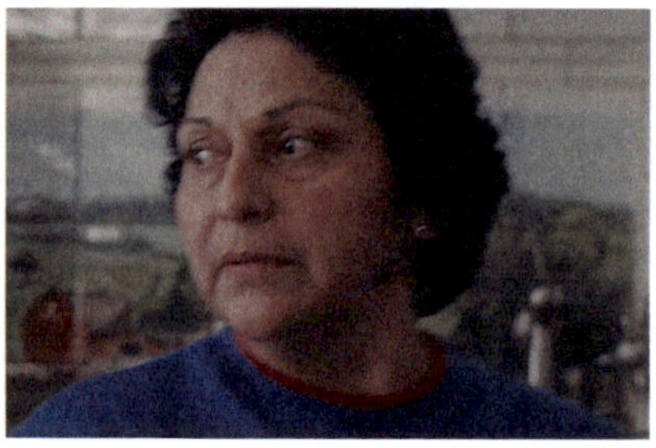
Maria

Asian woman

Daniel

Officer Hansen

Cameron

Farhad

1. *Cameron* – *probably descendant of slaves* – *slaves were brought to the North American colonies/the U. S. in the 17th and 18th centuries*	2. Hansen – probably descendant of settlers – 17th century – first settlers came to America in 1621	3. Kim Lee – 1880–1914 (3rd wave) made up of Chinese, Japanese + other Asians
reason: – *immigration was not a voluntary act, but organized by slave traders for economic reasons*	– settlers came to America to seek religious liberty	– more job opportunities – freedom of religion
4. Daniel – Fourth wave consisting of Europeans, Asians, Hispanics	5. Maria	6. Farhad – maybe refugees ??
– seeking better living conditions – job opportunities		

C2 a) The characters in C 1 provide a good cross-section of American society. Sociologists have used different metaphors to explain how people of different origins and from different cultures live together in one society. Look at these examples of such metaphors. Try to explain how the images function as metaphors for American society.

melting pot

pizza

salad bowl

quilt

US-American society – a melting pot or a salad bowl?

All the terms above have been used to describe US-American society. The melting pot metaphor – the oldest and most famous metaphor – reflects the idea of forming a new society consisting of people from various backgrounds. According to the melting pot metaphor American society is made up of immigrants who have fully assimilated not only by marrying immigrants from other countries, but also by giving up the traditions and culture of their native countries. They have developed an American way of life and an American identity, have adopted the English language and formed communities together with immigrants from other countries. This view of American society is expressed by the official motto of the US: *e pluribus unum* (= out of many, one). You can find this motto on the one-dollar bill and on the American coat of arms. The melting pot metaphor has often been criticized for not taking into account three major groups of Americans: Afro-Americans, Native Americans and immigrants from Southern and Eastern Europe. However, applied to immigrants from Northern and Western Europe only, the metaphor can be regarded as adequate.

According to the salad bowl metaphor (sometimes other metaphors are used: bouquet, quilt or pizza), US-American society is made up of people with different backgrounds who do not merge into a homogenous culture but keep their own distinct identities. For instance, they cherish traditions of their native countries, are married to immigrants from the same ethnic background, spend a lot of time among people from the same ethnic background and still speak the language of their native countries. What all these people have in common is that they live in the United States, usually speak English to some degree and regard themselves as Americans. The salad bowl metaphor is similar to the European concept of multiculturalism.

b) One characteristic of written English are participle constructions which are used to express something in an elegant and at the same time efficient way. The following participle constructions can be found in the text above. Rewrite these sentences without using a participle construction. Then compare the two versions and explain the function of the participle construction.

1. ... reflects the idea of forming a new society consisting of people from various backgrounds.

   that consists

2. ... immigrants who have fully assimilated not only by marrying immigrants from other countries, but also by giving up the traditions and culture of their native countries.

3. However, applied to immigrants from Northern and Western Europe only, the metaphor can be regarded as adequate.

   when it's applied

C3 a) Spider charts are a useful way to display multiple data within one diagram. They show or compare strengths and weaknesses between different things. Normally there is a scoring range from 0 (in the center) to 5 (at the edge), with 5 indicating the highest level.

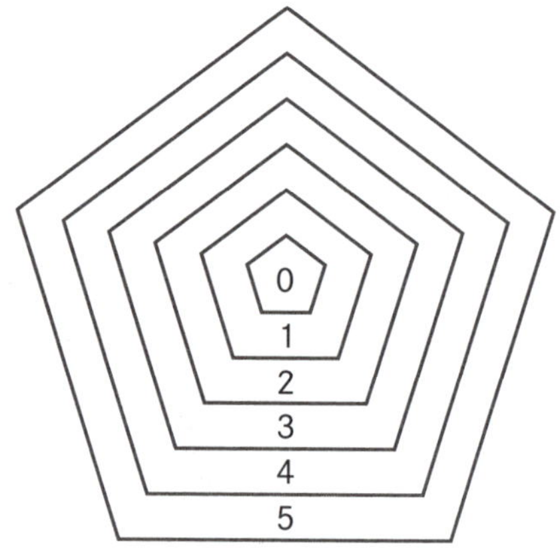

Diagram 1 visualizes the two concepts melting pot and salad bowl. The concept of the melting pot, for example, suggests that people have completely adopted the American way of life and speak English fluently. Explain the salad bowl concept as displayed in diagram 1.

Diagram 1: Melting pot and salad bowl

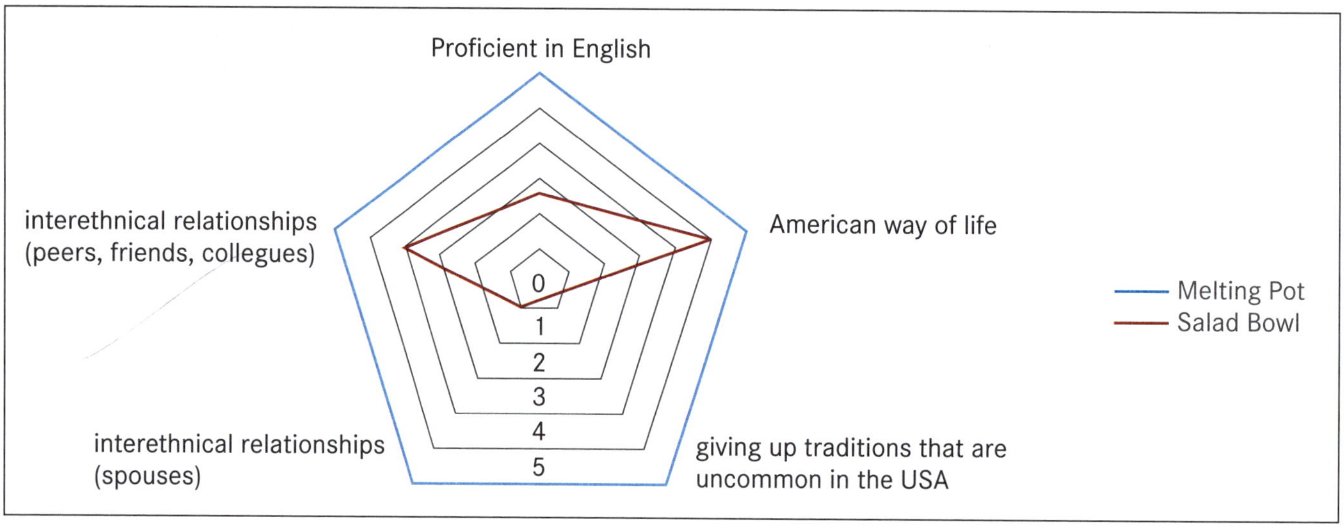

b) Examine the following characters from Crash – Jean, Daniel, Cameron and Farhad – to determine where they range and fill out diagram 2.

c) Taking your findings about Jean, Daniel, Cameron and Farhad into consideration, discuss which of the concepts above – melting pot or salad bowl – is most appropriate.

Diagram 2: Characters from Crash

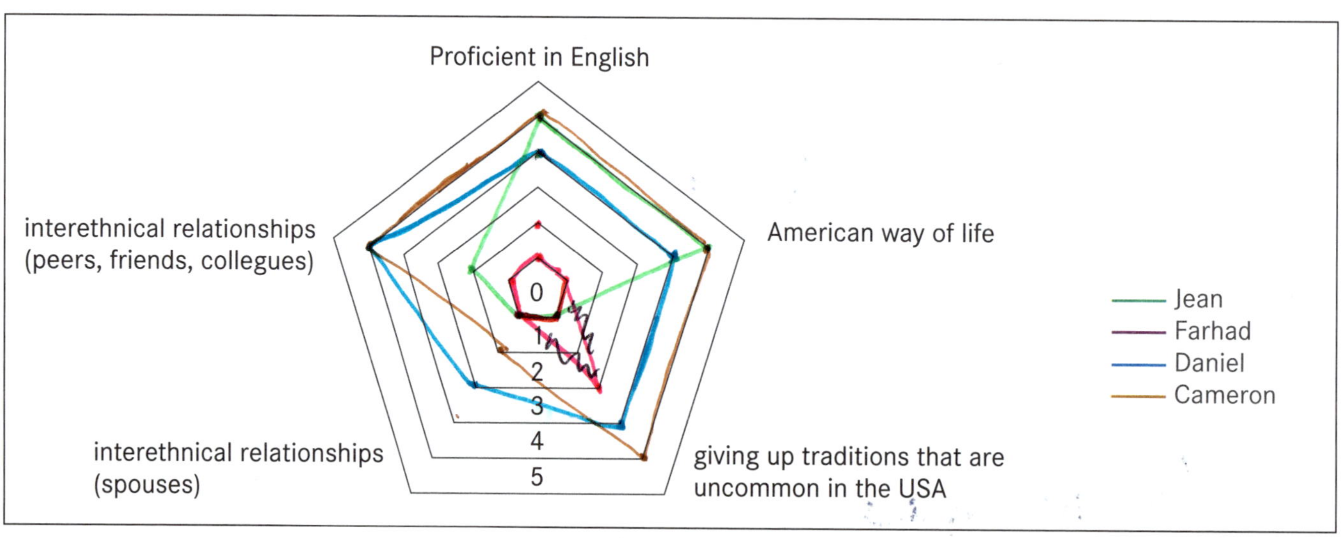

C4 Look at the cartoons on page 46 and write down which of the beliefs below the different cartoons comment on.

Beliefs of people who favor immigration	Beliefs of people who oppose immigration
Inexpensive labor	Immigrants take away jobs from American citizens
Immigrants do jobs other people do not want to do	Immigrants pose a threat to American culture
Helping the less fortunate is an American tradition	The immigrants' way of life seems strange
Accepting immigrants is a humanitarian duty and a civic virtue	Fear of terrorism
Almost all Americans are descended from immigrants	Immigrants will not assimilate
Immigrants contribute to America's multicultural society	Immigrants are a burden for the US taxpayer

Cartoon 1: – Immigrants Take away jobs from American citizens

Cartoon 2: – Fear of terrorism

Cartoon 3: – Immigrants pose a threat to American culture

Cartoon 4:

Cartoon 5:

Cartoon 6:

Cartoon 7: – Immigrants will not assimilate

The mortar of assimilation and the one element that won't mix. Puck, June 26, 1889.

annotations

riff-raff = an insulting word for people of low social class;

mortar = a substance used for joining bricks and stones to build walls

Viewing/Listening

D1 Watch the clip "What Are The True Costs And Benefits Of Illegal Immigration?" taken from the documentary "Crossing the Line: Border Stories" and fill out the table below.

groups of people	
winners	**reasons**
employers in industries, especially in the service industry/tourism,	
losers	
unclear	

Speaking

D2 Work with a partner. One of you (Partner 1) will present arguments in favor of allowing illegal immigrants to the United States to become US citizens. The other (Partner 2) will present arguments attacking the proposal.

Partner 1: In 2008 the Miller Center hosted a debate on immigration. The participants debated the motion: *Our national interests require a path to citizenship for the 12 million illegal immigrants presently here.* The following extract is taken from this debate. Eliseo Medina, International Executive Vice President of the Service Employees International Union, argues in favor of the motion.
Read the extract and fill out the relevant part of the graphic organizer on page 49. Then present your results to a partner and finish the graphic organizer with his/her information.

There is no question that our immigration system is broken. And it's not serving the interest of anyone – not the immigrants, not civic society, and not the interest of business. So we have a system today where 12 million people are living in the shadows, subject to exploitation, going to work every day in fear of being arrested and deported, leaving their children alone. We have hundreds of people who are dying in the desert every year, trying to get to America. And we have frustration [...] in our society in people who see the problem, but don't understand why our Congress cannot address it.
So I believe that it is crucial and it is in our best interest to fix this broken immigration system that we give the

undocumented immigrants among us the opportunity to legalize their status.
And I believe that for three very simple reasons.
Number one, it is impractical to deport 12 million people. It would cost us $200 billion and over 50 years and tens of thousands of law enforcement officials to go in and raid homes and businesses, community centers, looking to round up people in order to deport them; tens of thousands of police officers that could be working and keeping our communities safe and dealing with real crime, not nannies and gardeners and farm workers.
And this system is also creating a lot of pain and a lot of separation for families, and it's wrong. Number two, even if we were willing to pay the price, the unintended consequences for these families are incredible. They are living in blended families; they are married to U.S. citizens, they have U.S.-born children.
And if they get arrested and deported, who's going to take care of those millions of children who are going to be left alone? How much is it going to cost us in order to be able to create foster homes, orphanages or whatever instrument we need to be able to take care of these children, rather than having their parents with them?
And how about our economy? How are we going to replace that five percent of the work force in agriculture, in construction, in services, in health care? Who's going to pick our crops? Who's going to construct our homes? And who's going to take care of our elderly if they are not here?
So I believe that it is in our best interests of our society to ensure that, as a nation of immigrants, we continue to welcome people, but that we also have a way for people to come and be protected, to come in a safe, legal and orderly manner, and then, once here, they are not exploited and, in fact, respected for the contributions they make to our society.

Partner 2: In 2008 the Miller Center hosted a debate on immigration. The participants debated the proposed motion *Our national interests require a path to citizenship for the 12 million illegal immigrants presently here.* The following extract is taken from this debate. Mark Krikorian, Executive Director of the think-tank[1], the Center for Immigration Studies, argued against the motion.
Read the extract and fill out the relevant part of the graphic organizer on page 49. Then present your results to a partner and finish the graphic organizer with his/her information.

When we ask whether legalization, giving illegal immigrants legal status, which was what amnesty means or a path to citizenship, they're all different – they're all synonyms for the same thing. What would happen?[...]
The first thing that would happen is that 12 million applications would be dumped in the inbox of an agency that is incapable of dealing with the workload today.
The results are predictable. We've seen them before: massive fraud, fraud on a scale unprecedented in American history. We saw this with the last amnesty, where hundreds of thousands of people who should not have been legalized in fact were because the agency did not have the capacity to screen them out.
Secondly, the deal of enforcement tomorrow in exchange for legalization today [...] will not be followed through on. It's a bait-and-switch[2]. Because the legalization happens first, the promises of enforcement will be abandoned if the legalization happens first.
The result will be continued illegal immigration, and ten years from now we'll have another debate show asking what to do about the next 12 million illegal immigrants and whether we need to legalize them.
The only realistic approach, the only responsible approach is not legalization or, on the other hand, mass deportation, which we couldn't do if we wanted to – we don't have the capacity to do that; instead, the realistic approach is the middle way that's come to be called "attrition through enforcement."
And what the insight is, basically, is that the illegal population has a lot of churn[3] in it already, a lot of coming and going. And so, the solution is, reduce the number coming, increase the number going.
This is not just effected through border enforcement (...) It's also better enforcement at the worksite, et cetera, so that fewer new people come, more who are here, especially the more recently arrived, get the message that the party is over, and it's time for them to return home.
So that the result will be instead of the illegal population growing each year, the illegal population would start declining each year. This is a realistic approach to ...

annotations

[1] *think-tank* = a group of people who work together to produce new ideas on a particular subject

[2] *bait /beɪt/ and switch* = a sales tactic where a cheaply priced product is used to attract customers who are later expected to buy a similar, but more expensive product. In this case the "customer" referred to is the US immigration authorities

[3] *churn* = (here:) movement

Eliseo Medina: The immigration system is broken.

- It doesn't serve the interest of
  - → ______________
  - → *civic society*
  - → ______________
- In the system today we face the following problems
  - → ______________
  - → ______________
- It is crucial to fix the broken immigration system because
  - → ______________
  - → ______________

Should there be legalization of illegal immigrants?

Mark Krikorian

- What would happen after a legalization of immigrants?
  - *1.* ______________ → *result:* ______________
  - *2.* ______________ → *result:* ______________
- Responsible approach
  - *Not:*
    - → ______________
    - → ______________
  - *But:*
    - *Solution* → ______________
    - *How is this done?* → ______________
    - *Result: illegal population will* → ______________

Speaking

D3 Hold a panel discussion on the topic of "Immigration Challenges". The participants are: Farhad, Ria, an illegal immigrant from Asia, Lily Casey and the host. Read through this theme again and look for any points that might help you to present the position of your character. Note down any ideas you want to include.
⇨ skills: how to hold a panel discussion, pp. 117 – 118

Put yourself in the position of the **host** of the panel discussion who is chairing the discussion.

You should start the discussion and make sure you keep it moving. Prepare to ask other participants questions. It may be necessary to get them to explain points or clarify their positions if you can't understand what they are talking about.

The discussion should include the following parts.

Part 1: Participants introduce themselves and briefly talk about the challenges they have/had to face.
Part 2: Topic – Greatest challenges for immigrants and migrants.
Part 3: Topic – Do the United States still need immigrants and what should be done about illegal immigration?

Put yourself in the position of one of the **Asians in the truck** (an illegal immigrant) who has just arrived in L.A.

During the panel discussion you will have to:
1. introduce yourself and describe your reasons for leaving home
2. describe the challenges you are facing and the choices you have
3. criticize common points of views of immigration/immigrants
4. defend your desire for permanent residency and citizenship

Put yourself in the position of the Iranian shopkeeper, **Farhad**, a first generation immigrant and prepare for the panel discussion.

During the panel discussion you will have to:
1. introduce yourself and describe the challenges you are facing and the choices you have
2. criticize commonly held opinions about immigration/immigrants
3. state your opinion on illegal immigration

Put yourself in the position of an elderly **Lily** (Half Broke Horses). You will reflect on your history of migration and your family's ancestry.

During the panel discussion you will have to:
1. introduce yourself and describe your past challenges as a migrant as opposed to current challenges for immigrants
2. assess common points of view of immigration/immigrants
3. state your opinion on illegal immigration

Put yourself in the position of **Ria**, a policewoman of Hispanic origin and prepare for the panel discussion.

During the panel discussion you will have to:
1. introduce yourself and describe your situation as a Hispanic policewoman
2. criticize commonly held opinions about immigration/immigrants
3. state your opinion on illegal immigration

A1 Fill out the mind map using the words below. Look up the words you don't know.
Add any other words you can think of.

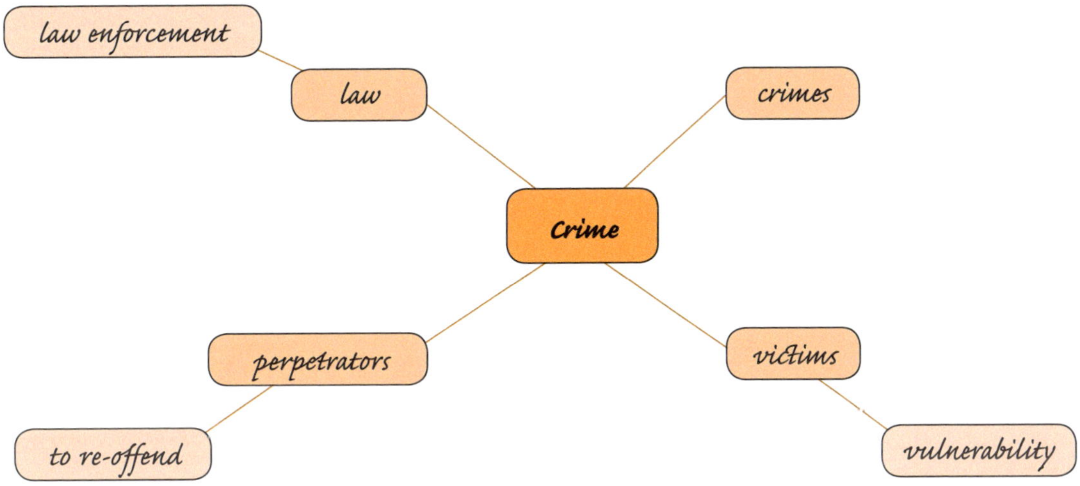

unknown suspect / investigation / assault / police department / to go into hiding / ~~law enforcement~~ / fraud / to arrest so. / brawl / to convict so. / to commit a crime / to conduct searches / ~~to re-offend~~ / to be attacked / to be threatened / thug / to protect so. / violation of the law / ~~vulnerability~~ / fire-arms / ammunition / to be traumatized / to be sentenced to / court / trial / to prevent a crime / intrude / to turn so. in / to be released / to release so. on bail / to take into custody

Mediation

A2 Read the following short articles and prepare to tell an American friend who doesn't know very much about Germany about your articles in English. Before you do that, underline the words and concepts that you think your friend won't understand and fill in the table below. ⇨ skills: how to mediate, p. 110

Einbruch bei EDEKA

1. In der Nacht zum Freitag ist ein Unbekannter in das Lager von EDEKA in Heilbronn eingebrochen und hat Leergut im Wert von ca. 500 Euro entwendet. Nach den bisherigen Ermittlungen der Polizei ist der Täter durch die Hintertür in das Lager gelangt und mit einem Lieferwagen der Marke Opel geflüchtet.

Nicht nur zu schnell gefahren

2. Nicht schlecht staunten zwei Beamte der Polizeiinspektion Stuttgart gestern. Sie wurden auf der Autobahn von einem VW Polo rechts überholt. Der Wagen fuhr 160 Stundenkilometer, obwohl nur 120 kmh erlaubt waren. Bei der anschließenden Kontrolle des Fahrers stellte sich dann die große Überraschung heraus – der Fahrer war erst 16 Jahre alt.

Polizeibericht: Schlägerei beim Fußballspiel

3. Beim Spiel zwischen dem VfB Stuttgart und dem Hamburger SV am vergangenen Samstag ging es nicht nur sportlich zu. Während des Spiels, das die Stuttgarter 2:0 gewannen, kam es laut Polizeibericht zu einer Schlägerei. Der Schläger – ein 38-jähriger Hartz IV Empfänger – wurde von der Polizei in Gewahrsam genommen.

Explosion am Zigarettenautomat

4. Ein 14-jähriger Realschüler ist in Werbach schwer verletzt worden, als er zusammen mit einem Bekannten am Samstag einen Zigarettenautomaten aufsprengen wollte. Durch die Wucht der Explosion wurde der Automat aus der Wandhalterung gerissen, durch die Luft geschleudert und stürzte dann auf den 14-jährigen, wie die Polizei in Tauber-Bischofsheim mitteilte.

Text	Word / Concept	Explanation	Does an American need the explanation / part of the explanation?
1	– *EDEKA* –	*German supermarket chain that mainly sells food and beverages*	*"supermarket" is sufficient*
2			
3			
4			

A3 Choose one police report and tell your American friend about the crime. Write down what you would say. You can use the mind map on page 51 for help.

A4 Read the following two texts that try to explain criminal behavior.

According to Roy F. Baumeister, a professor of psychology at Florida State University, there are four different causes of evil: instrumentality, threatened egotism, idealism and sadism.

Instrumentality: Evil acts are a means to an end. In order to get what they want some people turn to crime. What they want is typically not so different from what other people want. They want power, money, land and the like. If they cannot get what they want through legitimate means they commit criminal acts.

Threatened Egotism: Many criminals seem to have very favorable views of themselves. Baumeister believes that some people who think very positively of themselves become criminal if their image of themselves is being threatened or attacked. For them aggression and criminal acts are a strategy to deal with criticism and to avoid a loss of self-esteem.

Idealism: Criminals are motivated by the belief that they are doing something good. Idealists of both the left and the right have sometimes believed that their noble goals justify criminal means. The worst body counts of the twentieth century were perpetrated by people who believed that they were doing what was necessary to create a utopian society, whether this reflected a left-wing vision (as in the communist slaughters in China and the Soviet Union) or a right-wing one (as in the horrors perpetrated by Nazi Germany).

Sadism: Evil acts are motivated by the enjoyment of inflicting harm on others.

An important debate in the field of criminology is about the reasons why a person commits a crime. Over the years many different theories have emerged. Here are four of them.

The first one is the **rational choice theory**. According to this theory people weigh up costs and benefits of a crime. If the expected reward is higher than the potential risks (including getting caught and punished) a person commits a crime.

The **strain theory** says that while most people have similar desires they do not have the same abilities or opportunities. Those who fail to achieve their aspirations through socially accepted means - like hard work - may try to get what they want through crime.

According to the **social learning theory** people learn within a social context and role models are an important source of learning new behavior. Social behavior – including committing crimes – is supposed to be learned primarily by observing and imitating the actions of others. So if your role models commit crimes it is likely that you will adopt this behavior and become criminal yourself.

The **social control theory** assumes that if it weren't for controls that society places on individuals through institutions like churches, families, schools and workplaces people would commit crimes. So only social control prevents us all from becoming criminal.

A5 There are several crimes described in *Half Broke Horses* and *Crash*. Make a list of the crimes and discuss which of the theories above best explains the crime.

Crime	**Theory**
Half Broke Horses	
– *Lily selling bootleg alcohol*	*Rational Choice theory / Instrumentality*
–	
–	
Crash	
–	
–	
–	

Speaking

B1 a) Identify the crimes portrayed in the film stills. You can use the list in the word bank below.

b) Discuss the fears and insecurities that being exposed to the crimes in the film stills can cause in people.

Examples: fear of getting hurt, fear of losing one's belongings, loss of faith in law enforcement, fear of your children being exposed to negative influences ...

attempted murder -> fear of getting killed

word bank

homicide/murder = Mord	*robbery* = Raub	*sexual abuse* = sexueller Missbrauch
rape = Vergewaltigung	*housebreaking* = Einbruch	*attempted murder* = versuchter Mord
kidnapping = Entführung	*looting* = Plünderung	*drug abuse* = Drogenmissbrauch
theft = Diebstahl	*blackmail* = Erpressung	*hijacking* = Entführung von Dingen
willful damage of property = Sachbeschädigung	*to molest* = belästigen	*assault and battery* = Körperverletzung

B2 Talk about options individuals have to protect themselves. Use the pictures below.

B3 Imagine you are an American who has just moved into the suburb of a town in the United States. Your neighbor is a member of a neighborhood watch scheme and has asked you whether you would like to join the scheme. Read the following information about neighborhood watch schemes and write an email to your neighbor in which you explain your decision.

Neighborhood Watch

Decades ago crime rates across the US increased at an alarming pace. Citizens and law enforcement agencies focused on developing crime prevention programs to help reduce this growing trend. In 1972 The National Sheriff's Association organized the National Neighborhood Watch Program. This pilot program was funded by the Law Enforcement Assistance Administration of the US Department of Justice and was designed to enlist the participation of citizens with law enforcement to help reduce and prevent crime. Since then Neighborhood Watch has become one of the most effective means of fighting crime in our communities. This is because you and your neighbors are the ones who really know what is going on in your area, most likely to be the first to see a crime and call for help, and are in the best position to: (1) Report code violations, unsafe street conditions, etc. that degrade the quality of life in your area, (2) Take property owners to small claims court to abate nuisances, (3) Keep your block clean and free of graffiti, and (4) Provide a safe environment for your children.

What Is Neighborhood Watch?
Neighborhood Watch is a crime prevention program that enlists the active participation of residents in cooperation with law enforcement to reduce crime, solve problems, and improve the quality of life in your area. In it you will get to know and work with your neighbors, and learn how to:

- Recognize and report crimes and suspicious activities
- Protect yourself, your family, and your property,
- Protect your neighbor's family and property, and
- Identify crime and disorder problems in your area and work with SDPD[1] personnel to solve them.

[1] San Diego Police Department

B4 Look at the picture below and discuss whether you would like to live in a gated community like this.

Mediation

B5 a) Read the text on page 57 about gated communities. Imagine you have to tell an American friend about the article. Take notes on aspects you have to mention and aspects you can leave out.

Aspects you can leave out	Aspects you have to mention
Information about gated communities in Russia.	*Some neighbors in Germany are hostile towards gated communities.*

b) Go through the text again and underline words and concepts your American friend is probably not familiar with. Fill in the table below with your words and explanations.

word/concept	explanation

c) Compare your results with a partner.

22. Oktober 2009

Gated Communities: Todsicher in der Isolation

Von Julian Heissler, Spiegel Online 22.10.2009

In Deutschland etabliert sich eine neue Wohnform für Wohlhabende - Gated Communities und abgeschottete Stadthäuser. Sie bieten ihren vermögenden Einwohnern das Gefühl von Sicherheit: „Alles, was die Polizei empfiehlt, haben wir."

[...] Auch im alternativen Stadtteil Kreuzberg können sich die Besserverdienenden mittlerweile hinter dicke Mauern zurückziehen. Im „Carloft" in der Reichenberger Straße nehmen die Bewohner ihr Auto per Aufzug direkt mit in ihre Wohnung. In einer Gegend, in der dieses Jahr schon mehrfach Oberklasselimousinen in Flammen aufgegangen sind, ein mögliches Kaufargument.

Die Bauherren spielen mit der Furcht vor der Straße: „Angst vor Übergriffen ist für Sie Vergangenheit", heißt es auf der Webseite des Unternehmens. „Gefährdete Personen kommen direkt und ohne auszusteigen sicher in ihr Loft."

Widerstand gegen bewachten Wohnraum

Bisher wurden erst sieben der elf Wohnungen verkauft. Vielleicht auch, weil die Nachbarn dem Haus offen feindselig gegenüber stehen. Erst kürzlich gab es wieder eine Demonstration. Motto: „Carlofts zur Ruine machen!" Und nicht nur in Kreuzberg regt sich Widerstand gegen die bewachten Wohnräume.

Gerade die linke Szene sieht in den Reichenfestungen die hässlichste Ausdrucksform der sogenannten Gentrifizierung[1]. Farbanschläge und Demonstrationen begleiten die Neubauten der Luxuswohnanlagen - wohl auch, weil das Phänomen in Deutschland noch neu ist.

In anderen Ländern sind Gated Communities dagegen längst gang und gäbe. In den USA stehen mittlerweile über 40.000 überwachte Anlagen. Doch nicht nur dort ist die Wohnform verbreitet. Seit rund 30 Jahren gehören Gated Communities zum Bild südamerikanischer Städte. In Südafrika sind sie gerade seit dem Ende der Apartheid bei der weißen Bevölkerung beliebt. Und auch in Russland zieht sich die reiche Oberschicht zunehmend aus Städten zurück und sucht ihr Glück in umzäunten Wohnvierteln vor den Toren der Metropolen.

„Zunehmende Polarisierung"

„In Deutschland sind Gated Communities ein Ausdruck der zunehmenden Polarisierung zwischen Arm und Reich", sagt Ulrich Vogel-Sokolowsky, Soziologe an der Universität Bielefeld. „Die gesellschaftlichen Schichten haben sich in den vergangenen 40 Jahren voneinander entfernt." Diese zunehmende Distanz verursache bei den Eliten das Gefühl einer Bedrohung, die es „in dieser Form aber gar nicht gibt", wie die Statistik belege.

So ging die Zahl der Wohnungseinbrüche in Deutschland laut Bundeskriminalamt in den vergangenen zehn Jahren um fast ein Drittel zurück. Trotzdem bleibt Sicherheit das wichtigste Verkaufsargument für die bewachten Wohnräume.

[1] Gentrifizierung = Aufwertung eines Stadtteils durch dessen Sanierung oder Umbau mit der Folge, dass die dort ansässige Bevölkerung durch wohlhabenden Bevölkerungsschichten verdrängt wird.

d) Write down what you would tell your friend. ⇒ skills: how to mediate, p. 110

C1 Use the pictures to explain what options societies and governments have to protect people and discuss the effectiveness of the different approaches. Rank them from most to least effective in the diagram below.

1. Law enforcement / police presence

2. Social work

3. Boot Camps

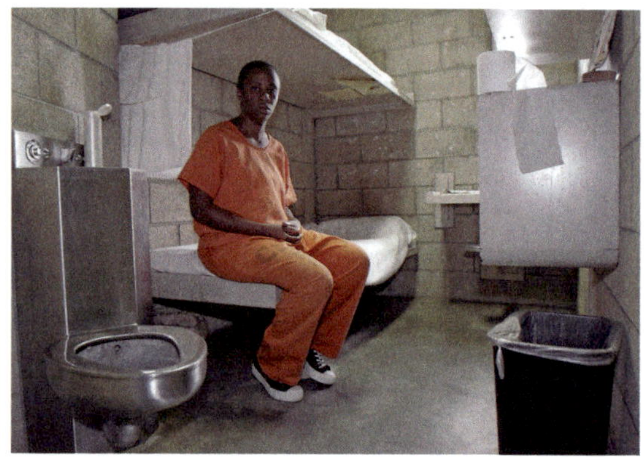

4. Prison

Most effective

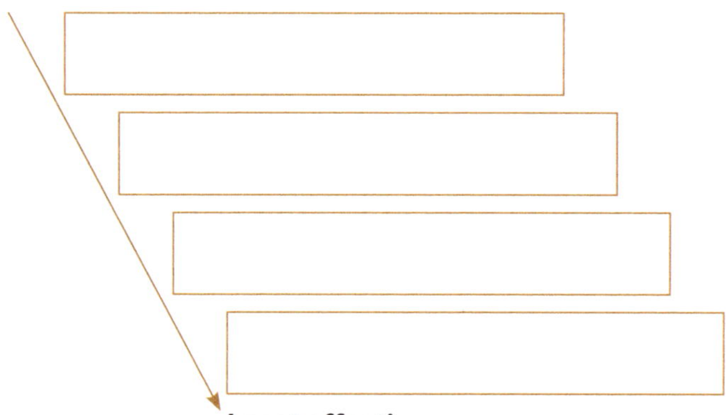

Least effective

C2 Discuss if imprisonment is an adequate way of dealing with crime. Consider the following statements/questions:

Criminals in prison cannot commit crimes.

What happens once a criminal gets released?

Society has to respect the dignity of the criminal

Info Boot camp

Boot camps are offered as a quick-fix solution for the parents of troubled teenagers. The programs use some of the same techniques as military recruit training camps. The principle is that the shock of incarceration and the rigorous activities that the children are forced to participate in will foster a respect for authority, a sense of discipline, an awareness of boundaries and an overall improvement in behavior.
However, the programmes used in private boot camps are not without controversy and there are strong doubts over their effectiveness. Research has not shown that boot camps succeed in any of their initial intentions and boot camp participants have a similar re-offending rate to former prison inmates. Although some surveys claim lower re-offence rates, others show no change when compared with offenders serving normal prison sentences. This inconsistency maintains the dispute, as supporters insist on the effectiveness of boot camps, while critics argue that that the emphasis on authority can be counter-productive, resulting in frustration, resentment, low self-esteem and increased aggression rather than respect.
Furthermore, the aggressive training has resulted in death in a number of circumstances. The New York Times reported that in 2001, there had been 31 known deaths of youths in U.S. boot camps since 1980.

Mediation

C3 You have just read a blog entry about boot camps in which the author praises boot camps as an effective means of dealing with young offenders. Open a new discussion thread in which you explain the different approach of Paidaia.

Der folgende Ausschnitt aus dem Artikel „Was in ihnen steckt" von Janette Otto aus der „Zeit" vom 06.06.2013 beschreibt die Arbeit des Vereins Paidaia, der mit jugendlichen Intensivtätern arbeitet.

Mit geballten Fäusten zogen sie, aneinandergereiht wie eine Mauer aus Wut und Gewalt, durch Ascheberg, eine 15.000-Seelen-Gemeinde im südlichen Münsterland. „Ein beschaulicher, wenig belasteter ländlicher Raum", wie Jugendamt und Polizei die Gegend beschreiben. Rote Backsteinhäuser, bunt bepflanzte Vorgärten, geringe Arbeitslosigkeit. Aber dann stand alle paar Tage ein neuer Artikel in der Lokalzeitung: Körperverletzung, Sachbeschädigung, Einbruch, Diebstahl, Raub, Beleidigung, Bedrohung, Waffen- und Drogenbesitz. Immer dieselben sieben steckten dahinter, sechs Jungen und ein Mädchen, zwischen 12 und 21 Jahren alt. Alle aus deutschen Familien. In ihrem Umfeld neun Mitläufer. 60 offiziell angezeigte Straftaten in etwas mehr als einem Jahr gingen auf das Konto der sieben „Intensivtäter", wie sie in Ascheberg schnell hießen – wobei die Polizei von weit mehr Vorfällen ausgeht. Wo sie auftauchten, wechselte man die Straßenseite, wo sie sich niederließen, wollte kein anderer sein. „Wir hatten immer Platz", sagt Marko.

[...]

In den vergangenen Jahren hat er [Ibrahim Ismail, Leiter des Vereins Paidaia] sich oft über die Rufe nach einem verschärften Jugendstrafrecht, stärkerem Durchgreifen und härteren Sanktionen geärgert. Er hält wenig davon, jugendliche Straftäter, egal, welcher Nationalität, in Box- oder Bootcamps umerziehen zu wollen, wo man vor allem auf Autorität und Disziplin setzt. Paidaia arbeitet auch mit Druck, klaren Ansagen und Selbstverpflichtungen, vor allem aber mit Achtung und Vertrauen.

„Die haben ganz normal mit uns geredet und wirklich zugehört", sagt Steven, dem es noch nicht oft passiert ist, dass ihn jemand ernst genommen hat. Gemeinsam mit den anderen hat er sich zu einer Art Seminar eingefunden. Sie reden über Jean-Paul Sartre. „Das Fremdbild wird irgendwann zum Selbstbild" steht unter einem Foto des Philosophen, das Ismail an die Wand projiziert hat. Er fragt in die Runde: „Was hat sich an eurem Selbstbild verändert?" – „Ich kann wieder durch die Straßen laufen, ohne dass die Leute einen großen Bogen um mich machen", sagt Steven. „Die Polizei ist nicht mehr mein Feind", sagt Marko.

„Ich war ein Arschloch"

Dass Bildung oder die „Stärkung der Geisteskraft", wie er es nennt, das Bewusstsein und damit die eigene Identität verändern kann, daran glaubt Ibrahim Ismail fest. Er kommt den Jugendlichen in seinen Vorträgen nicht nur mit Sartre. Er redet über Moral und Ethik, über Schopenhauer, Sokrates und Fromm. Und obwohl die Jugendlichen diese Namen noch nie gehört haben, erreicht er sie damit. Weil er es schafft, die Gedanken der Philosophen und Pädagogen auf ihr Leben in Ascheberg herunterzubrechen. „Es nützt ja nichts, Moralappelle von mir zu geben. Ich möchte, dass sie Erkenntnisse über sich selbst gewinnen und damit ihr Handeln verändern", sagt Ismail. Der erste Schritt in ein neues Leben beginnt dabei oft schmerzhaft: Das Paidaia-Team hält den Jugendlichen den Spiegel vor und fragt: Was hast du bisher gemacht, was hast du erreicht? Es sei hart, mit der Armseligkeit des eigenen Daseins konfrontiert zu werden. „Ich bin ein Monster", haben manche Jugendliche gesagt. „Mich liebt niemand", „Ich war ein Arschloch". – „In diesem Moment aber sagen wir ihnen: Wir sind an eurer Seite, wir helfen euch da raus." Ein zäher, aufreibender Prozess war das, der nicht nur einmal kurz vor dem Aus stand.

[...]

Kriminell aufgefallen sind sie nicht mehr. „Die Straftaten innerhalb der Gruppe sind auf nahezu null gesunken", sagt der zuständige Kriminalkommissar Thomas Hummels. „Ich war skeptisch und dachte nicht, dass eine so schnelle Trendwende möglich ist." Es habe sich aber gezeigt, wie empfänglich die Jugendlichen für Menschen seien, die sich intensiv um sie kümmerten.

Die große Nähe zu den Teammitgliedern von Paidaia war für die Jugendlichen der entscheidende Unterschied zu allen Hilfen, die man ihnen bis dahin angeboten hatte. Zum ersten Mal waren da Menschen, die mehr als nur ihre Defizite sahen. Marko sagt über seine Bezugsperson Hassan, er sei wie ein Vater für ihn geworden. „Die größte Strafe wäre es für mich, wenn Hassan mich nicht mehr besuchen würde."

C4 a) Read the following extract from *Half Broke Horses* and describe the influence that the radio has on Lily's life.

I worried constantly that someone might snatch my purse and make off with the check, so I kept the bag clutched to my chest when I walked through town. That was only one of a number of things I found myself worrying about in Phoenix. We had bought ourselves a radio that we could listen to all day long now that we were living in a house wired for electricity. At first I thought that was just grand, but it meant that for the first time I was also listening to the news every day, and about every day, it seemed, there was a report about some crime or another in town. People were always getting robbed or having their cars stolen or their houses burgled if they weren't getting raped, shot, or stabbed. A Phoenix woman named Winnie Ruth Judd – known as the "Blonde Butcher" and the "Trunk Murderess" because she'd killed two people and put their bodies in her luggage – kept escaping from the insane asylum she'd been sent to, and the news was always filled with accounts of possible Trunk Murderess sightings, along with warnings to the citizenry to lock all doors and windows. So I kept my pearl-handled revolver under my bed. I also bought a little twenty-two pistol to carry in my purse along with the check. Every night I made a point of bolting the doors, which we had never done at the ranch, and I slept on the outside of the bed I still shared with Rosemary, keeping her next to the wall so if anyone got through the locked doors and attacked us, I could fight them off while Rosemary escaped. "Mom, you've become such a worrywart," she said. Rosemary was right. On the ranch, we worried about the weather and the cattle and horses, but we never worried about ourselves. In Phoenix people worried about themselves all the time.

(Jeannette Walls: Half Broke Horses, Diesterweg Verlag, p. 280-1)

b) Join these jumbled sentence halves so that they make sense.

1. Lily heard about all the crime that occurred in Phoenix	because her house was wired for electricity.
2. In Phoenix people worried about themselves all the time	in case an attacker broke into the house.
3. She was able to listen to the radio at home all day	but on the ranch Lily's family only worried about the weather and the animals.
4. When she was in town Lily held her bag very close to her	in case someone tried to grab it and run away.
5. Lily kept her gun under her bed	because she listened to the news reports every day.

C5 Discuss if a general ban on reports about crimes would be better for society. Prepare by listing arguments.
⇨ skills: how to write an argumentative essay, pp. 125 – 126

Pro:	**Con:**

D1 Discuss what the pictures, texts and diagrams on pages 61 – 62 tell you about gun culture in the United States.

The 2nd Amendment

A well regulated militia, being necessary to the security of a free state, the right of the people to keep and bear arms, shall not be infringed.

Figure 1: Do you have a gun in your home?

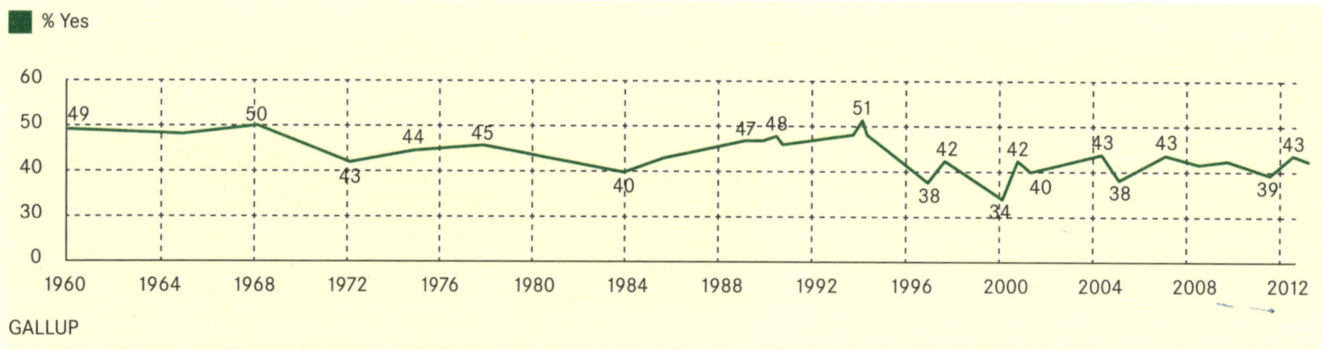

Figure 2: In general, do you feel that the laws covering the sale of firearms should be made more strict, less strict, or kept as they are now?

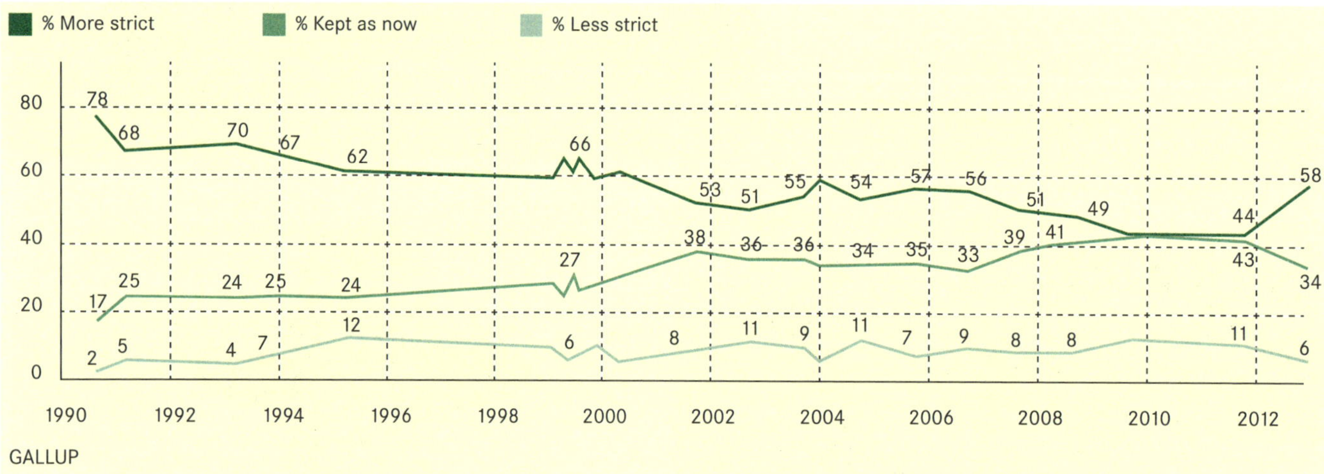

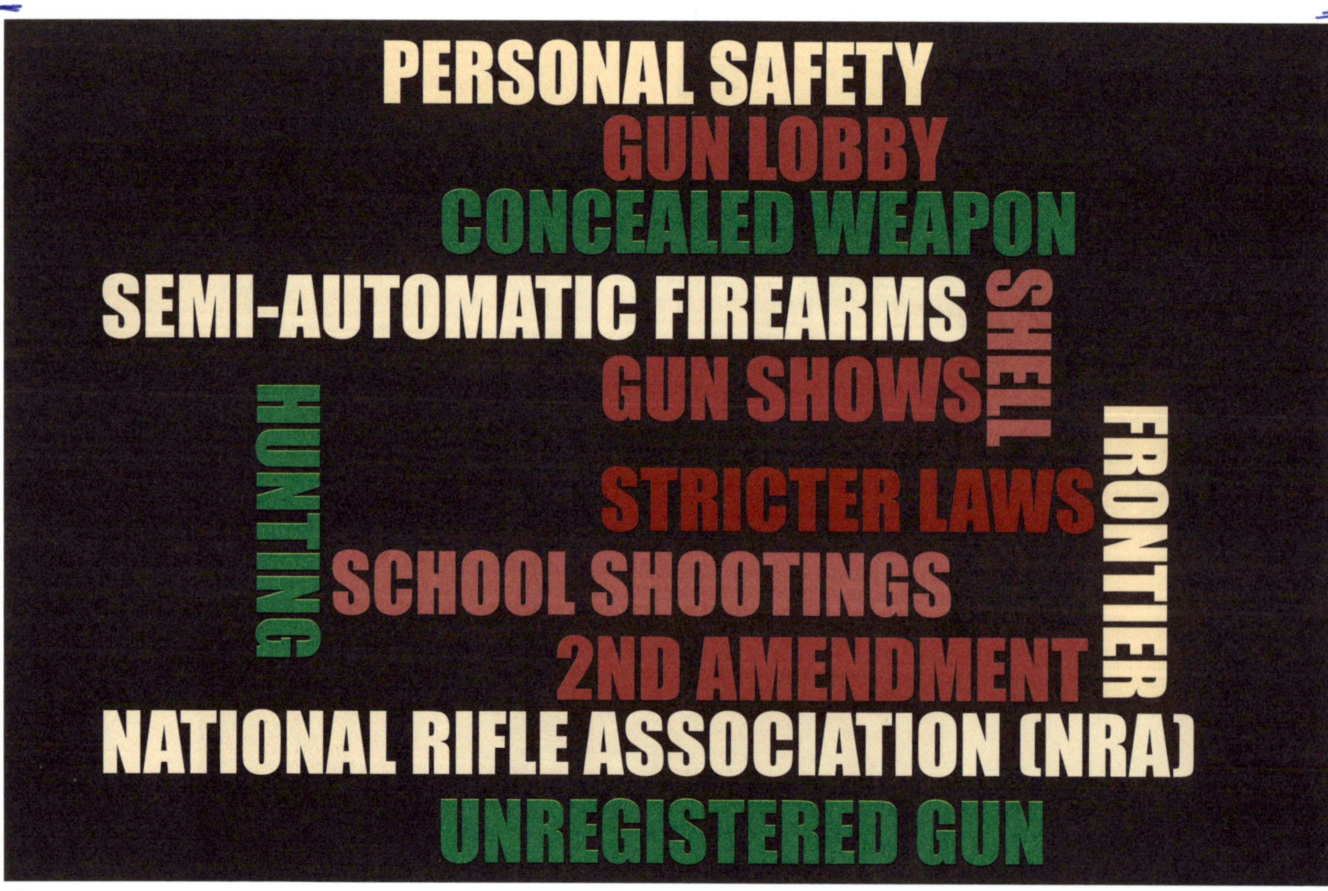

Speaking

D2 You are going to take part in a panel discussion on the following question:
"Does owning guns increase people's security?"
Study the material below and read through this theme again to find arguments for the discussion.
→ skills: how to hold a panel discussion, pp. 117 – 118

> Restrictive licensing of handguns was associated with a prompt decline in homicides and suicides by firearms in the District of Columbia. No such decline was observed for homicides and suicides in which guns were not used, and no decline was seen in adjacent metropolitan areas where restrictive licensing did not apply. Our data suggest that restrictions on access to guns in the District of Columbia prevented an average of 47 deaths each year after the law was implemented.

New England Journal of Medicine; 1991; 325: p. 1615 – 1620

> The truth is that our society is populated by an unknown number of genuine monsters – people so deranged, so evil, so possessed by voices and driven by demons that no sane person can possibly ever comprehend them. They walk among us every day. And does anybody really believe that the next Adam Lanza isn't planning his attack on a school he's already identified at this very moment?

(from a speech by Wayne LaPierre, Executive Vice-President of the National Rifle Association (NRA))

> As parents, we do everything we can to keep our children safe. It is now time for us to assume responsibility for their safety at school. The only way to stop a monster from killing our kids is to be personally involved and invested in a plan of absolute protection. The only thing that stops a bad guy with a gun is a good guy with a gun. Would you rather have your 911 call bring a good guy with a gun from a mile away ... or a minute away?

(from a speech by Wayne LaPierre)

> "I think everybody should have a gun. It levels the playing field."

(American citizen in "Armed America")

The Dangers Of Having A Gun In The Home

Posted in Uncategorized | July 13th, 2013

Although a gun is a way to keep your family safe, there are some dangers to having a gun in the house. If there are small children, they can possibly get the gun and accidentally shoot themselves or someone else. Teenagers in the home need to be monitored as well because if they know where the gun is, they can gain access to it and shoot someone in the home. Teenagers could also shoot themselves if they have depression issues. If someone tries to gain entrance in the home, then you have a way to shoot the person. The recent debate over gun safety has sparked more homeowners to keep guns in the home. This might be a good idea for someone who lives alone, but if you have a family, then you may want to rethink the decision.

Should civilian possession of handguns and other non-hunting guns be banned or severely restricted?

In a nutshell

Yes	No
1. Most violent crimes are committed with guns; thus, restricting gun ownership will likely reduce the number of such crimes. 2. Lunatics, bullied school kids, disgruntled workers, and others can inflict mass casualties with guns that otherwise wouldn't be possible. 3. A crime victim who has a gun may be in more danger than an unarmed person since the criminal may kill in perceived self-defense. 4. Suicides and crimes of passion are higher with gun availability, as it's much easier to act immediately on your impulses when a gun is available. 5. The 2nd Amendment of the Constitution was targeted towards militia, e.g. the National Guard, rather than individuals. 6. Crimes that may have been less harmful can be made more dangerous by adding a gun. 7. Legalized gun ownership means guns have a greater chance of falling into the hands of kids, potentially resulting in some deadly accidents. 8. Terrorism, school shootings, and other modern circumstances make guns more dangerous nowadays.	1. Criminals will always find a way to obtain their guns, leaving law-abiding citizens without any weapons to use in defense. 2. Crimes are often prevented by the deterrent effect of the possibility of victim gun possession. 3. The 2nd Amendment to the Constitution protects the individual's right to gun ownership. 4. Women and weaker individuals may have no means of self-defense from rape or other crimes, especially in the inner city. 5. Guns in the possession of citizens are an added protection against government tyranny. 6. Police are often too overwhelmed to protect all citizens from violent crime. 7. Banning guns will create another potentially large source of organized criminal revenue, as a black market for guns will surely develop. 8. Banning guns will take away yet another piece of our liberty, which is one more step to socialism and totalitarianism. 9. Reasonable gun control & education steps can be put in place, so an outright ban is unnecessary.

Put yourself in the position of a **spokesperson for the NRA (National Rifle Association)**. Your organization was founded in 1871 and since then has promoted the legal use of guns and gun safety in the U.S. and has defended U.S. citizens' constitutional right to own and bear firearms.
During the panel discussion you will have to
a) introduce yourself and the aims of your organization
b) bring forward arguments in favor of gun ownership
c) explain why you think legally owned guns are a contribution to people's security and well-being

Put yourself in the position of **Police Officer Hansen** from the Los Angeles Police Department (LAPD). Remember that he shot Peter Waters in a situation of perceived self-defense.
During the panel discussion you will have to
a) introduce yourself and the organization you work for
b) provide examples of situations in which firearms have been dangerous and in which they have been helpful
c) explain why you think guns in general are a threat to people's safety (in Britain even police officers are unarmed)

Put yourself in the position of a **father / mother whose child committed suicide with one of your guns**.
During the panel discussion you will have to
a) introduce yourself and your situation
b) explain why keeping guns in the house can be dangerous for your family and for yourself
c) why stricter gun laws would reduce the number of gun-related deaths and increase people's safety

Put yourself in the position of a **hunter and member of a gun club**.
During the panel discussion you will have to
a) introduce yourself and briefly explain why you enjoy shooting
b) bring forward arguments in favor of gun ownership
c) explain why stricter laws would have negative consequences for millions of law-abiding Americans who legally own guns

Put yourself in the position of **Dorri, Farhad's daughter**.
During the panel discussion you will have to
a) introduce yourself and briefly explain what happened to your father
b) argue in favor of stricter gun laws because of what your father did

Put yourself in the position of a **farmer**.
During the panel discussion you will have to
a) introduce yourself and your occupation
b) explain how guns help farmers and people in the country deal with wild animals (coyotes) that attack livestock (farm animals) or spread disease among livestock
c) explain why stricter gun laws would mean you risk losing a lot of livestock. Food prices would then have to increase as a result.

You are the **host** of the panel discussion.
You should start the discussion and make sure you keep it moving. Prepare to ask questions. It may be necessary to ask the participants to explain their points and positions. It may be helpful for the audience if you repeat the arguments that have been brought forward every once in a while.

A1 Read the following definitions of a myth. Assess to what extent these definitions apply to the pictures and the motto below. Then talk to a partner. You may use the words from the box at the bottom of the page as help.

> A myth is
> (i) something that many people believe in but that does not exist or is false
> (Oxford Advanced Learner's Dictionary)
>
> (ii) a popular belief or tradition that has grown up around something or someone; especially: one embodying the ideals and institutions of a society or segment of society
> (http://www.merriam-webster.com/dictionary/myth)

A2 Our image of the historical cowboy has been influenced by film, TV shows, dime novels and Wild West Shows. As a result, the figure of a cowboy is a mythical one. Describe other (American) myths you can think of.

> *individualistic, free, courageous, virile, strong, determined, selfish, independent, heroic, patriotic, lonely, selfless, good, powerful, brave, successful, disciplined, industrious, diligent, rugged*

Info The American Frontier

America seemed to offer people freedom, liberty and the chance of individuality. The Homestead Act of 1862 enabled anyone aged 21 or over, including immigrants, criminals, former slaves and single women, to own land there. An ever-increasing number of people were lured by the promise of this country that was so different from Europe and which offered unparalleled opportunity to so many. As a consequence, America's population continued to grow throughout the 19th century.

As more and more people arrived, there was an ever-increasing desire to explore the vast wilderness in the west. They wished to settle new territories and to bring them under their control, building new towns and expanding railways. However, the early settlers saw this as more than just a desire. They believed that they were God's chosen people. It was their right, their destiny and their duty to populate and possess the entire continent. This notion was known as "Manifest Destiny".

In addition to the moral obligation that the early settlers felt, the prospect of moving west was extremely attractive. The Homestead Act awarded applicants ownership of land at little or no cost. Under this law, a U.S. citizen could acquire 160 acres (about 64.75 hectares) of unoccupied land west of the Mississippi River and east of the Rocky Mountains simply by living on it for five years and making improvements to it. Thereafter, they could keep it. Between 1862 and 1934, about 10% of the total land in the United States was given to private owners in this way.

Despite the opportunities, the frontier which marked the border between civilization in the east and the lawlessness of the "Wild West" was often a difficult and inhospitable place to live. The way in which the settlers supposedly faced the challenges that arose from their choice to go westwards in search of a new life defined the ideals of American character and national mentality for decades. However, for many people the only source of their knowledge about life on the frontier was the idealized paintings of artists belonging to the Hudson River School, such as Albert Bierstadt, Frederic Edwin Church and Thomas Cole.

A3 a) People who lived at the frontier were often called pioneers. Talk to a partner about qualities that make people pioneers. Use the adjectives in the box below and agree on six characteristics.

curious, independent, clever, courageous, brave, rough, egoistic, strenuous, energetic, strong-willed, laid-back, conservative, relaxed, self-sufficient, traditional, coarse, self-reliant, self-restrained, determined, industrious, committed, eager, self-centered, self-assured, self-indulgent, inventive, creative, exceptional, class-conscious, heroic

b) Write a short definition:

A pioneer is someone who ______________________________

____

____

____

____

____

____

____

____

____

____

Speaking

A4 **Partner 1:** Study the painting on the left below and imagine you are one of the people in the painting who tells a friend about his life on the frontier. Write down keywords below. Prepare to tell your partner what you would say.

Thomas Cole, Home in the Woods, 1847

Emmanuel Leutze: Westward the course of the Empire takes its way, 1860

Partner 2: Study the painting on the right above and imagine you are one of the people in the painting who tells a friend about what kind of life he expects on the frontier. Write down keywords below. Prepare to tell your partner what you would say.

A5 Summarize the situations described in the texts and the photo. Focus on the challenges and insecurities faced by settlers living on the frontier.

May 8, 1880
Started early in the morning. Came past Colton and arrived at Sidney about noon, and camped with the intention of stopping over Sunday. Last night we had a shower and this morning was warm and pleasant; but after we were on the road awhile the wind commenced to blow, and I never saw a worse wind; the dust blew so that I could not see the wagon ahead of us. We could hardly see where to go. Sidney is, I think, the dirtiest town I ever saw; everything is thrown into the streets, and all around them the ground is covered with all kinds of cans, old shoes and dead cattle and horses, and everything you can think of. There is soldiers' barracks in this place – 1 company of Infantry and 2 companies of Cavalry. Saw several antelopes. Horse thieves in camp last night, and stampeded our horses, but did not get any; we were on the lookout for them.

Frank Stevens, Diary in:http://www.goldsbyfamily.info/frank_stevens_diary.ht

The tornado had missed the house, but it had plucked up the windmill and smashed it down on the roof. The house, made from wood that had already been busted apart once in that flood, was a total wreck. Dad started cussing up a blue streak. Life, he declared, had cheated him once again. "If I owned hell and west Texas," he said, "I do believe I'd sell west Texas and live in hell."

Jeannette Walls, Half Broke Horses, Diesterweg Verlag, p. 45

Lots of the folks homesteading in High Lonesome lived in dugouts because timber was so scarce in that part of Texas. Dad had made our home by shoveling out what was more or less a big hole on the side of the riverbank, using cedar branches as rafters and covering them over with sod. The dugout had one room, a packed earth floor, a wooden door, a waxed-paper window, and a cast-iron stove with a flue that jutted up through the sod roof.
The best thing about living in a dugout was that it was cool in the summer and not too cold in the winter. The worst thing about it was that, from time to time scorpions, lizards, snakes, gophers, centipedes, and moles wormed their way out of our walls and ceilings. [...]
Also, whenever it rained, the ceiling and walls in the dugout turned to mud. Sometimes clumps of that mud dropped from the ceiling and you had to pad it back in place.

Jeannette Walls, Half Broke Horses, Diesterweg Verlag, p. 19

challenges	*Extreme weather conditions*
insecurities	

A6 Compare and contrast the portrayal of the frontier in the paintings with the reality of life on the frontier as described in the texts and photos in A5. The following words may help you.

word bank

to mythologize = to construct or create a myth about sth.

to idealize = to consider or/and represent sth as being perfect

to distort = to twist or change facts and ideas so that they are no longer true

to exaggerate = make something seem larger, better, worse or more important

to portray events accurately = to show events the way they happened without exaggerating or distorting them

to deny = to say something is not true, to refuse to accept

Info The American Dream

In 1931, in the midst of the Great Depression, James Truslow Adams, an American historian, published a book called "The Epic of America", in which he dealt with what he described as the "American Dream". The concept itself had existed long before Adams and stood in stark contrast to the European concept of social hierarchy at that time (Ständegesellschaft). As early as 1630, John Winthrop envisioned his idea of a "city upon the hill", a city in which everybody had the chance to prosper and succeed in life, in a sermon to his fellow Puritan colonists. And in 1776, The Declaration of Independence emphasized the idea of everybody being entitled to "life, liberty and pursuit of happiness". Since 1931 the term has become a catchphrase for the lure and the promise of the new continent - whether it is real or simply a myth.

James Truslow Adams, The Epic of America

If (...) the things already listed were all we had had to contribute, America would have made no distinctive and unique gift to mankind. But there has been also the American dream, the dream of a land in which life should be better and richer and fuller for every man, with opportunity for each according to his ability or achievement. It is a difficult dream for the European upper classes to interpret adequately, and too many of us ourselves have grown weary and mistrustful of it. It is not a dream of motor cars and high wages merely, but a dream of a social order in which each man and each woman shall be able to attain to the fullest stature of which they are innately capable, and be recognized by others for what they are, regardless of the fortuitous circumstances of birth or position.

B1 From the sentences below, choose the one that sums up best what the paragraph is about.
The paragraph, from James Truslow Adams' The Epic of America, published in 1931, describes the "American Dream".

i) This is a society in which everyone has the opportunity to earn as much money as possible.
ii) This is a society in which everyone should realize their true potential in order to live as full a life as possible.
iii) This is a society in which people from lower social classes should be able to get to the top.

B2 a) The following word cloud includes aspects often associated with the American Dream. Work with a partner and agree on the five most important aspects for a successful life for both of you.

b) Identify any concepts in the word cloud that are represented in the painting *Stepping into the American Dream* by Xavier Cortada

B3 How can one achieve the different aspects of the American Dream? The following terms describe characteristics that were regarded as essential for a young person to have in order to succeed in life. Match the words from the box with the definitions in the table below.

> *perseverance – temperance – prudence – integrity – economy – courage – industry – punctuality – morality - honesty*

economy	the use of time, money, etc. that is available in a way that avoids waste
	the act of doing sth. at the arranged or correct time
	the ability to do sth. dangerous or face pain/oppression without showing fear
	the quality of continuing to try to achieve a particular aim despite difficulties
	a system of moral principles to be followed
	the practice of controlling your behavior, the amount you eat or drink etc. so that it is always reasonable
	the quality of always telling the truth and never stealing or cheating
	the quality of working hard
	the act of being sensible and careful when you make judgements and decisions, avoiding unnecessary risks
	the quality of being honest and having strong moral principles

B4 a) Describe and interpret the circled elements.

Ladder of Fortune, Nathaniel Currier and James Merritt Ives, 1875

book, sickle, apron, top hat
→ the different tools and clothing symbolize …

b) Summarize the message of the picture in two sentences.

B5 Explain what the quote below by Arnold Schwarzenegger tells you about the myth that is presented in the illustration above.

"Just remember, you can't climb the ladder of success with your hands in your pockets."

Info Arnold Schwarzenegger was born in Thal, Austria in 1947 into a rather poor family. He gained worldwide fame as a bodybuilding athlete, Hollywood actor and as governor of California.

Info **Occupy Wall Street** is a protest movement which began on September 17, 2011 as an organized protest in Zuccotti Park in New York City's Wall Street financial district and quickly spread to other cities across the US. The activists wanted to fight against corporate greed, the influence of corporations on government, social inequality, and the enormous gap between the rich and poor. Their protest slogan *We are the 99%* aims at showing the wealth distribution between the richest 1% and the rest of the population in the United States. The eviction of Zuccotti Park in November 2011 and various ensuing events led to worldwide media awareness. Protests have continued until today.

C1 Describe what impression of the movement you get from the pictures.

C2 Explain the idea of success as presented in the photos below and compare it with the illustration "Ladder of Success" by Currier and Ives.

C3 At a campaign stop on 29 November 2011, Newt Gingrich, a candidate for the 2012 Republican Party presidential nomination, commented on the Occupy movement saying:

"I repudiate, and I call on the president to repudiate, the concept of the 99 and the 1. It is un-American, it is divisive, it is historically false ..."

Using what you know about American myths and American realities, discuss this quote.

➩ skills: how to write an argumentative essay, pp. 125 – 126

Mediation

C4 **Situation**

You are staying in the US as an exchange student. Your social studies class has been working on the topic "Social mobility in the US". You have just read an article by Jana Simon, a German author, about her impressions of Los Angeles and are to give a presentation of her view of the American Dream.
Remember:
a) you are summarizing the author's, not your own opinion;
b) you are a guest in the USA.
Before you write down the text for your presentation, use the right-hand column to take notes in English on the relevant aspects mentioned by the author.

➩ skills: how to mediate, p. 110

Mein armes Amerika von Jana Simon, ZEITmagazin No44/2011

Los Angeles ist ein Ort, von dem jeder eine Vorstellung hat, und immer ist es eine angenehme. Wir haben L.A. in Hunderten Filmen gesehen. Surfer, Skater, Schauspieler – wir glauben die kalifornische Lebenskultur gut zu kennen. Unser Bild von L.A. ist von Hollywood geprägt: Sonne, Stars, Schönheit. Die westliche Welt hat L.A. als Ziel ihrer Sehnsüchte auserwählt. Die Stadt der Hoffnung, die Ruhm und Unsterblichkeit verleihen kann. Vielleicht ist es die amerikanischste aller Städte, weil hier der amerikanische Traum am intensivsten erstrebt wird. Und jeder hat das Gefühl, er kann mitreden, wenn es um L.A. geht, auch wenn er nie dort gewesen ist. Los Angeles ist die bekannte Unbekannte. Auch ich habe diese Vorstellungen von Luxus und Glamour verinnerlicht und bin mit meinem Mann und meiner Tochter gekommen, um sieben Monate in L.A., in den USA, zu leben, zu schreiben, zu arbeiten.

(...) Warum sind wir hier? Herr Schindler ist schuld, mein Geografielehrer an der Dr. Richard Sorge-Schule im Ost-Berlin der achtziger Jahre. In der neunten Klasse nahmen wir die USA durch, wir sahen Karten an, auf denen Bodenschätze verzeichnet waren, und dann zeigte Herr Schindler uns Dias von New York. Ich konnte meinen Blick nicht von den Hochhäusern lösen. Ich weiß nicht, ob Herr Schindler vorhatte, uns abzuschrecken und uns Wolkenkratzer als krasse Symbole des Imperialismus vorzuführen. Ich glaube eher, er empfand ähnlich wie ich. Mir stiegen Tränen in die Augen, mein Magen fühlte sich hohl an, der Tag war gelaufen. Ich hatte mich in den Klassenfeind verliebt.

(...) Meine erste große Reise nach dem Mauerfall machte ich 1991 nach New York. Ich war gerade 18. Meine Mutter war nicht begeistert, und ich durfte noch nicht einmal legal Alkohol trinken. Ich wohnte allein auf der Upper West Side in einer Wohnung von Freunden und ging, auch allein, auf ein Konzert im Central Park. New York war der Inbegriff der neuen Welt, der neuen Freiheit, meines neuen Lebens. Ich war im Rausch.

(...) Zwei Blocks von unserem Haus entfernt beginnt homeless country, das Land der Obdachlosen. Hunderte, Tausende Menschen in allen Stadien des Verfalls leben auf der Straße in Zelten. Sie sind krank, verrückt, auf Drogen oder anderweitig nicht mehr in der Lage, ein normales Leben zu führen. Als wir einmal morgens durch das Viertel fahren, können wir beobachten,

everybody has an idea of L.A.: it is always a pleasant one
our image of L.A. is characterized by stars, surfers, skaters

wie sich eine Stadt buchstäblich aus dem Asphalt erhebt. Manchmal liegen Menschen auch auf dem Bürgersteig, und es ist nicht klar, ob sie überhaupt noch leben. Aber niemand wählt 911.

Ich war oft in den USA und in vielen armen Ländern dieser Erde. Diesmal ist es anders, existenzieller. Immer wenn ich amerikanischen Bekannten erzähle, wie geschockt ich von der Armut in einem der reichsten Länder der Welt bin, in dem es als fast selbstverständlich gilt, dass Familien zwei riesige Autos zu fahren, schauen sie mich an, als erzählte ich etwas Unanständiges. Das Thema ist unangenehm, nicht Small-Talk-geeignet. Oft antworten sie, es liege an unserem Wohnort Downtown. Anderswo würden wir die Obdachlosen nicht so wahrnehmen. Aber das stimmt nicht, sie sind überall, selbst in Beverly Hills und am Strand. Freunde behaupten, dass viele Obdachlose auf der Straße leben wollten, es ihre eigene Entscheidung sei. Für mich klingt das wie ein Angriff auf meine Intelligenz. Zu Beginn habe ich auch die Plakate von Feeding America, der größten nationalen Organisation zur Bekämpfung des Hungers, für eine Kunstaktion oder die Vorankündigung einer historischen Ausstellung gehalten. Bis mir klar wurde: Das Zwanziger-Jahre-Design soll auf ein sehr gegenwärtiges Problem aufmerksam machen: Jeder sechste Amerikaner leidet tatsächlich Hunger.

(...) Je länger ich in den Vereinigten Staaten, in Los Angeles, bin, desto mehr bekomme ich das Gefühl, dass eine Gemeinschaft, wie ich sie kenne, hier nicht mehr existiert. Die amerikanische Idee basierte immer auf der Freiheit des Einzelnen, nicht auf Gleichheit, nicht auf Solidarität. Das funktioniert, solange es dem Land gut geht. Wenn es in eine Krise gerät, wie jetzt, pervertiert dieses Freiheitsprinzip. Das soziale Gewissen wird ausgelagert, privaten Stiftungen und Wohltätigkeitsvereinen überlassen.

Los Angeles ist eine Ansammlung von Individuen, die nebeneinanderher leben. Das Zentrum des Narzissmus.

(...) Die Bindungslosigkeit hat auch etwas Rauschhaftes. Es ist egal, ob man sich trifft oder nicht. Für nichts ist man verantwortlich, nur für sich selbst. Es ist das Gefühl der totalen Freiheit. Nur scheint es den Amerikanern dabei nicht besonders gut zu gehen. Noch nie habe ich so viele Anzeigen für Antidepressiva gesehen, als versinke eine ganze Stadt in Schwermut. Die Träume in L.A. sind intensiv – wenn sie sich nicht erfüllen, darf man kein Mitleid erwarten.

(...) Auf der Suche nach dem Glamour mache ich mich auf den Weg nach Hollywood. Der Hollywood Boulevard empfängt mich graugesichtig, am Walk of Fame bieten Ramschläden Levi's-Jeans an, ein paar bemitleidenswerte Gestalten haben sich als Batman und Mickey Mouse verkleidet, an ihnen donnern die Autos vorbei. Das Kodak Theatre, der Oscar-Palast, ist in Wirklichkeit ein Einkaufscenter, in dem viele Läden leer stehen. Es kommt der Augenblick, in dem ich das Gefühl habe, mich in einem einzigartigen Fake, in einer Scheinwelt zu bewegen. Eine riesige Werbe-Medien-Maschine vermarktet seit Jahren etwas, das es so nicht gibt. Die Studios sitzen bis auf eines schon längst nicht mehr in Hollywood. L.A. lebt mit dem glanzvollen Bild von einst und hat beschlossen, nicht mehr in den Spiegel zu blicken.

(...) Für viele wäre es schlicht nicht auszuhalten, wenn sich alle ihre Anstrengungen als sinnlos erwiesen. Wenn sich herausstellte, dass der Amerikanische Traum gar nicht so traumhaft ist.

(...) Als wir nach sieben Monaten USA im Sommer nach Berlin zurückkehren, wirkt die Stadt im Vergleich zu Los Angeles wie ein Ferienort – die Berliner verbringen endlose entspannte Tage draußen in Straßencafés, genießen genetisch unbedenkliches Essen und viel Wein. Ein paar Wochen später beginnen in New York die Anti-Wall-Street-Demonstrationen. Im Fernsehen sehe ich nun Amerikaner, die in Schlafsäcken im Zuccotti-Park mitten im Börsenviertel kampieren und gegen die soziale Ungerechtigkeit protestieren. Ein Bild prägt sich mir besonders ein: An einem Zaun hängt ein Plakat, es ist ein wenig zerfleddert und vom Regen durchweicht, »Kapitalismus funktioniert nicht« steht darauf. Die Ratlosigkeit ist niederschmetternd. Ich habe schon einmal miterlebt, wie ein System untergegangen ist, nur was sollte diesmal die Alternative sein?

D1 Read the extracts from the speeches by Bill Clinton and Barack Obama below and complete the tasks on page 77.

Clinton and Obama on American myths and realities

My fellow Americans, all of us in this grand hall and everybody watching at home, when we vote in this election, we'll be deciding what kind of country we want to live in. If you want a winner-take-all, you're-on-your-own society, you should support the Republican ticket. But if you want a country of shared opportunities and shared responsibility, a we're-all-in-this-together society, you should vote for Barack Obama and Joe Biden.
(...) And if you think – if you think the president was right to open the doors of American opportunity to all those young immigrants brought here when they were young so they can serve in the military or go to college, you must vote for Barack Obama. If you want a future of shared prosperity, where the middle class is growing and poverty's declining, where the American dream is really alive and well again, and where the United States maintains its leadership as a force for peace and justice and prosperity in this highly competitive world, you have to vote for Barack Obama.
Look, I love our country so much. And I know we're coming back. For more than 200 years, through every crisis, we've always come back. People have predicted our demise ever since George Washington was criticized for being a mediocre surveyor with a bad set of wooden, false teeth. And so far every single person that's bet against America has lost money, because we always come back. We've come through every fire a little stronger and a little better. And we do it because, in the end, we decide to champion the cause for which our founders pledged their lives, their fortunes, their sacred honor, the cause of forming a more perfect union.

Bill Clinton, *Speech at the Democratic National Convention on September 5, 2012.*

For we, the people, understand that our country cannot succeed when a shrinking few do very well and a growing many barely make it. We believe that America's prosperity must rest upon the broad shoulders of a rising middle class. We know that America thrives when every person can find independence and pride in their work; when the wages of honest labor liberate families from the brink of hardship. We are true to our creed when a little girl born into the bleakest poverty knows that she has the same chance to succeed as anybody else, because she is an American; she is free, and she is equal, not just in the eyes of God but also in our own. (...)
We, the people, declare today that the most evident of truths – that all of us are created equal – is the star that guides us still; just as it guided our forebears through Seneca Falls, and Selma, and Stonewall; just as it guided all those men and women, sung and unsung, who left footprints along this great Mall, to hear a preacher say that we cannot walk alone; to hear a King proclaim that our individual freedom is inextricably bound to the freedom of every soul on Earth.
It is now our generation's task to carry on what those pioneers began. For our journey is not complete until our wives, our mothers and daughters can earn a living equal to their efforts. Our journey is not complete until our gay brothers and sisters are treated like anyone else under the law – for if we are truly created equal, then surely the love we commit to one another must be equal as well. Our journey is not complete until no citizen is forced to wait for hours to exercise the right to vote. Our journey is not complete until we find a better way to welcome the striving, hopeful immigrants who still see America as a land of opportunity – until bright young students and engineers are enlisted in our workforce rather than expelled from our country. Our journey is not complete until all our children, from the streets of Detroit to the hills of Appalachia, to the quiet lanes of Newtown, know that they are cared for and cherished and always safe from harm.
That is our generation's task – to make these words, these rights, these values of life and liberty and the pursuit of happiness real for every American. Being true to our founding documents does not require us to agree on every contour of life. It does not mean we all define liberty in exactly the same way or follow the same precise path to happiness.

Barack Obama, *Second Inaugural Address, January 21, 2013*

a) Complete the sentences.

(i) In his speech, Bill Clinton
- ☐ favors the idea of individualism.
- ☐ encourages people to climb the ladder of success.
- ☐ calls for a society in which people feel responsible for each other.

l. ____________________

(ii) Bill Clinton tells his audience to
- ☐ vote Republican if they are in favor of the new immigration policy.
- ☐ vote for Obama if they are willing to share their wealth with others.
- ☐ vote for Obama if they believe in self-sufficiency, self-reliance and competition.

l. ____________________

b) True or false? Tick the correct answer.
Do not forget to support your choice with evidence from the text. Write down the line numbers.

In his speech Obama ...	true	false
says that the number of poor people is declining and the number of rich people is growing. l. _______		
demands that work should be adequately paid for. l. _______		
shows his solidarity with homosexuals. l. _______		
says that their shared past asks for everyone to be of the same opinion. l. _______		

D2 a) Underline aspects of American myths that Clinton and Obama criticize and the aspects they want to revive. Use different colors to do so.
b) Explain what kind of society Clinton and Obama envision. In your answer refer to American myths and American realities.

D3 Discuss if the American Dream is reality or just a myth.
⇨ skills: how to write an argumentative essay, pp. 125 – 126

Info **Abraham Harold Maslow** (April 1, 1908 – June 8, 1970) was an American psychologist and one of the founders of humanistic psychology. When working with monkeys he found out that certain needs for them take precedence over others. In 1943, on the basis of his observations, he published a paper entitled "A Theory of Human Motivation" in which he outlined this theory of a "hierarchy of needs". He used five different needs that he regarded as being fundamental for human beings wanting to exploit their full potential. Those needs can be divided into two different groups: on the one hand the so-called survival or deficit needs which stem from a lack of something and which need to be satisfied if negative feelings are to be avoided, and on the other hand the being-needs which stem from a desire to grow as a person and are therefore also called growth needs.

A1 a) Have a look at the needs identified by Maslow and decide on your own hierarchy of needs. Write down the needs in the pyramid below. Give reasons for your choice.

esteem needs: achievement, status, reputation, respect of others etc.

safety needs: protection, physical security, health and property, order, law, steady employment, stability etc.

biological and physiological needs: food, water, air, shelter, warmth, sleep etc.

belongingness and love needs: family, friendship, sexual intimacy, work group, etc.

self-actualisation: morality, creativity, problem solving, personal growth, self-fulfillment etc.

b) Exchange your results with a partner. Together discuss which needs can be met by the individual on his/her own and which needs can only be met if others are involved.

word bank

to find personal fulfillment · to be held in high esteem by so. · to meet a need/demand · to be provided with sth. · to live up to sth. · to enable so. to do sth. · to gain influence/power/access · to achieve an aim · to participate in sth. · basic requirement · to stem from sth.

A2 a) Read the following extracts and note down below each one what they tell you about the relationship between the individual and society/government.

Even before Old Man Pucket had shot the dogs, we'd had our differences. Like most folks on the Rio Hondo, he did what he could to get by, and if that meant encroaching on someone else's land or diverting a creek onto his property, he was prepared to do it. Dad called him a dirt farmer, but I thought of him as a scrapper who understood that sometimes, instead of asking another person's permission, you were best off doing what needed to be done, defending it with bluster, and then apologizing later – if and when it came to that. "Payment acknowledged," I said, and shook his hand. Unlike Dad, I saw no point in carrying a grudge with a neighbor. You never knew when you might need someone's help.

Jeannette Walls, Half Broke Horses, Diesterweg Verlag 2013, p. 67

I could tell life at the ranch was going to be a lot of hard work. We were too far from town to count on anyone else for anything. Jim and I would have to be our own veterinarian, farrier, mechanic, butcher, cook, as well as cattle driver, ranch manager, husband and wife, and mother and father of two little children. But Jim and I both knew how to roll up our sleeves, and in times like these, I knew how lucky we were not just to have work but to be our own bosses doing something we were good at doing.

Jeannette Walls, Half Broke Horses, Diesterweg Verlag 2013, p. 169

We the People of the United States, in order to form a more perfect Union, establish Justice, insure domestic Tranquility, provide for the common defense, promote the general Welfare, and secure the Blessings of Liberty to ourselves and our Posterity, do ordain and establish this Constitution for the United States of America.

American Constitution

We hold these truths to be self-evident, that all men are created equal, that they are endowed by their Creator with certain unalienable Rights, that among these are Life, Liberty and the pursuit of Happiness. – That to secure these rights, Governments are instituted among Men, deriving their just powers from the consent of the governed, – That whenever any Form of Government becomes destructive of these ends, it is the Right of the People to alter or to abolish it, and to institute new Government, laying its foundation on such principles and organizing its powers in such form, as to them shall seem most likely to effect their Safety and Happiness.

Declaration of Independence

Individuals must control their governments. Governments are supposed to serve and depend on individuals, not the other way round.

The right of the people to be secure in their persons, houses, papers, and effects, against unreasonable searches and seizures, shall not be violated, and no Warrants shall issue, but upon probable cause, supported by Oath or affirmation, and particularly describing the place to be searched, and the persons or things to be seized.

Bill of Rights, Fourth Amendment

b) The Founding Fathers of the United States, political leaders and statesmen who were the authors of the last three documents above, had thought long and hard about the ideal relationship between the individual and government. Assess their vision of an ideal community from your present day point of view taking into consideration what Maslow says about fundamental human needs.

Info **Ron Paul** is a Republican politician from Texas who served as U.S. Representative for Texas and sought the American presidency three times. In January 2013 he retired from service in Congress. The extract at hand is taken from his farewell address to Congress and can be seen as an example of the basic principles Paul stands for, especially the belief in unrestricted personal liberty, unregulated free markets, personal responsibility and a limited federal government.

A3 a) Read the extract of Ron Paul's Farewell Address to Congress, delivered on November 14, 2012, and summarize its contents in three sentences using the following words:

adherence – self-reliance – abuse of power – to deny so. sth. – to limit sth.

This may well be the last time I speak on the House Floor. At the end of the year I'll leave Congress after 23 years in office over a 36 year period. My goals in 1976 were the same as they are today: promote peace and prosperity by a strict adherence to the principles of individual liberty.

It was my opinion, that the course the U.S. embarked on in the latter part of the 20th Century would bring us a major financial crisis and engulf us in a foreign policy that would overextend us and undermine our national security. To achieve the goals I sought, government would have had to shrink in size and scope, reduce spending, change the monetary system, and reject the unsustainable[1] costs of policing the world and expanding the American Empire. (...)

I have a few thoughts as to why the people of a country like ours, once the freest and most prosperous, allowed the conditions to deteriorate[2] to the degree that they have. Freedom, private property, and enforceable voluntary contracts, generate wealth. In our early history we were very much aware of this. (...) The majority of Americans and many government officials agreed that sacrificing some liberty was necessary to carry out what some claimed to be "progressive" ideas. Pure democracy became acceptable. They failed to recognize that what they were doing was exactly opposite of what the colonists were seeking when they broke away from the British. (...)

Everyone claims support for freedom. But too often it's for one's own freedom and not for others. Too many believe that there must be limits on freedom. They argue that freedom must be directed and managed to achieve fairness and equality thus making it acceptable to curtail[3], through force, certain liberties. Some decide what and whose freedoms are to be limited. These are the politicians whose goal in life is power. Their success depends on gaining support from special interests.

The great news is the answer is not to be found in more "isms." The answers are to be found in more liberty which cost so much less. Under these circumstances spending goes down, wealth production goes up, and the quality of life improves. Just this recognition – especially if we move in this direction – increases optimism which in itself is beneficial. The follow through with sound policies are required which must be understood and supported by the people.

But there is good evidence that the generation coming of age at the present time is supportive of moving in the direction of more liberty and self-reliance. The more this change in direction and the solutions become known, the quicker will be the return of optimism. Our job, for those of us who believe that a different system than the one that we have had for the last 100 years, has driven us to this unsustainable crisis, is to be more convincing that there is a wonderful, uncomplicated, and moral system that provides the answers. We had a taste of it in our early history. We need not give up on the notion of advancing this cause. It worked, but we allowed our leaders to concentrate on the material abundance that freedom generates, while ignoring freedom itself. Now we have neither, but the door is open, out of necessity, for an answer. The answer available is based on the Constitution, individual liberty and prohibiting the use of government force to provide privileges and benefits to all special interests.

After over 100 years we face a society quite different from the one that was intended by the Founders. In many ways their efforts to protect future generations with the Constitution from this danger has failed. Skeptics, at the time the Constitution was written in 1787, warned us of today's possible outcome. The insidious[4] nature of the erosion of our liberties and the reassurance our great abundance gave us, allowed the process to evolve into the dangerous period in which we now live. (...)

Today we face a dependency on government largesse[5] for almost every need. Our liberties are restricted and government operates outside the rule of law, protecting and rewarding those who buy or coerce government into satisfying their demands. Here are a few examples: (...)

- The Patriot Act and FISA legislation passed without much debate have resulted in a steady erosion of our 4th Amendment rights.

- Tragically our government engages in preemptive war, otherwise known as aggression, with no complaints from the American people.
- The drone warfare we are pursuing worldwide is destined to end badly for us as the hatred builds for innocent lives lost and the international laws flaunted. Once we are financially weakened and militarily challenged, there will be a lot of resentment thrown our way.
- It's now the law of the land that the military can arrest American citizens, hold them indefinitely, without charges or a trial. (...)

Liberty can only be achieved when government is denied the aggressive use of force. If one seeks liberty, a precise type of government is needed. To achieve it, more than lip service is required.

Two choices are available.

1. A government designed to protect liberty – a natural right – as its sole objective. The people are expected to care for themselves and reject the use of any force for interfering with another person's liberty. Government is given a strictly limited authority to enforce contracts, property ownership, settle disputes, and defend against foreign aggression.
2. A government that pretends to protect liberty but is granted power to arbitrarily[6] use force over the people and foreign nations. Though the grant of power many times is meant to be small and limited, it inevitably metastasizes into an omnipotent political cancer. This is the problem for which the world has suffered throughout the ages. Though meant to be limited it nevertheless is a 100% sacrifice of a principle that would-be-tyrants find irresistible. It is used vigorously – though incrementally and insidiously. Granting power to government officials always proves the adage that: "power corrupts."

Once government gets a limited concession for the use of force to mold people's habits and plan the economy, it causes a steady move toward tyrannical government. Only a revolutionary spirit can reverse the process and deny to the government this arbitrary use of aggression. There's no in-between. Sacrificing a little liberty for imaginary safety always ends badly.

Today's mess is a result of Americans accepting option #2, even though the Founders attempted to give us option #1. (...) Ultimately, the people have to decide which form of government they want; option #1 or option #2. There is no other choice. Claiming there is a choice of a "little" tyranny is like describing pregnancy as a "touch of pregnancy." (...)

Our Constitution, which was intended to limit government power and abuse, has failed. The Founders warned that a free society depends on a virtuous and moral people. The current crisis reflects that their concerns were justified. (...) I have come to one firm conviction after these many years of trying to figure out "the plain truth of things." The best chance for achieving peace and prosperity, for the maximum number of people worldwide, is to pursue the cause of LIBERTY.

If you find this to be a worthwhile message, spread it throughout the land.

http://www.campaignforliberty.org/national-blog/transcript-of-farewell-address/

annotations

[1] *unsustainable* = untragbar, unhaltbar

[2] *to deteriorate* = to become worse

[3] *to curtail* = to limit sth. or make it last for a shorter time

[4] *insidious* = spreading gradually or without being noticed, but causing serious harm

[5] *largesse* = the act or quality of being generous with money

[6] *arbitrary* = willkürlich

b) Decide whether the following statements are true or false. Quote the exact lines from the text to support your answer.

	true	false
1. Ron Paul is an advocate of limited government. quote: "To achieve the goals I sought, government would have had to shrink in size and scope."	X	
2. Those politicians who believe that freedom needs restrictions only focus on their own interests. quote:		

3. Personal liberty and independence seem to be important for the younger generation. *quote:* ______________________ ______________________		
4. The government is law-abiding. *quote:* ______________________ ______________________		
5. The Founding Fathers emphasized the importance of self-reliance, the rejection of any forceful interference in other people's liberty and the limited authority of government *quote:* ______________________ ______________________		
6. There are times when it is necessary to limit liberty in order to increase safety. *quote:* ______________________ ______________________		

c) In his speech Paul claims that the relationship between the people and the federal government has developed in a way that was not intended by the Founding Fathers. Find five examples that Paul gives to support his claim. At the same time he mentions alternatives. Note them down too.

examples supporting his claim	**alternatives**
– *politicians whose goal in life is power (l. 36)*	– *government would have to shrink in size and scope (l. 12)*

d) The following text was written by a student whose task it was to analyze Ron Paul's speech.

(i) Read the analysis that has not been paragraphed. Mark the paragraphs in the text by using the following symbol ⌋. Note down the function of the different parts, e.g. introduction, first stylistic device, conclusion.
(ii) Highlight the stylistic devices and their effects mentioned in the analysis.
(iii) Use a different colour to highlight expressions that are useful for writing a speech analysis.

➩ skills: how to analyze a speech, pp. 119 – 121

Unrestricted personal liberty, unregulated free markets, personal responsibility and a limited authority of government are the themes Ron Paul, a Republican congressman from Texas, focuses on in the speech at hand. Delivered on 14 November 2012, it is his farewell address to Congress after a 36 year period in politics and is primarily addressed to the members of Congress. ⌋ *Since the fight for unrestricted personal liberty and limited influence of the government has been an important objective in his political career, he, for the last time, aims at convincing his fellow congressmen of the importance of these goals. Not only in his opening words but throughout his speech he emphasizes the importance of these goals as well as his continuing fight for them by comparing the current political situation with the vision the Founding Fathers had of society. He criticizes the restriction of liberty and a dependency on government largesse which, from his point of view, have brought the Americans a financial crisis and a loss of national security and finishes his speech by strongly recommending people to follow the "cause of liberty" (l. 140). Ron Paul uses different stylistic devices to convince his audience. The frequent use of personal pronouns such as "we" and "our" in sentences like "Our job ... is to be more convincing" (ll 51 – 55) or "We need not give up on the notion of advancing this cause" (ll. 57 – 58) establishes a feeling of togetherness, a group feeling. It is not only him, who is responsible for the course of the country, but it is everyone. When Paul alludes to events and famous people in the past, like he does in the following sentence: "They failed to recognize that what they were doing was exactly the opposite of what the colonists were seeking when they broke away from the British." (ll. 25 – 28), he can be sure of the audience's attention. The allusions are easily recognizable and remind his fellow congressmen of their responsibility for the country, especially when contrasting the goals of the Founding Fathers of the United States with present day politicians. He thereby triggers emotions and appeals to his listeners' conscience. The use of superlatives when referring to the nation in the past as "once the freest and most prosperous" (l. 17) emphasizes the contrast between past and present even more. Whereas words such as "deteriorate" (l. 18), "unsustainable" (ll. 13 – 14), "curtail through force" (ll. 33 – 34), "insidious" (l. 71) or "today's mess" (l. 125), which are used for current politics, carry negative connotations, the past is described in the most positive way. When reminding the audience of the Founders' warnings about the possible outcome of wrong priorities (ll. 66 – 71), their role as a model as well as the antithesis between past and present are once again emphasized. Since a speech is only heard once, the speaker needs to make a lasting impression by repeating certain terms or ideas that are central to it. For Paul the terms "liberty" and "freedom" are essential and therefore he constantly repeats them. But it is not only special words that he uses again and again, he also employs the group of three (or the so-called tricolon) to make his speech and its content more memorable. One example can be found in lines 40 – 42, where he claims: "Under these circumstances spending goes down(1), wealth production goes up(2), and the quality of life improves(3)." At the same time one might interpret this device as a climax, since the improvement of quality of life in general seems to be the most desirable goal. All in all, Paul focuses on the difference between past and present to make his audience aware of the problem the gradual loss of liberty brings. He displays strong conviction as well as passion for this topic and therefore is, from my point of view, quite convincing. The speech made me think about the degree of influence governments should have on our lives and how much liberty means to me.*

introduction

Info The following extract is taken from the novel "Falling Man" by Don DeLillo. It was published in May 2007 and tells the story of a survivor of the 9/11 attacks. Keith Neudecker is a lawyer working for an insurance company at the World Trade Center. He managed to escape from the collapsing building only slightly injured. The day has a lasting influence on his life – as a result of the traumatic experience he tries to reunite with his estranged wife but doesn't succeed. He starts an affair with a woman, who like he himself survived the attacks, turns to spending more and more of his time playing poker and finally becomes a professional player. The extract here presents the opening passage of the novel.

B1 a) "It was not a street anymore but a world, a time and space of falling ash and near night."
This is the sentence the novel "Falling Man" by Don DeLillo starts with. Explain what it tells you about the impact of 9/11.

b) Now read the extract and choose five adjectives from the box to describe the atmosphere conveyed in the text. Note them down in the box below and explain your choice. Exchange results with a partner. Together agree on five adjectives.

tense · hostile · cosy · thrilling · melancholic · desperate · intense · mysterious · hopeless · awkward · threatening · cold · friendly · eerie · unreal · quiet · alarming · chaotic · hectic · overwhelming · frightening · soothing · distant · nauseating

adjective	explanation
e.g. distant	*... because of the perspective chosen ("he"): the protagonist doesn't even have a name*

Extract from "Falling Man" by Don DeLillo

It was not a street anymore but a world, a time and space of falling ash and near night. He was walking north through rubble[1] and mud and there were people running past holding towels to their faces or jackets over their heads. They had handkerchiefs pressed to their mouths. They had shoes in their hands, a woman with a shoe in each hand, running past him. They ran and fell, some of them, confused and ungainly[2], with debris coming down around them, and there were people taking shelter under cars. The roar[3] was still in the air, the buckling rumble of the fall. This was the world now. Smoke and ash came rolling down streets and turning corners, busting around corners, seismic tides of smoke, with office paper flashing past, standard sheets with cutting edge, skimming, whipping past, otherworldly things in the morning pall. He wore a suit and carried a briefcase. There was glass in his hair and face, marbled bolls of blood and light. He walked past a Breakfast Special sign and they went running by, city cops and security guards running, hands pressed down on gun butts to keep the weapons steady. Things inside were distant and still, where he was supposed to be. It happened everywhere around him, a

car half buried in debris, windows smashed and noises coming out, radio voices scratching at the wreckage. He saw people shedding water as they ran, clothes and bodies drenched from sprinkler systems. There were shoes discarded in the street, handbags and laptops, a man seated on the sidewalk coughing blood. (...)
The world was this as well, figures in windows a thousand feet up, dropping into free space, and the stink of fuel fire, and the steady rip of sirens in the air. (...)
He kept on walking. (...) He saw two women sobbing in their reverse march, looking past him, both in running shoes, faces in collapse. (...)
In time he heard the sound of the second fall. He crossed Canal Street and began to see things, somehow differently. Things did not seem charged in the usual ways, the cobbled street, the cast-iron buildings. There was something critically missing from the things around him (...).

annotations

[1] *rubble* = bits of broken stone, rock or brickwork

[2] *ungainly* = clumsy, awkward

[3] *roar* = loud, deep sound as of a lion, of thunder, of a person in pain, etc.

c) The novel is called "Falling Man". Explain the title.

B2 a) Together with a partner talk about what you know about 9/11. Use the pictures below.

b) Read the info about 9/11. Think of reasons why the terrorists might have chosen these targets.

Info 9/11

The terrorist attacks of 9/11 were a series of four co-ordinated attacks launched by al-Qaeda on the United States, specifically in New York City and the Washington D.C. area, on Tuesday September 11 2001. Al-Qaeda and its erstwhile principal spokesman, Osama bin Laden (11.3.1957 – 2.5.2011) are the radical, extremist fringe of modern Islamic militancy. In addition to 9/11, al-Qaeda has also claimed responsibility for numerous other attacks against civilian and military targets, which resulted in mass casualties.
On the morning of 9/11, four airliners were hijacked by 19 al-Qaeda members. Between 8:46 and 9:03 am two of those planes – American Airlines Flight 11 and United Airlines Flight 175 – crashed respectively into the North and South towers of the World Trade Center in New York. Within two hours, both towers collapsed. The debris and resulting fires caused partial or complete collapse of all other buildings in the World Trade Center complex, as well as major damage to other structures nearby. A third plane – American Airlines Flight 77 – was crashed into the Pen-

tagon, which is the headquarters of the United States Department of Defense. The crash lead to a partial collapse in the building's west side. The fourth and final plane also had Washington D.C. as its objective, but crashed into a field near Shanksville in Pennsylvania after its passengers had tried to overpower the hijackers.

Osama bin Laden

Almost 3,000 people died in the attacks in total, including the 227 civilians and 19 hijackers aboard the four airliners. More than 90% of the fatalities were workers and visitors who had been at, or above, the planes' point of impact. In the North Tower alone, 1,355 people were trapped and died of smoke inhalation, were killed in the building's eventual collapse, fell, or jumped from the tower to escape the flames.
On September 14, 2001, the U.S. Congress passed the Authorization for Use of Military Force Against Terrorists (AUMF). Still in effect to this day, it grants the President the authority to use all "necessary and appropriate force" against those whom he determines "planned, authorized, committed or aided" the 9/11 attacks. This includes force against those who harbored said persons or groups.
The war on terror began in Afghanistan on October 7, 2001, when U.S. and British forces began bombing Taliban and al-Qaeda camps from the air. They later invaded Afghanistan with ground troops of the Special Forces. From 2001 until 2011 one of the chief objectives of the war on terror was to kill or capture Osama bin Laden and a price of $25 million was placed on his head by the FBI. On May 2, 2011, bin Laden was found and killed in Pakistan in an operation ordered by U.S. President Barack Obama.

B3 a) On 7 October 2001, Osama Bin Laden, referring to the 9/11 attacks, issued a strongly-worded warning to the United States which was broadcasted on Al-Jazeera TV. Read the extract taken from this speech.

(...) God Almighty hit the United States at its most vulnerable spot. He destroyed its greatest buildings. Praise be to God. Here is the United States. It was filled with terror from its north to its south and from its east to its west. Praise be to God.
What the United States tastes today is a very small thing compared to what we have tasted for tens of years. Our nation has been tasting this humiliation and contempt for more than 80 years. Its sons are being killed, its blood is being shed, its holy places are being attacked, and it is not being ruled according to what God has decreed[1]. Despite this, nobody cares.
But if the sword falls on the United States after 80 years, hypocrisy raises its head lamenting the deaths of these killers who tampered[2] with the blood, honour, and holy places of the Muslims. The least that one can describe these people is that they are morally depraved. They champion falsehood, support the butcher against the victim, the oppressor against the innocent child. (...)
In the aftermath of this event and now that senior US officials have spoken, beginning with Bush, the head of the world's infidels[3], and whoever supports him, every Muslim should rush to defend his religion. They came out in arrogance with their men and horses and instigated even those countries that belong to Islam against us. They came out to fight this group of people who declared their faith in God and refused to abandon their religion. They came out to fight Islam in the name of terrorism. (...)
These incidents divided the entire world into two regions – one of faith where there is no hypocrisy and another of infidelity, from which we hope God will protect us. The winds of faith and change have blown to remove falsehood from the [Arabian] peninsula of Prophet Mohammed, may God's prayers be upon him.
As for the United States, I tell it and its people these few words: I swear by Almighty God who raised the heavens without pillars that neither the United States nor he who lives in the United States will enjoy security before we can see it as a reality in Palestine and before all the infidel armies leave the land of Mohammed, may God's peace and blessing be upon him.
God is great and glory to Islam. May God's peace, mercy, and blessings be upon you.

annotations

[1] *to decree* = to issue an order/law

[2] *to tamper with* = to meddle or interfere with, to make unauthorized changes in

[3] *infidels* = people with no belief in a specific religion, esp. in what is considered to be the true religion, "Ungläubige"

b) Summarize how Bin Laden justifies the attacks and describe the future he envisions for the US.

justification			future
– humiliation and contempt	→	**9/11 attack** →	

Info **George Walker Bush** (born July 6, 1946) was the 43rd President of the United States of America from 2001 to 2009 and the 46th Governor of Texas from 1995 to 2000. Being a former president's son himself, Bush was elected president in 2000 after a close and controversial election, since he received fewer popular votes nationwide than his opponent.
When the terrorist attacks occurred, George W. Bush was eight months into his first term as president. On the night of September 11, the president addressed the nation in a first reaction to the attacks. The speech below, entitled "Address to a Terrified Nation", is a crisis speech which was delivered nine days after the attacks on the country addressing Congress, the American people and the world alike.

Writing

B4 a) Before you start reading the speech Bush delivered nine days after the attacks on September 20, 2001, speculate about what kind of message he wanted to get across to his audience.

b) Read the speech and find a title for each paragraph.

c) Highlight essential stylistic devices and note down their effects in the box below.

stylistic device	effect
frequent use of personal pronouns → ll. 5, 6, 7, 9	creates a feeling of togetherness, the president and the nation being one – in their sorrow as well as in their wish to fight those who are responsible for the attacks

d) Write an analysis of Bush's speech.

➩ skills: how to analyze a speech, pp. 119 – 121

Mr. Speaker, Mr. President Pro Tempore, members of Congress, and fellow Americans:

In the normal course of events, Presidents come to this chamber to report on the state of the Union. Tonight, no such report is needed. It has already been delivered by the American people. We have seen it in the courage of passengers, who rushed terrorists to save others on the ground. (...) We have seen the state of our Union in the endurance of rescuers, working past exhaustion. We have seen the unfurling[1] of flags, the lighting of candles, the giving of blood, the saying of prayers – in English, Hebrew, and Arabic. We have seen the decency of a loving and giving people who have made the grief of strangers their own. My fellow citizens, for the last nine days, the entire world has seen for itself the state of our Union - and it is strong.

Tonight we are a country awakened to danger and called to defend freedom. Our grief has turned to anger, and anger to resolution. Whether we bring our enemies to justice, or bring justice to our enemies, justice will be done. I thank the Congress for its leadership at such an important time. (...)

On September the 11th, enemies of freedom committed an act of war against our country. Americans have known wars – but for the past 136 years, they have been wars on foreign soil, except for one Sunday in 1941. Americans have known the casualties of war – but not at the center of a great city on a peaceful morning. Americans have known surprise attacks – but never before on thousands of civilians. All of this was brought upon us in a single day – and night fell on a different world, a world where freedom itself is under attack.

Americans have many questions tonight. Americans are asking: Who attacked our country? The evidence we have gathered all points to a collection of loosely affiliated[2] terrorist organizations known as al-Qaeda. They are the same murderers indicted for bombing American embassies in Tanzania and Kenya, and responsible for bombing the USS Cole. Al-Qaeda is to terror what the mafia is to crime. But its goal is not making money; its goal is remaking the world – and imposing its radical beliefs on people everywhere.The terrorists practice a fringe[3] form of Islamic extremism that has been rejected by Muslim scholars and the vast majority of Muslim clerics - a fringe movement that perverts the peaceful teachings of Islam. The terrorists' directive commands them to kill Christians and Jews, to kill all Americans, and make no distinction among military and civilians, including women and children. (...)

And tonight, the United States of America makes the following demands on the Taliban: deliver to United States authorities all the leaders of al-Qaeda who hide in your land. Release all foreign nationals, including American citizens, you have unjustly imprisoned. Protect foreign journalists, diplomats and aid workers in your country. Close immediately and permanently every terrorist training camp in Afghanistan, and hand over every terrorist, and every person in their support structure, to appropriate authorities. (Applause.) Give the United States full access to terrorist training camps, so we can make sure they are no longer operating.

These demands are not open to negotiation or discussion. (...)

The terrorists are traitors to their own faith, trying, in effect, to hijack Islam itself. The enemy of America is not our many Muslim friends; it is not our many Arab friends. Our enemy is a radical network of terrorists, and every government that supports them. Our war on terror begins with al-Qaeda, but it does not end there. It will not end until every terrorist group of global reach has been found, stopped and defeated.

Americans are asking, why do they hate us? They hate what we see right here in this chamber – a democratically elected government. Their leaders are self-appointed. They hate our freedoms - our freedom of religion, our freedom of speech, our freedom to vote and assemble and disagree with each other. (...)

Americans are asking: How will we fight and win this war? We will direct every resource at our command - every means of diplomacy, every tool of intelligence, every instrument of law enforcement, every financial influence, and every necessary weapon of war - to the disruption and to the defeat of the global terror network.

introduction

(...) Our response involves far more than instant retaliation[4] and isolated strikes. Americans should not expect one battle, but a lengthy campaign, unlike any other we have ever seen. It may include dramatic strikes, visible on TV, and covert operations, secret even in success. We will starve terrorists of funding, turn them one against another, drive them from place to place, until there is no refuge or no rest. And we will pursue nations that provide aid or safe haven to terrorism. Every nation, in every region, now has a decision to make. Either you are with us, or you are with the terrorists. From this day forward, any nation that continues to harbor or support terrorism will be regarded by the United States as a hostile regime. (...) the only way to defeat terrorism as a threat to our way of life is to stop it, eliminate it, and destroy it where it grows.

This is not, however, just America's fight. And what is at stake is not just America's freedom. This is the world's fight. This is civilization's fight. This is the fight of all who believe in progress and pluralism, tolerance and freedom. We ask every nation to join us. (...)

After all that has just passed – all the lives taken, and all the possibilities and hopes that died with them – it is natural to wonder if America's future is one of fear. Some speak of an age of terror. I know there are struggles ahead, and dangers to face. But this country will define our times, not be defined by them. As long as the United States of America is determined and strong, this will not be an age of terror; this will be an age of liberty, here and across the world.

Great harm has been done to us. We have suffered great loss. And in our grief and anger we have found our mission and our moment. Freedom and fear are at war. The advance of human freedom – the great achievement of our time, and the great hope of every time – now depends on us. Our nation – this generation – will lift a dark threat of violence from our people and our future. We will rally the world to this cause by our efforts, by our courage. We will not tire, we will not falter, and we will not fail. (...)

I will not forget this wound to our country or those who inflicted it. I will not yield; I will not rest; I will not relent[5] in waging this struggle for freedom and security for the American people. The course of this conflict is not known, yet its outcome is certain. Freedom and fear, justice and cruelty, have always been at war, and we know that God is not neutral between them.

Fellow citizens, we'll meet violence with patient justice – assured of the rightness of our cause, and confident of the victories to come. In all that lies before us, may God grant us wisdom, and may He watch over the United States of America.

Thank you.

annotations

1 *unfurling* = unrolling of the flag

2 *affiliated* = loosely connected

3 *fringe* = a form that is not part of the main group/the outer edge of a group

4 *retaliation* = revenge

5 *to relent* = to give in

B5 a) Compare the two speeches. Take notes on how the speakers portray their respective enemies and their deeds as well as their respective victims in the US, or the Arab world. List the actions and consequences each of them announces.
Then talk to a partner about what you find striking/interesting/surprising about your results.

	Osama Bin Laden	**George W. Bush**
enemies	*– hypocritical killers (l. 15)*	*– murderers (l. 25)*
victims		
actions/consequences		

b) Some people have claimed that *George W. Bush is no better than Osama bin Laden*.
Write a text arguing against this point of view. Take into consideration aspects such as terrorism, legitimacy, leadership, democracy, international law and human rights. Before you start writing, make notes.

terrorism

legitimacy

leadership

democracy

international law

human rights

word bank

to target so. · retaliation · to wage war against so. · innocent bystander · to hijack a plane · to prevent sth. from happening · to be committed to doing sth. · to culminate in sth. · to escalate tension · to come to so.'s aid · to act in one's own interest · lack of understanding · to threaten · to intervene · to ensure security · to result in sth.

C1 Discuss the message of the following quote.

Quote by Benjamin Franklin (1706–1790)

"Any society that would give up a little liberty to gain a little security will deserve neither and lose both."

C2 Match the words/phrases below with the definitions/translations in the table.

resolution / to authorize / to conduct a study / to amount to / detention camp / to establish / to detain / suspect / to be entitled to something / trial / to grant something / to release / to give an account / law enforcement agency / to disclose / to obtain / to comprise

	to consist of, to be made up of
resolution	a formal expression of opinion or intention agreed on by a legislative body
	to get, acquire or secure
	to carry out
	to give official permission for
	to make known, to allow to be seen
	a place where suspects are interned
	sich beziffern auf
	an institution that enforces the law, examples: the police, the FBI
	to set up on a permanent basis
	to provide a report or description of an event
	to keep someone in official custody
	to set someone free, typically prisoners
	bewilligen, gewähren
	Prozess, Verhandlung
	Verdächtige(r)
	to have or be given the legal right

Info **Reactions to the attacks on September 11th, 2001**

On September 14th, 2001 the House of Representatives and the Senate passed a resolution authorizing the United States Armed Forces to use military force against those responsible for the attacks on September 11th, 2001. Only one person out of the 435 Representatives and 100 Senators – Representative Barbara Lee from California - voted against this resolution. The military operation that has followed is known as the **war on terror**. Usually referred to as AUMF (Authorization for Use of Military Force), this joint resolution has formed the legal basis for the war on terror up to this day. According to a study conducted by the Watson Institute for International Studies at Brown University the costs for the war on terror amounted to at least 2.3 trillion dollars at the end of 2011. A large amount of this money was spent by the military on sophisticated technology such as drones.

As part of the war on terror, the Bush administration established a detention camp in Cuba on **Guantanamo Bay** Naval Base, where they detained people who were suspected of being terrorists or of supporting terrorism. Because the camp was located outside the USA, detainees were not entitled to a regular trial, something which is guaranteed by the Sixth Amendment to the Constitution. They were not even granted the protection that prisoners of war are usually granted under the Geneva Convention. Some detainees have spent years in the camp without any trial. After being released many former terror suspects gave detailed accounts of torture and abuse.

On October 23rd, 2001, the House of Representatives passed the **USA PATRIOT Act**. Just one day later the Act passed the Senate. It was signed into law by President George W. Bush on October 26th. USA PATRIOT is an acronym that stands for Uniting (and) Strengthening America (by) Providing Appropriate Tools Required (to) Intercept (and) Obstruct Terrorism Act of 2001. Comprising 10 Titles on over 340 pages the law generally broadens the power of law enforcement agencies and intelligence agencies such as the NSA giving them, for example, the right to order Internet service providers to disclose IP addresses and login times of persons related to terrorist activities. It also regulates authorities' power to obtain information about bank accounts and cut off the financial support of terrorist groups.

The creation of the United States Department of **Homeland Security** was another consequence of the attacks of September 11th. It comprises 22 agencies such as the U.S. Secret Service, the Transportation Security Administration (TSA) and the U.S. customs service. Many of these agencies exercise the powers given to them by the USA PATRIOT Act.

C3 Find all the participle constructions and shortened relative clauses in the text above. Mark them, write them in the table below and rephrase them.

participle constructions	
... passed a resolution authorizing the United States Armed Forces to ...	*... passed a resolution and authorized the United States Armed Forces to ...*

shortened relative clauses	
According to a study conducted by the ...	*According to a study that was conduc*

C4 Look at the diagram and read the quotes as well as the extracts from the Federalist Papers. Then write down why the Founding Fathers limited the power of the government and how they did it.

When people are given authority they tend to expand their power -> different branches which control each other -> danger of abuse is reduced

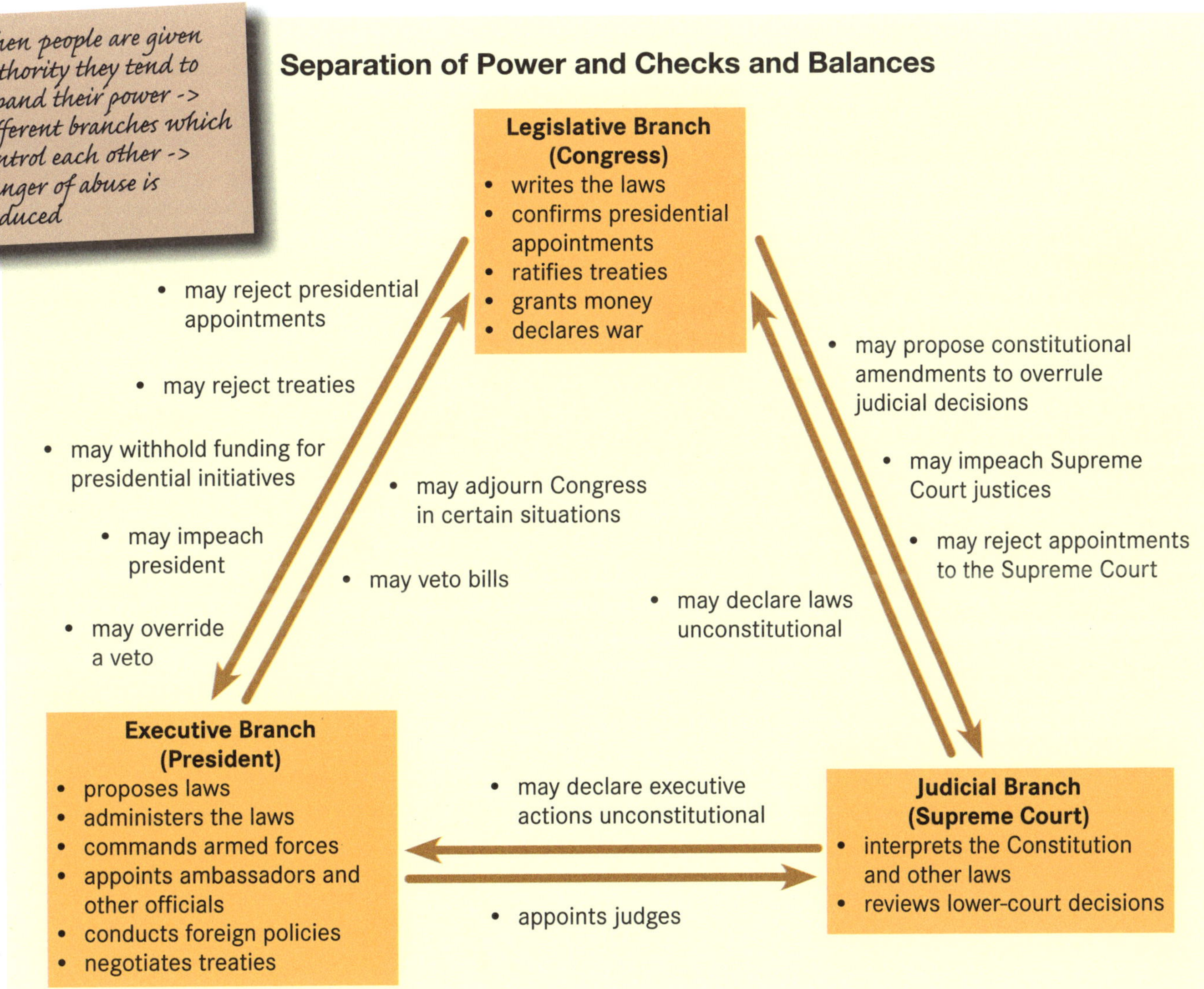

Quotes by James Madison:

Wherever the real power in a Government lies, there is the danger of oppression.

I believe there are more instances of the abridgment of the freedom[1] of the people by gradual and silent encroachments[2] of those in power, than by violent and sudden usurpations[3].

Info **James Madison** (1751 – 1836) was the fourth President of the United States and is known as the father of the United States Constitution. He was a close friend of Thomas Jefferson.

Quotes by Thomas Jefferson:

When the people fear their government, there is tyranny; when the government fears the people, there is liberty.

What country can preserve its liberties if its rulers are not warned from time to time that their people preserve the spirit of resistance?

Info **Thomas Jefferson** (1743 – 1826) was the third President of the United States and is known as the author of the Declaration of Independence and as one of the Founding Fathers.

annotations

[1] *abridgment of the freedom* = Beschneidung der Freiheit

[2] *encroachment* = Übergriff, Eingriff

[3] *usurpation* = Usurpation, widerrechtliche Aneignung

The ***Federalist Papers*** *are a series of 85 articles and essays written by Alexander Hamilton, James Madison and John Jay promoting the ratification of the United States Constitution. The following extracts are taken from article 51, published in the* Independent Journal *in 1788 and entitled:* The Structure of the Government Must Furnish the Proper Checks and Balances Between the Different Departments. *The article's author is James Madison.*

If men were angels, no government would be necessary. If angels were to govern men, neither external nor internal controls on government would be necessary. In framing a government which is to be administered by men over men, the great difficulty lies in this: you must first enable the government to control the governed; and in the next place oblige it to control itself. A dependence on the people is, no doubt, the primary control on the government; but experience has taught mankind the necessity of auxiliary precautions.

But it is not possible to give to each department an equal power of self-defense. In republican government, the legislative authority necessarily predominates[1]. The remedy[2] for this inconveniency is to divide the legislature into different branches[3]; and to render them, by different modes of election and different principles of action, as little connected with each other as the nature of their common functions and their common dependence on the society will admit.

annotations

[1] *to predominate* = be the strongest or main element

[2] *remedy* = Abhilfe, Gegenmittel

[3] *branch* = Ast, Zweig, Gewalt (z. B. legislative Gewalt)

Writing

C5 Choose ONE of the following tasks. Look back through this theme for more information.

(i) Analyse in what ways the various political reactions to the attacks of 9/11 violated the constitution as well as the system of checks and balances.

(ii) Analyse the cartoon below. First describe the circled elements and think about their functions.

Nick Anderson,
Three branches of government

George W. Bush, American President who signed the USA Patriot Act in 2001. He is portrayed as a cowboy …

D1 How do the pictures on the right make you feel? Talk to a partner.

word bank

surveillance camera · to be kept under constant surveillance/observation · surveillance of known troublemakers · to be under surveillance - to monitor sth. / so. closely · drones · unmanned spy planes · a widespread use of sth. · to suspect so. of doing sth. · to be suspicious of/about so./sth. · to grow incensed/angry/indignant · to uncover a plot · to take measures to do sth. · civil liberties (usu. pl.) · regardless of sth. · to come at a price

Info **NSA** – The NSA (National Security Agency) was established in 1952 and is currently the largest of U.S. intelligence organizations. Being part of the Department of Defense its main function is the collection, decoding, translation and analysis of data for intelligence purposes by electronic or other means. The NSA is the most secret of all intelligence agencies. Its headquarters are in Maryland. It operates additional stations in many countries around the world, including Wiesbaden / Germany. The wider public became aware of the NSA and its actions in 2013, when Edward Snowden, a former employee of the NSA, published secret documents. They revealed information about the immense extent of data collection from public institutions as well as ordinary citizens whose mobile phone and internet data were monitored on a massive scale.

D2 a) Look at the poll below that was conducted in the United States in June 2013 and discuss if the numbers surprise you or not.

Public reaction to NSA monitoring

Q: What do think is more important right now for the federal government: to investigate possible terrorist threats, even if that intrudes on personal privacy OR not to intrude on personal privacy, even if that limits its ability to investigate possible terrorist threats?

Don't intrude on privacy	Investigate threats	*No opinion*
34%	62%	4%

Q: As you may know, it has been reported that the National Security agency has been getting secret court orders to track telephone record of millions of Americans in an effort to investigate terrorism. Would you consider this access to telephone call records an acceptable or unacceptable way for the federal government to investigate terrorism?

56% Acceptable ◄		► 41% Unacceptable		*No opinion*
30%	26%	14%	27%	2%
Strongly	Somewhat	Somewhat	Strongly	

Q: Do you think the U.S. government should be able to monitor everyone's email and other online activities if officials say this might prevent future terrorist attacks? (Based on interviews from June 7 to 9 only)

Yes	No	*No opinion*
45%	52%	3%

This poll was conducted by telephone June 6 to 9, 2013, among a random sample of 1, 004 adults. The results have a margin of sampling error of plus or minus 3.5. percentage points. The question asked from June 7 to 9 is based on 743 interviews with an error margin of 4.5 percentage points. This survey was produced for The Washington Post by Capital Insight, with sampling data collection and tabulation by PSRAI of Princeton, N.J.

b) While many Americans seem to agree with the methods of the NSA, criticism and warnings of possible abuses can also be found. Assess the following abuses and rank them from most to least dramatic. Compare your ranking with a partner and discuss.

A The NSA intrudes into people's private spheres without informing them about it.	B Danger of accidents: innocent people become terror suspects.
C Loss of control of private information: the NSA might sell the data or the data might leak to institutions and people that use it for purposes other than protecting people's safety. For example, the information might be used by companies to target customers with advertising.	D On the basis of the collected data, the NSA can create profiles of people and try and predict behavior. Depending on the prediction law enforcement authorities might apprehend people and detain them even though they haven't committed any crime.

Reading

D3 a) Get together in groups of four. Study your material, fill in the table on page 100 and then report your findings to each other.

Material 1

The Guardian, Thursday 6 June 2013

NSA collecting phone records of millions of Verizon[1] customers daily

Exclusive: Top secret court order[2] requiring Verizon to hand over all call data shows scale of domestic surveillance under Obama
by **Glenn Greenwald**

The National Security Agency is currently collecting the telephone records[3] of millions of US customers of Verizon, one of America's largest providers, under a top secret court order issued in April. The order, a copy of which has been obtained by the Guardian, requires Verizon on an "ongoing, daily basis" to give the NSA information on all telephone calls in its systems, both within the US and between the US and other countries.
The document shows for the first time that under the Obama administration the communication records of millions of US citizens are being collected indiscriminately and in bulk – regardless of whether they are suspected of any wrongdoing. The secret Foreign Intelligence Surveillance Court (FISA) granted the order to the FBI on April 25, giving the government unlimited authority to obtain the data for a specified three-month period ending on July 19. (...)
Under the Bush administration, officials in security agencies had disclosed[4] to reporters the large-scale collection of call records data by the NSA, but this is the first time significant and top-secret documents have revealed the continuation of the practice on a massive scale under President Obama. The unlimited nature of the records being handed over to the NSA is extremely unusual. FISA court orders typically direct the production of records pertaining to a specific named target who is suspected of being an agent of a terrorist group or foreign state, or a finite set of individually named targets. (...)
The court order appears to explain the numerous cryptic public warnings by two US senators, Ron Wyden and Mark Udall, about the scope of the Obama administration's surveillance activities. For roughly two years, the two Democrats have been stridently advising the public that the US government is relying on "secret legal interpretations" to claim surveillance powers so broad that the American public would be "stunned" to learn of the kind of domestic spying being conducted. Because those activities are classified[5], the senators, both members of the Senate intelligence committee[6], have been prevented from specifying which domestic[7] surveillance programs they find so alarming. (...)
The NSA, as part of a program secretly authorized by President Bush on 4 October 2001, implemented a bulk collection program of domestic telephone, internet and email records. A furore erupted in 2006 when USA Today reported that the NSA had "been secretly collecting the phone call records of tens of millions of Americans, using data provided by AT&T, Verizon and BellSouth" and was "using the data to analyze calling patterns in an effort to detect terrorist activity." Until now, there has been no indication that the Obama administration implemented a similar program. (...)
In the mid-1970s, Congress, for the first time, investigated[8] the surveillance activities of the US government. Back then, the mandate of the NSA was that it would never direct its surveillance apparatus domestically. At

the conclusion of that investigation, Frank Church, the Democratic senator from Idaho who chaired the investigative committee, warned: "The NSA's capability at any time could be turned around on the American people, and no American would have any privacy left, such is the capability to monitor everything: telephone conversations, telegrams, it doesn't matter."

annotations

[1] *Verizon* = Verizon Communications Inc. is one of the largest American broadband and telecommunications company

[2] *court order* = Gerichtsbeschluss, Anordnung

[3] *record* = Aufzeichnung, Mitschrift

[4] *to disclose* = offenlegen, enthüllen

[5] *classified* = designated as officially secret

[6] *Senate intelligence committee* = Ausschuss des Senats, der zuständig ist für die Geheimdienste

[7] *domestic* = existing inside a particular country (opposite: foreign)

[8] *investigate* = carry out a systematic examination

Material 2

The Guardian, Friday 7 June 2013

NSA Prism program taps in to user data of Apple, Google and others

Top-secret Prism program claims direct access to servers of firms including Google, Apple and Facebook • Companies deny any knowledge of program in operation since 2007

by **Glenn Greenwald, Ewen MacAskill**

The National Security Agency has obtained direct access[1] to the systems of Google, Facebook, and other US giants, according to a top secret document obtained by the Guardian. The access was enabled by changes to US surveillance law introduced under President Bush and renewed under Obama in December 2012.

The program facilitates extensive, in-depth surveillance on live communications and stored information. The law allows for the targeting[2] of any customers of participating firms who live outside the US, or those Americans whose communications include people outside the US. It also opens the possibility of communications made entirely within the US being collected without warrants[3].

Disclosure[4] of the Prism program follows a leak[5] to the Guardian on Wednesday of a top-secret court order compelling provider Verizon to turn over the telephone records of millions of US customers.

annotations

[1] *direct access* = direkter Zugriff

[2] *to target* = ins Visier nehmen

[3] *warrant* = Vollmacht, Durchsuchungsbeschluss

[4] *disclosure* = Enthüllung

[5] *leak* = here: intentional disclosure of secret information

Material 3

USA TODAY 12:14 a.m. EDT June 19, 2013

NSA director: Surveillance foiled 50 terror plots

WASHINGTON – National Security Agency Director Keith Alexander told a House committee[1] Tuesday that more than 50 terror threats throughout the world have been disrupted with the assistance of two secret surveillance programs that were recently disclosed[2] by former defense contractor Edward Snowden.

More than 10 of the plots targeted the U.S. homeland, Alexander told the House Intelligence Committee, including a plot to attack the New York Stock Exchange. (...)

At the rare open committee hearing, Alexander and Deputy Attorney General Jim Cole told lawmakers[3] that both surveillance operations – a domestic telephone tracking system that collects records of millions of Americans and an Internet monitoring program targeting non-citizens

outside the U.S. – have been subject to[4] rigorous oversight to guard against privacy abuses[5]. "This isn't some rogue[6] operation that some guys at the NSA are operating," said Alexander, also an Army general.
Deputy FBI Director Sean Joyce described another threat Tuesday that was neutralized by the surveillance programs: Investigators used the phone tracking system to identify an operative in San Diego who was providing support to terrorists in Somalia. Joyce also referred to two disrupted plots that were disclosed last week as having been thwarted[7] by the surveillance operations, including a 2009 plan to bomb the New York subway system. In that case, authorities used its Internet monitoring program to identify overseas communications involving Najibullah Zazi in Colorado, who was later convicted in connection with the subway attack plan.
"This is not a program that is off the books," Cole said, outlining the executive, legislative and judicial controls attached to both surveillance operations. (...)
Lawmakers raised few questions about the intelligence officials' authority to conduct the operations, despite the heated national privacy debate that was prompted by Snowden's disclosures. Rep. Mike Rogers, R-Mich., the panel's chairman, said the programs were "designed" to protect Americans. "Trust can wane when faced with so many inaccuracies," Rogers said, noting the "misperceptions" about the surveillance operations caused by "wrong" news reports.
Maryland Rep. Dutch Ruppersberger, the committee's ranking Democrat, said Snowden's unauthorized disclosures "put our country and allies in danger." "We need to seal this crack in the system," Ruppersberger said.
Alexander said intelligence officials have "significant concerns" about the access[8] to such sensitive information. He said about 1,000 so-called system administrators have access similar to Snowden. And a majority, like Snowden, are contractors. "We do have significant concerns in this area and it is something we need to look at," Alexander said. Joyce said a criminal investigation into Snowden's disclosures is continuing. Asked what he expected to result from that inquiry, Joyce offered a blunt assessment. "Justice."

annotations

1 *House committee* = Ausschuss des Repräsentantenhauses (House of Representatives)

2 *to disclose* = enthüllen, offenlegen

3 *lawmaker* = Parlamentarier

4 *to be subject to* = unterliegen

5 *abuse* = Missbrauch

6 *rogue* = Schurke

7 *to thwart* = vereiteln, verhindern

8 *access* = Zugang

Material 4

Two slides from the presentation on PRISM that Edward Snowden handed over to GUARDIAN Journalist Glenn Greenwald. The presentation was obviously used to train agents and was not meant to be disclosed to the public.

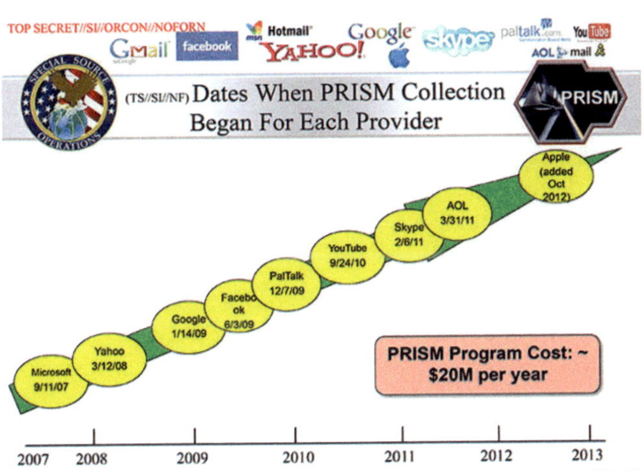

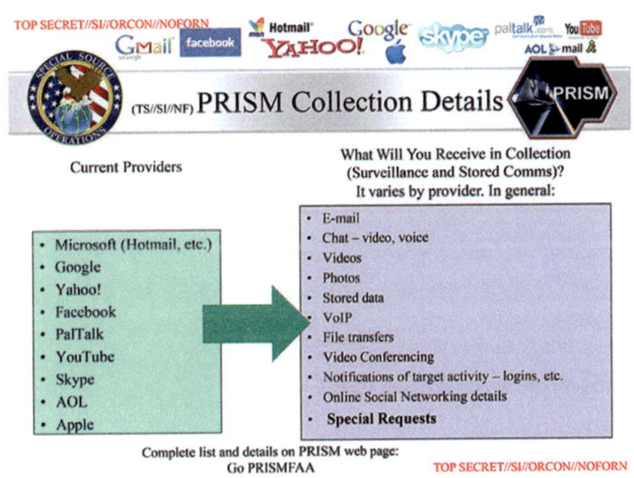

The following pages show the FISA court order that forms the legal basis of the surveillance of Verizon customers and is one the documents that Edward Snowden handed over to the GUARDIAN.

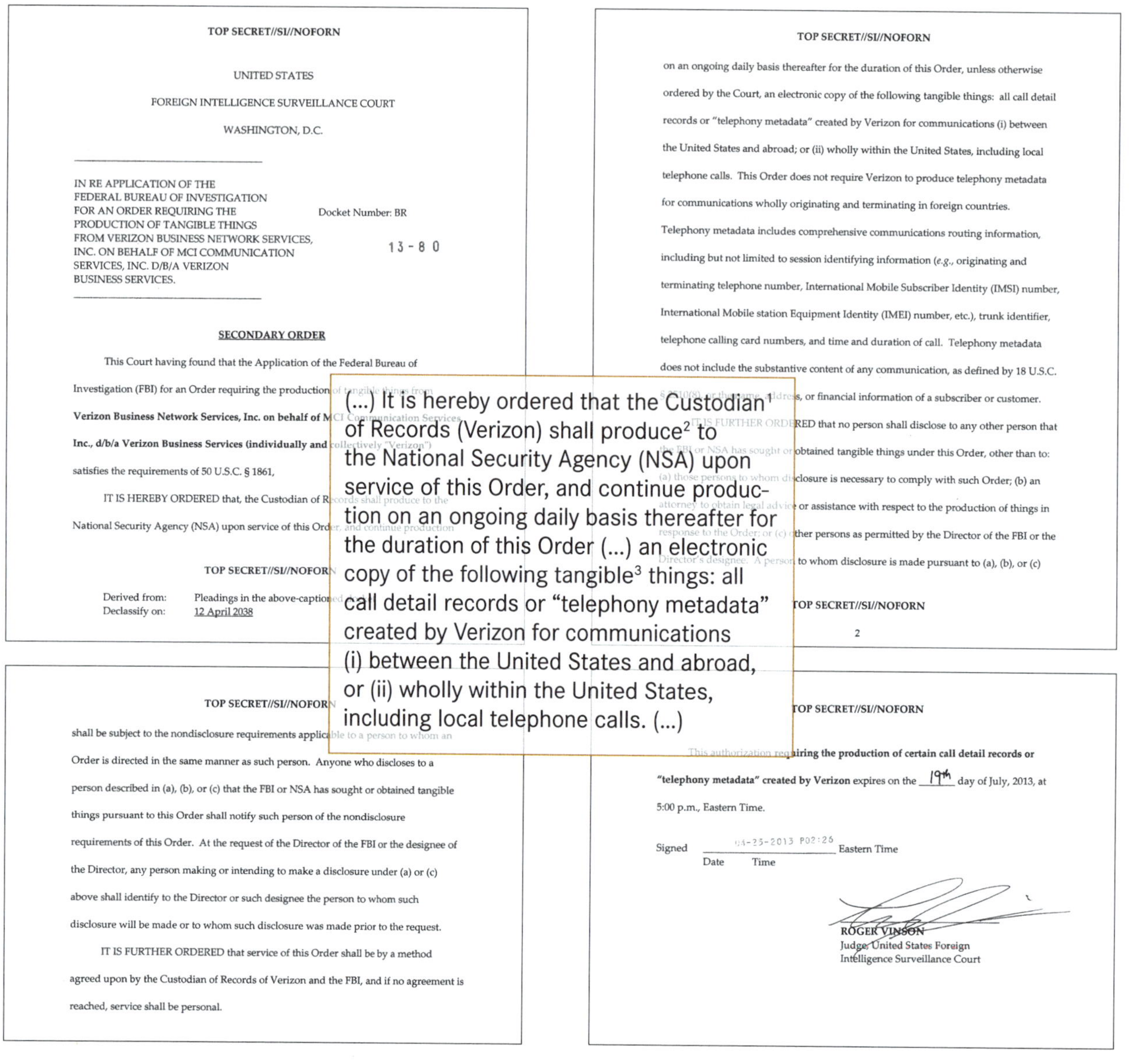

TOP SECRET//SI//NOFORN

UNITED STATES
FOREIGN INTELLIGENCE SURVEILLANCE COURT
WASHINGTON, D.C.

IN RE APPLICATION OF THE FEDERAL BUREAU OF INVESTIGATION FOR AN ORDER REQUIRING THE PRODUCTION OF TANGIBLE THINGS FROM VERIZON BUSINESS NETWORK SERVICES, INC. ON BEHALF OF MCI COMMUNICATION SERVICES, INC. D/B/A VERIZON BUSINESS SERVICES.

Docket Number: BR 13-80

SECONDARY ORDER

This Court having found that the Application of the Federal Bureau of Investigation (FBI) for an Order requiring the production of tangible things from **Verizon Business Network Services, Inc. on behalf of MCI Communication Services Inc., d/b/a Verizon Business Services (individually and collectively "Verizon")** satisfies the requirements of 50 U.S.C. § 1861,

IT IS HEREBY ORDERED that, the Custodian of Records shall produce to the National Security Agency (NSA) upon service of this Order, and continue production

TOP SECRET//SI//NOFORN

Derived from: Pleadings in the above-captioned docket
Declassify on: 12 April 2038

TOP SECRET//SI//NOFORN

on an ongoing daily basis thereafter for the duration of this Order, unless otherwise ordered by the Court, an electronic copy of the following tangible things: all call detail records or "telephony metadata" created by Verizon for communications (i) between the United States and abroad; or (ii) wholly within the United States, including local telephone calls. This Order does not require Verizon to produce telephony metadata for communications wholly originating and terminating in foreign countries. Telephony metadata includes comprehensive communications routing information, including but not limited to session identifying information (*e.g.*, originating and terminating telephone number, International Mobile Subscriber Identity (IMSI) number, International Mobile station Equipment Identity (IMEI) number, etc.), trunk identifier, telephone calling card numbers, and time and duration of call. Telephony metadata does not include the substantive content of any communication, as defined by 18 U.S.C. § 2510(8), or the name, address, or financial information of a subscriber or customer.

IT IS FURTHER ORDERED that no person shall disclose to any other person that the FBI or NSA has sought or obtained tangible things under this Order, other than to: (a) those persons to whom disclosure is necessary to comply with such Order; (b) an attorney to obtain legal advice or assistance with respect to the production of things in response to the Order; or (c) other persons as permitted by the Director of the FBI or the Director's designee. A person to whom disclosure is made pursuant to (a), (b), or (c)

TOP SECRET//SI//NOFORN

2

TOP SECRET//SI//NOFORN

shall be subject to the nondisclosure requirements applicable to a person to whom an Order is directed in the same manner as such person. Anyone who discloses to a person described in (a), (b), or (c) that the FBI or NSA has sought or obtained tangible things pursuant to this Order shall notify such person of the nondisclosure requirements of this Order. At the request of the Director of the FBI or the designee of the Director, any person making or intending to make a disclosure under (a) or (c) above shall identify to the Director or such designee the person to whom such disclosure will be made or to whom such disclosure was made prior to the request.

IT IS FURTHER ORDERED that service of this Order shall be by a method agreed upon by the Custodian of Records of Verizon and the FBI, and if no agreement is reached, service shall be personal.

TOP SECRET//SI//NOFORN

This authorization requiring the production of certain call detail records or "telephony metadata" created by Verizon expires on the 19th day of July, 2013, at 5:00 p.m., Eastern Time.

Signed 04-25-2013 P02:26 Eastern Time
Date Time

ROGER VINSON
Judge, United States Foreign Intelligence Surveillance Court

(...) It is hereby ordered that the Custodian[1] of Records (Verizon) shall produce[2] to the National Security Agency (NSA) upon service of this Order, and continue production on an ongoing daily basis thereafter for the duration of this Order (...) an electronic copy of the following tangible[3] things: all call detail records or "telephony metadata" created by Verizon for communications (i) between the United States and abroad, or (ii) wholly within the United States, including local telephone calls. (...)

annotations

[1] *custodian* = Verwahrer, Treuhänder

[2] *to produce* = to provide or show

[3] *tangible things* = Section 215 of the USA PATRIOT Act defines tangible things as follows: "books, records, papers, documents, and other items", Section 215 deals with the role of FISA regarding the access of authorities to records

What type of material is it?	
Who is the author?	
Who is meant to read the material?	

Speaking

b) As a group talk about the challenges that readers face regarding the different types of documents and regarding the information about the NSA that has been available in newspapers and on the Internet. One aspect you should discuss is the degree of credibility of the different materials / sources.

D4 A whistleblower is a person who reveals details of corruption or wrongdoing. Describe what the following cartoon tells you about whistleblowers.

Brian Narelle, Whistleblower's Point

D5 a) Read the newspaper article about Edward Snowden and list the reasons why he became a whistleblower.

The Guardian, Monday 10 June 2013

Edward Snowden: the whistleblower behind the NSA surveillance revelations

The 29-year-old source behind the biggest intelligence leak in the NSA's history explains his motives, his uncertain future and why he never intended on hiding in the shadows by **Glenn Greenwald, Ewen MacAskill and Laura Poitras**

The individual responsible for one of the most significant leaks in US political history is a 29-year-old former technical assistant for the CIA and current employee[1] of the defence contractor Booz Allen Hamilton. Snowden has been working at the National Security Agency for the last four years as an employee of various outside contractors, including Booz Allen and Dell. The Guardian, after several days of interviews, is revealing his identity at his request.

From the moment he decided to disclose numerous top-secret documents to the public, he was determined not to opt for the protection of anonymity. "I have no intention of hiding who I am because I know I have done nothing wrong," he said.

Snowden will go down in history as one of America's most consequential whistleblowers, alongside Daniel Ellsberg and Bradley Manning. He is responsible for handing over material from one of the world's most secretive organisations - the NSA. In a note accompanying the first set of documents he provided, he wrote: "I understand that I will be made to suffer for my actions," but "I will be satisfied if the federation of secret law, unequal pardon and irresistible[2] executive powers that rule the world that I love are revealed even for an instant."

Despite his determination[3] to be publicly unveiled[4], he repeatedly insisted that he wants to avoid the media spotlight. "I don't want public attention because I don't want the story to be about me. I want it to be about what the US government is doing." He does not fear the consequences of going public, he said, only that doing so will distract[5] attention from the issues raised by his disclosures. "I know the media likes to personalise political debates, and I know the government will demonise me."

Despite these fears, he remained hopeful his outing will not divert attention from the substance of his disclosures[6]. "I really want the focus to be on these documents and the debate which I hope this will trigger[7] among citizens around the globe about what kind of world we want to live in." He added: "My sole motive is to inform the public as to that which is done in their name and that which is done against them."

He has had "a very comfortable life" that included a salary of roughly $200,000, a girlfriend with whom he shared a home in Hawaii, a stable career, and a family he loves. "I'm willing to sacrifice[8] all of that because I can't in good conscience allow the US government to destroy privacy, internet freedom and basic liberties for people around the world with this massive surveillance machine they're secretly building." (...)

Snowden did not always believe the US government posed a threat to his political values. (...) In 2003, he enlisted in the US army and began a training program to join the Special Forces. Invoking the same principles that he now cites to justify his leaks, he said: "I wanted to fight in the Iraq war because I felt like I had an obligation as a human being to help free people from oppression". (...)

By 2007, the CIA stationed him with diplomatic cover in Geneva, Switzerland. His responsibility for maintaining computer network security meant he had clearance to access a wide array of classified documents.

That access[9], along with the almost three years he spent around CIA officers, led him to begin seriously questioning the rightness of what he saw. He described as formative an incident in which he claimed CIA operatives were attempting to recruit a Swiss banker to obtain secret banking information. Snowden said they achieved this by purposely getting the banker drunk and encouraging him to drive home in his car. When the banker was arrested for drunk driving, the undercover agent seeking to befriend him offered to help, and a bond was formed that led to successful recruitment. "Much of what I saw in Geneva really disillusioned me about how my government functions and what its impact is in the world," he says. "I realised that I was part of something that was doing far more harm[10] than good."

He said it was during his CIA stint in Geneva that he thought for the first time about exposing government secrets. But, at the time, he chose not to for two reasons. First, he said: "Most of the secrets the CIA has are about people, not machines and systems, so I didn't feel comfortable with disclosures that I thought could endanger anyone". Secondly, the election of Barack Obama in 2008 gave him hope that there would be real reforms, rendering disclosures unnecessary. (...) The primary lesson from this experience was that "you can't wait around for someone else to act. I had been looking for leaders, but I realised that leadership is about being the first to act." (...) He described how he once viewed the internet as "the most important invention in all of human history". As an adolescent, he spent days at a time "speaking to people with all sorts of views that I would never have encountered on my own". But he believed that the value of the internet, along with basic privacy, is being rapidly destroyed by ubiquitous[11] surveillance. "I don't see myself as a hero," he said, "because what I'm doing is self-interested: I don't want to live in a world where there's no privacy and therefore no room for intellectual exploration and creativity."

Once he reached the conclusion that the NSA's surveillance net would soon be irrevocable[12], he said it was just a matter of time before he chose to act. "What they're doing" poses "an existential threat to democracy", he said. As strong as those beliefs are, there still remains the question: why did he do it? Giving up his freedom and a privileged lifestyle? "There are more important things than money. If I were motivated by money, I could have sold these documents to any number of countries and gotten very rich."

For him, it is a matter of principle. "The government has granted itself power it is not entitled[13] to. There is no public oversight. The result is people like myself have the latitude to go further than they are allowed to," he said. (...)

Snowden said that he admires both Ellsberg and Manning, but argues that there is one important distinction between himself and the army private, whose trial coincidentally began the week Snowden's leaks began to make news. "I carefully evaluated every single document I disclosed to ensure that each was legitimately in the public interest," he said. "There are all sorts of documents that would have made a big impact that I didn't turn over, because harming people isn't my goal. Transparency is." (...)

annotations

1 *employee* = Angestellter
2 *irresistible* = unwiderstehlich
3 *determination* = Entschlossenheit
4 *to unveil* = enthüllen
5 *to distract* = ablenken
6 *disclosure* = Enthüllung
7 *to trigger* = auslösen
8 *to sacrifice* = opfern
9 *access* = Zugang
10 *harm* = damage
11 *ubiquituous* = allgegenwärtig
12 *irrevocable* = not able to be changed or reversed
13 *to be entitled to sth.* = berechtigt sein zu etw.

b) Write down the challenges, choices and insecurities that Edward Snowden has been facing over the past six years.

challenges	
choices	
insecurities	

D6 a) The following quote is taken from the speech by Ron Paul you dealt with earlier.

"Our Constitution, which was intended to limit government power and abuse, has failed. The Founders warned that a free society depends on a virtuous and moral people. The current crisis reflects that their concerns were justified."

According to Ron Paul's definition, Edward Snowden could be called a "virtuous and moral" person who has disclosed government wrongdoing. But opinions are divided. Read the following article that expresses a critical attitude towards Snowden.

There is no evidence to indicate that Snowden pursued appropriate whistleblowing channels within the government. The Department of Defense and the Central Intelligence Agency both have robust protections for whistleblowers; and if those paths didn't yield any results, Snowden easily could have contacted one of the committees in Congress charged with overseeing intelligence activities. If he had, he would have realized that those committees were fully aware of PRISM, and that they exercised rigorous oversight of how the program was used. Congress is not popular these days, but in a contest between congressional overseers – more than a few of whom are on the left side of the political spectrum – and a high school dropout systems administrator, I'd trust the judgment of the former any day of the week.

Philip Lohaus, "Edward Snowden is no hero", published on The Daily Caller, an online news platform on June 16th, 2013.

b) React to the article by writing a letter to the editor in which you discuss the question whether Edward Snowden is a traitor or a hero.

➩ skills: how to write a letter to the editor, p. 124

A1 These are the first two definitions of *insecurity* you find in Webster's dictionary:

1: not adequately guarded: UNSAFE <an *insecure* investment>

2: not confident or sure: UNCERTAIN <feeling somewhat *insecure* about his reception>

Identify the different insecurities dealt with in *Crash*, *Half Broke Horses* and the themes in this book and list the situations.

	Definition 1: unsafe	**Definition 2: uncertain**
Crash		*Officer Hansen feels insecure after witnessing Officer Ryan sexually abusing Cameron's wife. At first he doesn't know how to react.*
Half Broke Horses		
Themes in this book	*Some people feel insecure in their neighborhood because they are afraid of becoming a victim of crime.*	

A2 Compare your results with a partner and together think of other insecurities that we have not dealt with but which people are nevertheless confronted with.

Speaking

A3 **Partner 1:**

a) Why is the feeling of uncertainty rapidly increasing? Read through the following material and find an answer to this question. When you are ready, present your findings to a partner.

The tyranny of choice
If you can have everything in 57 varieties, making decisions becomes hard work

Dec 16th 2010 | PARIS | The Economist

Choice seduces the modern consumer at every turn. Lattes come tall, short, skinny, decaf, flavoured, iced, spiced or frappé. Jeans come flared, bootlegged, skinny, cropped, straight, low-rise, bleach-rinsed, dark-washed or distressed. Moisturiser nourishes, lifts, smooths, revitalises, conditions, firms, refreshes and rejuvenates. Tropicana, another part of PepsiCo, turns out freshly pulped juice in more than 20 different varieties, up from just six in 2004; it says there could be as many as 30 in the next decade.

Thanks to a mix of modern medicine, technology and social change, choice has expanded from the grocery shelf to areas that once had few or none. Faces, noses, wrinkles, breasts and bellies can be remodelled, plumped or tucked. America in 2008 alone saw 2.5 million Botox injections, 355,671 breast implants, 341,144 liposuction treatments, 195,104 eyelid lifts and 147,392 stomach tucks, according to the American Society for Aesthetic Plastic Surgery.

Teenagers can choose to surf, chat, tweet, zap or poke in ways that their parents can barely fathom. Moving pictures and music can be viewed, recorded, downloaded or streamed on all manner of screens or devices. The internet has handed huge power to the consumer to research options, whether of medical procedures or weekend breaks.

[...] But amid all the dizzying possibilities, a nagging question lurks: is so much extra choice unambiguously a good thing?

[...]

As options multiply, there may be a point at which the effort required to obtain enough information to be able to distinguish sensibly between alternatives outweighs the benefit to the consumer of the extra choice. "At this point", writes Barry Schwartz in "The Paradox of Choice", "choice no longer liberates, but debilitates. It might even be said to tyrannise." In other words, as Mr Schwartz puts it, "the fact that *some* choice is good doesn't necessarily mean that *more* choice is better."

[...]

Daniel McFadden, an economist at the University of California, Berkeley, says that consumers find too many options troubling because of the "risk of misperception and miscalculation, of misunderstanding the available alternatives, of misreading one's own tastes, of yielding to a moment's whim and regretting it afterwards", combined with "the stress of information acquisition". Indeed, the expectation of indecision can prompt panic and a failure to choose at all. Too many options means too much effort to make a sensible decision: better to bury your head under a pillow, or have somebody else pick for you.

b) "Worry about the right things." Talk about the things that worry you and assess to what extent they are the right things to worry about.

c) "*Some* choice is good doesn't necessarily mean that *more* choice is better." Discuss.

Partner 2:

a) American citizens live in a rather safe world. The perception, however, is different and many Americans feel insecure. Read through the following material and find out why. When you are ready, present your findings to a partner.

b) "Worry about the right things." Talk about the things that worry you and assess to what extent they are the right things to worry about.

c) "*Some* choice is good doesn't necessarily mean that *more* choice is better." Discuss.

The 'Fear Industrial Complex'

Feb 23th 2007 | By JOHN STOSSEL and NATALIE D. JAQUEZ via

From the faces of missing children on posters that cry "Have You Seen Me?" to public service announcements about cancer and other illnesses; from the terrorist attacks splashed across daily headlines to the reports of mad cow disease and avian flu on nightly newscasts, the media provide the public with no shortage of things to fear. The message is clear: The world is a scary place, and you should be worried.

A Time magazine cover in April 2006 said it outright: "Be Worried. Be Very Worried." The media aren't the only purveyors of fear, however.

"I think there is a fear industrial complex," said Barry Glassner, author of "The Culture of Fear: Why Americans Are Afraid of the Wrong Things." (...) He said the fear industrial complex is composed of politicians, activist groups and corporations that all sell us on the idea that they can provide safety from the very dangers they are scaring us about.

[...] The reason we scare people is simple: "Fear gets your eyeballs," said Dr Edward Hallowell [...]. For broadcast media, eyeballs equal ratings. For politicians, eyeballs equal votes. For activists, eyeballs equal support for their causes. For corporations, eyeballs equal sales. The bottom line: worry and fear sell.

In the case of the media, they provide plenty to worry about, like shark attacks being on the rise, killer bees attacking, flesh-eating bacteria and countless other threats. But they are rarely reported with any real perspective on the actual risk involved. Suddenly, the public starts to panic over something that poses minimal risk at most.

"We often worry about things that ... are not very dangerous, but which seem it. And the reason they seem it is because of ... the media who show images and tell stories about terrible, terrible things that happen," said Stephen Dubner, co-author of "Freakonomics." "People see those things and they think that they are the norm, and in fact, they are a great exception."

[...]

Relax ... A Little

We live in about the safest place, about the safest times in human history, and yet we're terrified of everything.

[...] "You should worry about whatever is causing you a problem ... whatever it is that happens to be in your life worth worrying about, like a mole on your forearm, like a debt that continues to rise. "Marc Siegel, author of "False Alarm: The Truth about the Epidemic of Fear," has similar advice about worrying.

"Our message isn't, 'Don't worry about anything,'" he said. "Our message is, 'Worry about the right things. Worry about things that can really harm your health.'"

Local TV news coverage analyzed by topic (2009)

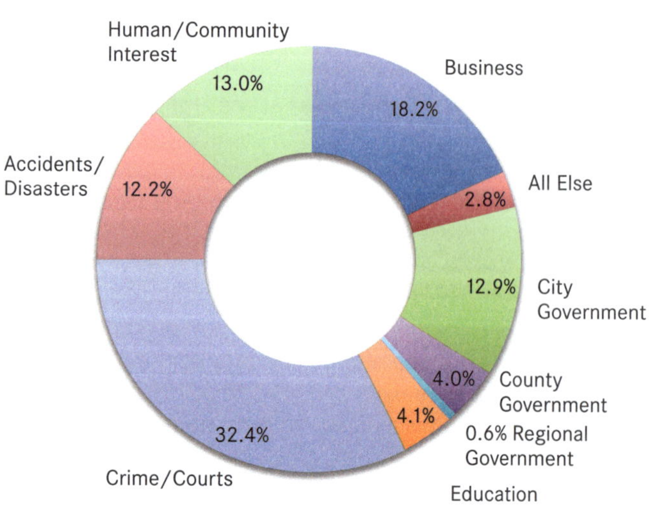

Mediation

A4 An American friend of yours wants to know more about the situation of German high school graduates. Write an e-mail in which you tell him about what you found out from the following material.

Ziemlich planlos vor der Reifeprüfung

Von Christoph Titz, Spiegel Online 24.04.2009

Es ist ein großer Aufbruch – und der wirft reichlich Fragen auf. Ein Drittel der Abiturienten weiß nicht recht, wie es nach den Prüfungen weitergehen soll: Uni, Lehre, etwas ganz anderes? Zudem befürchten viele Schüler, dass sie sich ein Studium nicht leisten können.

Das Abitur ist eine anstrengende Zeit – aber auch eine schöne. In der Oberstufe haben die meisten Schüler schon so viele Punkte eingesammelt, dass sie sich ums Bestehen oder Durchfallen nicht mehr arg viele Sorgen machen müssen. Aber um die Abi-Endnote schon, denn die ist ein Türöffner fürs Studium. Um besonders viel geht es bei den letzten Prüfungen für alle, die schon ein zugangsbeschränktes Fach fest anvisiert haben.
Wissen, was man nach dem Abi nicht will, ist eine Sache – aber wie soll die eigene Zukunft aussehen? In dieser Zeit der Verheißung und der Unsicherheit haben Forscher für die Hochschulinformations-System GmbH (HIS) die Schüler des Abi-Jahrgangs des Winters 2007/2008 befragt, wie schon in den Vorjahren.
Die größte Sorge der deutschen Abiturienten 2008 galt der unabsehbaren Entwicklung auf dem Arbeitsmarkt. Vier von zehn Abiturienten gaben diesen Grund als besonderes persönliches Problem bei der Wahl der künftigen Richtung ihrer Ausbildung an. Die massive Rezession, in der Deutschland wohl auch im kommenden Jahr noch stecken wird, hat dieses Ergebnis allerdings im Befragungszeitraum von Ende 2007 bis Anfang 2008 noch nicht beeinflusst – eine aktuelle Befragung fiele in diesem Punkt wohl dramatischer aus.

Was soll ich nur tun? Und was kann ich überhaupt?
Fast auf dem gleichen Rang wie die Sorgen um die Berufschancen landet die Unsicherheit angesichts des Überangebots an Möglichkeiten, die sich nach dem Abi bieten - ein Ergebnis, das auch mit dem Zulassungschaos an den deutschen Hochschulen in den vergangenen Jahren zusammenhängen dürfte.
Mache ich eine Lehre, oder studiere ich an einer Hochschule? Soll es eine Uni oder eine FH sein, und wenn ich das weiß, welches Fach? Nur ein Viertel der Oberstufenschüler fühlt sich über die Möglichkeiten nach dem Abi gut informiert, ein Drittel nennt die Vorbereitung dagegen unzureichend. Ein knappes Drittel ist sich unklar über die persönliche Eignung für den einen oder anderen Weg.
[...]

Writing

A5 Put yourself into the position of an American high school student. You have been selected to give the graduation speech. Write a speech on the topic of "Challenges and choices in an insecure world".
- Think of aspects you could talk about, e.g. self-actualization, money ...
  Create a handwritten wordle (see page 5). Remember that the size of the words indicates their importance.
- Consider your audience. Think about what you have to keep in mind when addressing them.

Audience:

teachers, ______________________________

- Write down an effective lead-in to grab the audience's attention.

____

____

____

____

____

____

– As speakers use many rhetorical devices in speeches, match the following devices, definitions and examples in preparation for your own speech.

alliteration | metaphor | use of pronouns | anaphora | parallelism | antithesis | rhetorical question | climax | hyperbole | repetition

Am I talking to a wall? | What you see is what you get. | A kleptomaniac is a person who helps himself because he can't help himself. | Mad world! Mad kings! Mad composition! | Betty Botter bought some butter. | For we, all of us, will be judged by the dreams and deeds we pass on to our children. | Give every man thy ear, but few thy voice. | I came, I saw, I conquered | My heart is broken. | This cat weighs a ton!

device	definition	example
alliteration	a repetition of the same letter/ sound at the beginning of words that are close together	*Betty Botter bought some butter.*
	a repetition of words or phrases at the beginning of successive sentences	
	a contrast between two things	
	a row of statements from weakest to strongest	
	an exaggeration	
	a comparison between two things that are not alike at all with no words of comparison (*like, as*)	
	the repetition of similar phrases/ sentences structures in neighboring sentences/paragraphs	
	the use of a word or a phrase more than once	
	a question that need not be answered since the answer is obvious	
	the use of a pronoun that refers to a particular person, group, or thing	

A6 Write the speech and make use of at least three stylistic devices. ⇒ skills: how to write a speech p. 122

How to write a comment

In a comment you express your opinion on a certain topic or statement in a coherent form. You might, for example, be asked to state your opinion on a quotation. So you have to decide whether you agree or disagree with it. In your comment you then try to convince the reader of your opinion by presenting arguments and giving examples that support your arguments. It is essential that you have a sound knowledge of the topic or statement you write about.

Before you start writing read the task carefully, then collect and organise your thoughts / arguments and the relevant examples.

Your comment should be made up of three parts: the introduction, the main part (body) and the conclusion. Use paragraphs for each part. Your thesis should either be part of the introduction or the conclusion.

Introduction	
· Write a clear introduction in which you mention the topic / statement and explain what it means for you. · Attract the reader's attention with the help of a recent event or a personal experience that illustrates the topic and / or shows its significance.	→ *The problem of ... has met with a lot of attention lately, As far as I understand/can see ...; There are many reasons for ...; There is no doubt that*
· Mention your thesis in the introduction if you think this attracts the reader's attention.	→ *... claims that ... . I strongly disagree with him/her.* → *... claims that ... . I fully agree with him / her and in this comment I will show why ...*
Body	
· Use a sentence that connects the introduction and the main part.	→ *In the following I shall be concerned with ...; I intend to present arguments in favour of ...*
· Provide arguments in favour of your opinion	→ *Firstly, ... secondly, ... another point, in addition, besides ..., furthermore ..., on top of that*
· Give examples (numbers, statistics, events, etc.) which illustrate or explain arguments.	→ *for example, for instance, such as, e.g., to illustrate this idea, I would like to ...; This idea can best be demonstrated by an example*
· You can also mention arguments against your thesis / opinion in order to show to the reader that you aren't ignoring these arguments. If you do so, you should present a strong counterargument in the same paragraph. · Use one paragraph for each single argument. · Start each paragraph with a topic sentence which expresses what the whole paragraph is about.	→ *There are sceptics who say ...; I am fully aware that there are people who ..., but ...; You may have heard of people who claim ..., but ...*
Conclusion	
· Briefly refer to the original question and repeat your opinion.	→ *In conclusion, I would like to say that ...; I would like to conclude by saying that ...; After having read and assessed the arguments carefully I'm sure you agree that ...; The conclusion I draw is as follows: ...; I think it has become obvious that ...*
· You can also refer to the event or personal experience you mentioned at the beginning or speculate about the significance of the topic / statement in the near future. · Make sure that you do not introduce any new ideas in your conclusion.	
Language	
· Use connectives within the text, e.g. *This means that ..., Thus ..., As a consequence ...* · Avoid imprecise and overused adjectives/adverbs, i.e. not: *good, bad, happy, sad, ...* but: *convincing, positive, helpful, harmful, negative, ...* · Avoid generalizations and be as precise as possible. The following words and phrases might be useful: *... tends to be ..., many, a considerable number of, almost, at least, particularly, rather,* etc. · Vary your sentence structure. For example, use participle constructions, subordinate clauses, etc.	

How to mediate

What is mediation? It is a technique used to enable communication between people who do not speak the same language by transferring information from one language into another. The material you have to mediate might be a printed text, audio material such as an interview or visuals (e.g. cartoon, statistics). Unlike translation, it is more than just simply putting a text into a different language as exactly as possible. It is not enough just to summarize the basic information given in another language. Instead, mediation requires intercultural knowledge, since it not only depends on the text itself but also on the context and situative factors, such as the text type you are dealing with, the situation in general, the addressee, the relationship between author, mediator and reader and the purpose of the mediation.

Preparation
· Identify the source your material was taken from. · Skim and scan the text carefully, look for important keywords and get the gist of the text.
Content
· Keep in mind the situation you are in and use the correct form to present your material (e.g. presentation, summary, letter). · Focus on the main aspects of the task at hand. · Be precise and avoid redundancy. · Do not stuck to the original literally but try to understand the meaning and intention of the given material.
Addressee
· Always keep in mind your addressee. Provide additional material to clarify certain aspects for your addressee if necessary. For instance, your addressee may need additional background information about certain aspects of your culture, like institutions. · Use intercultural knowledge to decide how to present your material. · Leave out information that is not relevant for the addressee.
Structure
· Structure your ideas in a logical way.
Language
· Use your own words (no quotes!). · Adapt your language to the situation and the addressee. · Avoid overused words. · Employ connectives. · Vary your sentence structure by using subordinate clauses and participle constructions.

How to analyze and interpret statistics

Statistics collect, organize and present data in different forms. The most frequent forms are tables, line graphs, pie charts or bar charts. Whether a table is used or a pie chart depends on the focus of the presentation. Line graphs, for example, can show developments over a period of time, tables present raw data, bar charts compare two or more figures and pie charts show percentages of 100%.

a	b	c
2	1	6
3	3	2
1	2	3

table

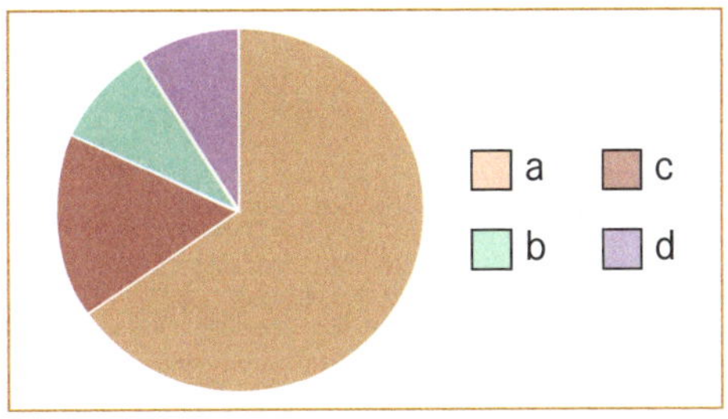

pie chart

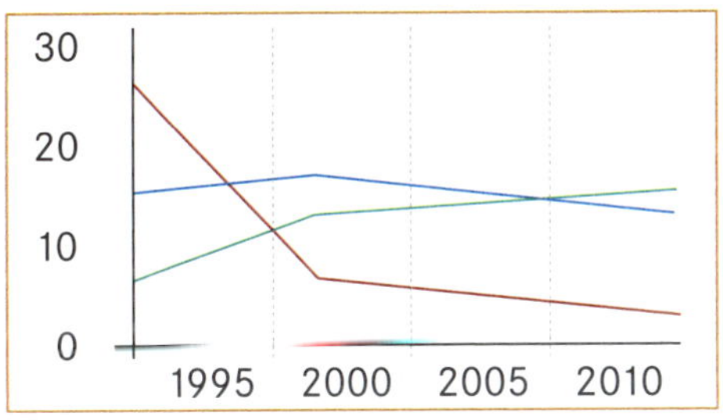

line graph

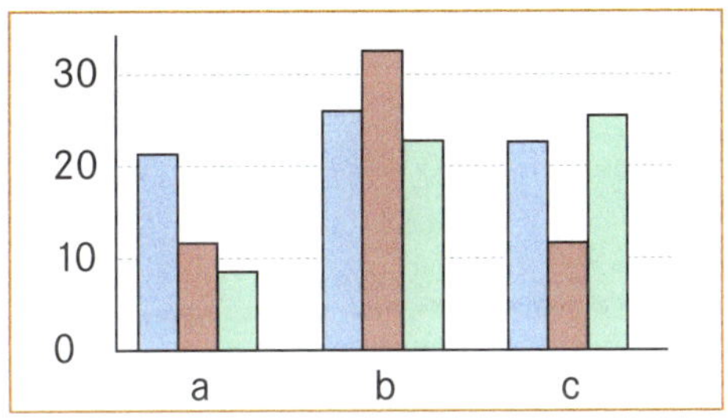

bar chart

Before you start analyzing statistics, study the graph, the chart or the table carefully.
Look at the title and the key thoroughly and highlight any surprising/interesting or sudden features.

Introduction	
· Mention the origin/source, the author, the date · Roughly outline what the statistic depicts in general	→ *the survey at hand carried out by … and published in … focuses on/deals with …* → *this table shows/is about/provides information about …*
Formal components	
· Explain the formal components of the presentation (table, chart, graph) · general structure · period of time covered · axes labels · information on the units	→ *The chart consists of …* → *It covers the years from … to …* → *the vertical/horizontal axis represents …* → *… in percent/millimeters/kilograms/absolute numbers*
Description	
· Describe developments/changes over time · Describe peaks and lows · Describe relationships and connections · Describe in a systematic way (e.g. mention the most important aspects first) and concentrate on the most remarkable data · Consider why the data is presented in a table, chart or diagram	→ *Between … and … there is an increase/decrease in …* → *… reaches a peak/a low point in …; an all-time high* → *The majority of …/Nearly half of …/Compared to …*
Interpretation/Conclusion	
· Draw conclusions from the numbers	→ *As you can see from the diagram, …; This development clearly shows/indicates that …; The path of the curve reveals …; As a result of …; … suggests a relation between … and …; So it is easy/difficult to estimate/judge/make precise comments; All in all, the statistics for … reveal/show that …*

· Explain your conclusions with your background knowledge of the topic · Be critical about the form of the presentation: e.g. easily understandable form? Reliable source? Up-to-date figures? · Discuss how the figures are presented – in a positive, negative or neutral light · Put your conclusion in a larger context	→ *The chart underlines the fact that ...; The data confirm/contradict/are not consistent with ...* → *The chart is more/less effective than ... because ...*
Structure	
· Structure the text: introduction, main part, conclusion · Make sensible paragraphs within the main part; use topic sentences	
Language	
· Use connectives within the text · Use phrases that are essential for this text type · Avoid imprecise and overused adjectives/adverbs · Vary your sentence structure (e.g. use participle constructions)	

How to analyze and interpret pictures

Pictures/photos/drawing can be compared with texts. They were created with a purpose and in order to be able to interpret what they are supposed to tell the viewer, you need a systematic approach. It is important to have a close look at a picture's details and to consider its context: when was it painted/drawn? Where was it published? Who was it made for?

When dealing with photographs, keep in mind that there are different kinds (documentary photographs, snap shots, staged photographs). Some photographs try to show a situation as authentically as possible, others are taken by accident and show realistic situations without any changes while others may have been digitally altered with a special effect in mind.

A systematic approach can be divided into the following four steps:

Introduction	
· Mention the name of the photographer/artist and when/where the picture/photo/drawing was taken (if the information is available). · Roughly outline what the visual depicts in general.	→ *The photo by ... was published in ...* → *The photo was probably taken in/at/to ...* → *The picture refers to .../deals with ...* → *The topic of the photo is ...* → *The picture shows/illustrates ...* → *This is a reference to ...* → *It wants us to ...* → *The situation reminds me of ...*
· State your first response to the visual.	→ *My first thought when I saw the drawing was ...* → *The photo is shocking/disgusting/ amazing/spectacular/special ...*
Description	
· Describe the visual clearly and concentrate on the relevant aspects only.	→ *In the center, there is/are* → *The field size is a close-up* (very close to an object/ person)*/a medium shot/a long shot* (persons/objects + surroundings) → *The focus of attention is on ...*
· Describe in a systematic way – start with the dominant image/the main aspect and describe it in detail without forgetting the aspects in the background. · If there are lots of different things in the visual or if there is no difference between foreground and background, work from top to bottom, from left to right.	→ *What strikes the eye is ...* → *In the background, one can see ...* → *... is displayed in the right-hand corner*
· Describe the technique the artist/painter/photographer used (e.g. light, colour).	→ *The artist used water colour/oil /bright colours ...* → *The photographer used black and white/colour/a sharp focus ...* → *to be out of focus/to be blurred* → *There is a contrast between light and dark ...* → *X seems to be sad/distracted/angry/embarrassed ... because ...*
· Describe body language and facial expressions and speculate about who the people are and what their relationship is like.	
Analysis/Interpretation	
· State what the artist is trying to say and how he/she does it.	→ *The artist criticizes/wants to point out ...* → *The photo is meant to criticize ...* → *According to the photographer, ...*
· Speculate about the possible addressee; it might be useful to keep in mind the source of the visual (e.g. age, biased source).	→ *Since it was published in ..., one might assume that...*
· State whether the picture was taken with a special intention (i.e. snap shot ↔ staged photograph).	→ *The photo was staged to achieve a certain effect ... It is a realistic picture of ...*

· If it is a staged or a manipulated photograph, assess the effect on the viewer. · Discuss how the characters are presented: in a positive, negative light or neutral light? How is this done? · Explain the (intended) effect on the viewer and the way it is achieved (e.g. use pictorial elements which back up the message as 'evidence'). · Wrap up your interpretation in a final statement.	→ *... is represented as ... / comes across as being ...* → *The characters are presented in a positive light. This is due to their facial expressions/gestures/what they are saying* → *The photo comes across as ...; This is achieved by ...* → *The colors support the impression that ...* → *The atmosphere in the picture seems rather ... since the artist uses ...* → *All in all/In general, the painter/photographer wants to make the reader aware of the fact that ...*
Evaluation	
· Explain the effect the visual has on you. · Evaluate the artist's presentation, his/her message and the situation he/she depicts. · Assess the success of the message: is it presented convincingly?	→ *Personally, I like/do not like the photo, because ...; The photo touches me/leaves me cold because ...* → *My initial reaction to the picture was ..., but on second glance I think that ...* → *In my opinion, the artist has successfully shown that ...* → *The picture does not reach the intended target group because ...* → *The photo is (not) effective in its presentation of ...* → *It could have been more effective if it had ...*
tips	
· Structure your text well and make sensible use of paragraphs. · Use connectives as well as phrases that are essential for this type of text. · Vary your sentence structure.	

How to analyze and interpret cartoons

Cartoons are drawings, often either simplified or exaggerated, which comment on current topics or criticize well-known people as well as institutions in a humorous, mostly satirical way.

In order to understand a cartoon, it is essential to have a close look at its details and to pay special attention to the combination between the drawing itself and the text (e.g. caption or speech bubbles). Moreover, it is important to consider its context (when was it originally drawn? Where was it published? Who was it made for?)

A systematic approach would comprise the following four steps:

Introduction	
· Mention the name of the cartoonist and when/where the cartoon was published. · Roughly outline what the cartoon depicts in general. · Give your first response to the cartoon. · State possible reasons for the representation provided.	→ *The cartoon by ... was published in ...* → *The cartoon refers to .../deals with ...* → *The topic of the cartoon is ...* → *The situation reminds me of ...* → *My first thought when I saw the cartoon was ...*
Description	
· Start with the most important elements, but make sure that you do not forget those in the background. · Describe the cartoon in detail but make sure that you concentrate on the relevant aspects only. · Identify the current events/people/institutions referred to. · If your cartoon includes texts, link them to the drawing. · Describe artistic techniques the cartoonist used.	→ *The focus of attention is ...; What strikes the eye is ...* → *The cartoon depicts/shows...* → *In the center, there is/are* → *In the background, one can see ...* → *... is displayed in the right-hand corner* → *The figure in the foreground bears a likeness to ...; ... shows X as a ...* → *There is a caption at/on/in ...* → *The speech bubble contains ...* → *The caption says ...* → *The cartoonist used color / showed the subject close up*
Analysis/Interpretation	
· State what the cartoonist is trying to say. Use the context of the cartoon as well as a possible addressee. Think about the source it was published in and base your interpretation on this. · Examine whether the issues/persons/institutions are presented in a positive or negative light and explain how this is done. Pay attention to the devices used, such as the use of exaggeration, irony, puns and symbols and consider whether you can take the message at face value or not. · Explain the (intended) effect on the viewer and the way it is achieved (e.g. mention pictorial elements that back up the message as 'evidence'). · Wrap up your interpretation: what is the cartoonist trying to say/criticize ?	→ *The cartoon refers to/deals with ...* → *The artist is criticizing/wants to point out ...* → *Since it was published in ..., one might assume that ...* → *The cartoon comes across as ... This is achieved by ...* → *The characters are presented in a positive light. This is due to their facial expressions/gestures/what they are saying* → *According to the cartoonist, ...* → *The overall atmosphere is rather ...* → *Although/Even though..., the real point the cartoon seems to be making is ...* → *The cartoonist wants to ridicule/make fun of ...* → *In general, what the cartoonist wants to make the reader aware of is ...* → *By presenting ..., the cartoonist ...* → *All in all, the cartoonist wants to make the viewer aware of the fact that ...*

Evaluation	
· Mention your personal opinion regarding the artist's representation and its message. · Outline the effect the cartoon has on you and explain why you like/do not like it.	→ *Personally, I do/do not like the cartoon, because ...* → *The cartoon touches me/leaves me cold because ...* → *In my opinion, the cartoonist has successfully shown that ...*
· Evaluate the artist's presentation from your point of view and assess the success of the message: is it presented convincingly?	→ *The cartoonist has failed to ...* → *The cartoon is (not) effective in its presentation of ...*

tips
· Structure your text well and make sensible use of paragraphs. · Use connectives as well as phrases that are essential for this type of text. · Vary your sentence structure.

How to hold a panel discussion

In a panel discussion you have to slip into a role that is assigned to you. From this person's point of view you have to present and defend a certain position.

You should think about the following aspects:
- Make sure that you understand what the controversy at hand is about.
- Collect ideas and information about the topic.
  → What are the most important aspects for your position?
  → What are arguments for the opposing view and ways to refute them?
- Structure your points from least to most important.
- Make sure that you can give evidence for each argument.
- Think about what is essential in your role to come across credibly.
- Listen carefully to what other participants say.
- Always express yourself politely and respectfully. Only attack arguments but not people.

The following phrases have different communicative functions and may help you in a discussion.

giving an opinion	expressing agreement
→ *In my opinion/view, …* → *To my mind, …* → *Personally, I think …* → *If you ask me, …* → *I firmly believe that …* → *I am convinced that …* → *As far as I'm concerned …* → *It goes without saying that …*	→ *You are right.* → *Absolutely/Exactly/Precisely.* → *I think you are right to a point.* → *I totally agree.* → *I fully support your point of view.* → *That sounds very convincing.* → *I think X is absolutely right when saying …*
expressing disagreement	**adding aspects/arguments**
→ *I am sorry but I don't agree at all.* → *I am afraid I think you are wrong here.* → *I completely disagree with you on …* → *I would question that argument.* → *I believe that is possibly a mistaken view.* → *This may be true to a certain extent, but …* → *I take the opposite view, unfortunately.* → *With respect, I see the situation differently.*	→ *Firstly, …secondly, … thirdly, …* → *In the first place, …* → *Furthermore/Moreover, …* → *In addition/Additionally, …* → *I'd like to add that …* → *Another reason/convincing argument is that …* → *Finally, I wish to point out that …* → *And last but not least, …* → *To conclude, …*
giving evidence	**interrupting politely**
→ *Let me give you an example of what I mean by …* → *Take …, for example.* → *Statistics/Surveys show …* → *There is strong evidence that …* → *For instance, look at …* → *Looking at facts and figures, it is clear …*	→ *May I interrupt you for a second/a moment, please?* → *Sorry, can I just make a point?* → *Sorry to interrupt you, but …* → *Can I just come/jump in here?* → *Excuse me, but can I stop you for a moment?*
checking understanding	**involving a partner**
→ *If I understand you correctly, …* → *What do you exactly mean by that?* → *Do you really mean to say that …?* → *Excuse me, I didn't quite catch your point about …* → *So, what you are saying is …*	→ *What do you think about …?* → *Is there anything you would like to add?* → *How about you?* → *Would you agree with that?*
correcting misunderstandings	**introducing a new aspect**
→ *You've got the wrong impression, I'm afraid.* → *Please let me repeat what I actually said.* → *I wonder if I may explain again what I mean.* → *Don't get me wrong. What I meant was …*	→ *That reminds me of …* → *Talking of …* → *What we haven't discussed yet is the question whether …* → *We should also discuss …* → *I would like to raise another point.*

showing results	summing up
→ *Therefore, ...* → *That is why ...* → *This leads to ...* → *Consequently/As a consequence, ...* → *As a result, ...*	→ *To sum up, ...* → *In brief ...* → *To cut a long story short ...* → *We have heard that ...* → *The general trend seems to be ...*

How to analyze a speech

In a speech, a speaker expresses his opinion on a certain topic in front of an audience. Since the audience usually only listens to a speech once, the speaker has to make sure that the audience immediately comprehends what he/she is trying to say.

Basically, there are four different types of speeches, depending on the speaker's goal: the **informative speech** which serves to provide information to the audience, the **demonstrative speech** which informs but also teaches the audience something, the **persuasive speech** which aims to win over and persuade the audience to change something and the **entertaining speech** which provides pleasure to make the audience laugh. However, speeches can also be a mixture of all these types. Knowing the speaker's objective is critical to analyzing the speech, and should therefore influence how you study it.

Moreover, you should keep in mind the audience itself. A speaker will use different strategies to connect with an audience of 2000 than with an audience of only 20. The same is true for the key demographic features of the audience such as age, background, knowledge and position.

Your speech analysis should be made up of three parts: the introduction, the main part (body) and the conclusion. Use paragraphs for each part and make sensible paragraphs within the main part.

Introduction	
· Write an introduction in which you mention the speaker, his/her role at that time and the relevant circumstances in which the speech was delivered. · Identify the type of speech.	→ *The speech "..." delivered in ... on ... by ..., at that time ...., deals with ....; The speech is addressed to ...; it is an election speech/address/a state of the nation speech ...*
· Summarize the topic as well as the speaker's supposed intention.	→ *The focus is on ...; The speaker wants to/is aiming to/is trying to ...; The speaker is canvassing for ...; The speaker wishes to stir/persuade his audience ...*
Main part	
· Describe the structure of the speech.	→ *The speech can be divided into ...; In his opening words ...; Halfway through the speech ...; Towards the end of the speech ...*
· List different stylistic devices/strategies in order of importance.	→ *One of the most effective devices the speaker employs is ...; The most powerful strategy ...; At one point in his/her speech he/she makes use of ...; A recurrent rhetorical device ...; A striking rhetorical device is ...; One of the most efficient devices is ...*
· Use quotes to exemplify the devices/strategies employed.	→ *In line ..., the speaker argues/illustrates/claims that "...": As the speaker observes in line ...*
· Explain their intended effect (first in general, then in the context of the speech).	→ *to establish a personal relationship with ...; to make the audience aware of ...; to make the audience feel understood; to trigger off emotions; to engage the listener effectively; to create immediacy and urgency; to make a lasting impression by ...; to involve the difference between A and B; to deceive an audience; to avoid offense; to heighten the audience's attention; to make a speech more memorable; to make easily recognizable references; to emphasize sth; to make the listeners aware of the extent of the problem; to arouse interest; to simplify complicated matters by referring to everyday experiences; to launch into a polemic against ...; to appeal to the listeners' conscience; to leave no room for doubt; to impose one's opinion on ...; to increase intensity; to create the illusion of mutual understanding; to win over so.*

Conclusion	
· Briefly summarize your results.	→ *All in all, it can be said that ...., In conclusion, I would like to say that ...; I would like to conclude by saying that ..., To put it into a nutshell, ...; The message of the speech is clear and simple: ...*
· Evaluate the effect with reference to the speaker's supposed intention.	→ *In my opinion, the speaker displays a thorough/intimate/superficial knowledge of ...; The speaker twists/perverts the truth by ...; From my point of view the speech is convincing, because ...* → *The speech deeply moved me/left me cold/made me laugh ...; The speech made me think about ...*

tips
· structure the text in three main part and use sensible paragraphs · write topic sentences · use connectives within the text · use phrases that are essential for this text form · vary your sentence structure (e.g. use participle constructions and subordinate clauses).

Info: Stylistic/rhetorical devices

Stylistic/rhetorical devices are frequently used in speeches to convince the listeners of the speaker's idea. The most frequently used devices are the following:

devices	definition	example
alliteration	a repetition of the same letter/sound at the beginning of words that are close together	*Peter Piper picked a peck of pickled pepper.*
allusion	an indirect reference to a famous person/event/theme ...	*"I violated the Noah rule: predicting rain doesn't count; building arks does."* Warren Buffett
anaphora	a repetition of words or phrases at the beginning of successive sentences	*"I needed a drink, I needed a lot of life insurance, I needed a vacation, I needed a home in the country."* Raymond Chandler, Farewell, My Lovely
antithesis	a contrast between two things	*"Tonight you voted for action, not politics as usual. You elected us to focus on your jobs, not ours."* Barack Obama
climax	a row of statements from weakest to strongest	*"Friends, Romans, countrymen!"* Shakespeare, *Julius Caesar*
direct address	a construction in which a speaker or writer directly addresses another individual	*Peter, my friend, you look tired today.*
euphemism	the use of positive or polite words for sth. that is unpleasant/ embarrassing/ frightening	*to pass away* instead of *to die*
hyperbole	an exaggeration	*I am so hungry that I could eat a horse.*
metaphor	a comparison between two things that are not alike at all with no words of comparison (*like, as*)	*Life is but a walking shadow.* Shakespeare, *Macbeth*
parallelism	the repetition of similar phrases/sentences structures in neighboring sentences/paragraphs	*"When you are right you cannot be too radical; when you are wrong, you cannot be too conservative."* Martin Luther King, Jr.
personification	the presentation of things/animals/ideas as if they were human being/possessed human qualities	*Fear knocked on the door.*

repetition	the use of a word or a phrase more than once	*Tomorrow and tomorrow and tomorrow, creeps in this petty pace from day to day.* Shakespeare, *Macbeth*
rhetorical question	a question that need not be answered since the answer is obvious	*Don't we all hate war?*
simile	a comparison between two things that are not like one another.	*He fought like a lion.*
symbol	sth. concrete that stands for sth. abstract	*scales for justice*
tricolon	a row of three statements/ideas (often climactic)	*Eye it, try it, buy it.*
use of pronouns	the use of a pronoun that refers to a particular person, group, or thing	*For we, all of us, will be judged by the dreams and deeds we pass on to our children.* Bill Clinton

↓

Stylistic devices can be divided into different categories (sense or sound). The speaker might use them for the following reasons:

Effects	
· to grab the audience's attention · to produce a rhythm · to evoke/trigger off positive/negative feelings · to establish a feeling of togetherness · to make the reader aware of the importance of the topic · to make the audience feel understood by the speaker	· to establish a good speaker-audience relationship · to engage the listener effectively · to make a lasting impression · to simplify a complex issue · to avoid offense · to heighten the audience's attention · to emphasize a certain aspect · to hammer home a point

How to write a speech

Apart from analysing a speech, you might also be given the task of writing a speech. In order to produce a good speech, you should consider the following aspects.

Preparation	
· Carefully read your assignment: What is the topic of your speech? Do you have to refer to other material (e.g. a newspaper article, a certain event, another speech?) · If you have to take a role, take into consideration what this person is like (age, knowledge, position, relationship to others ...). · Think about the purpose of your speech. Do you want to inform, demonstrate, persuade or entertain? · Think about the audience (e.g. background, age, knowledge, interests). What do they already know about the topic? · After researching the topic, list aspects you could talk about. Then structure your ideas logically.	
Introduction	
· Directly address the audience with a note of welcome.	→ *Ladies and gentlemen, fellow students, my friends, members of ..., my fellow countrymen ...; It's an honour for me to be here today at ...; I really appreciate being here with you today ...; I feel greatly honoured by your invitation ...*
· Create an effective lead-in to grab the listeners' attention by using, for example, a provocative statement, a surprising fact, a new discovery, an anecdote, a rhetorical question or a quotation. · Present the topic/problem.	→ *In the following I shall be concerned with/deal with the problem/subject/issue of ...; As some of you might know, ...; We are here today to ...; I intend to present arguments in favour of/against ...*
Main part	
· Develop your ideas step by step and organize your speech according to the structure of a comment. · Concentrate on the most important aspects (no more than five) and be specific and direct instead of giving too many ideas. · Start with the least important point and work up to the most important point; alternatively, you can start with your most important one and then work progressively from the least important point up to the second most important one. · Provide background information if necessary.	→ *Undoubtedly, this is a time of ... but at the same time it is also a period of ...; It is generally believed that ...; At first sight this seems to be true but ...*
· Support your point of view with examples/facts/statistics.	→ *Take for example ...; There is some evidence to suggest that ...*
· Use stylistic devices to emphasize the main message (e.g. repetition, contrast, rhetorical questions, metaphors and similes).	
· Link ideas and arguments. · Repeat the most important ideas, emphasize phrases or passages.	→ *Now let us return to ...; This brings me to the next point; In addition to this point I want to stress that ...; Take for example ...; There seems to be a contradiction here ...; Hence, ...; The result of this is as follows ...; Having discussed ... it is now appropriate to mention ...*
· Establish contact with the audience by addressing them directly/flattering them/using the first-person plural/appealing to shared experiences.	→ *We all know that ...*
· Show your conviction.	→ *Undoubtedly/certainly/indeed/strangely enough/first and foremost*

Conclusion	
· Briefly summarize your main points.	→ *All in all, I think it can be said that ...; To put it in a nutshell, ...; In conclusion, I would like to say that ...; Let me conclude with the words of ...; Looking at all the facts and figures, I have to draw the conclusion that ...; What it all boils down to is the following: ...*
· Call for action, look into the future, use a relevant quotation or a promise. · Clearly finish your speech and thank the audience for their attention.	→ *Let us all work together to ...; We have to ensure that ...; In the near future ...; In the long run ...; We are confident that ...; We should take on new roles.*

Structure
· Structure your speech into three parts: introduction, body, conclusion. · Make sensible use of paragraphs within the main part.

Language
· Incorporate transitions and connectives (e.g. *additionally, however, ...; that is why ...; in short, ...*). · Use a mixture of mostly short and only a few long sentences. · Use striking adjectives and adverbs. · Employ the appropriate register and tone (e.g. formal, informal, entertaining, serious, witty etc.).

Presentation
· Rehearse your speech before you deliver it. · Speak clearly and at a moderate speed. · Modulate your voice (volume, speed). · Stress important words to emphasize your key points. · Establish contact with the audience and maintain eye contact. · Use helpful body language (gestures, facial expression).

How to write a letter to the editor

A letter to the editor is a formal letter in which a reader states his or her opinion concerning an article in a newspaper/magazine or a problem which is of public interest. The letter can either criticize or support an article, a radio or television programme, but it can also express a personal opinion concerning a topic which has recently been discussed in public. Moreover, a letter to the editor may attract the attention of other readers to a topic worthy of attention.

This type of letter has a few differences from other formal letters.

Content	
· In the reference line say exactly which article you are referring to. · Start your letter with "Sir or Madam".	→ *"Edward Snowden is no hero", June 16th, 2013*
· At the beginning of your letter, name the article/recent event/public statement etc. you are referring to.	→ *In his article of 13th August 2013, "..." (title/heading) the author "..." mentioned/said/wrote that ...; With reference to your article of 13th August 2013 ..., I would like to ...; I am writing in response to your article ...; Having read your article "...", I would like to ...*
· In the opening sentence you give your reason for writing (e.g. support, criticism, information).	→ *I would like to object to ...; I utterly agree with you that ...; I would like to point out that ...; I would like to congratulate you on....; As a firm believer of ...; I think you are mistaken if you believe ...; After carefully studying your suggestions, I am sorry to say that ...; Please allow me to voice my criticism of ...; I would appreciate more objectivity when ...; I would like to express doubts about ...; With all due respect ...; I was hoping for a more objective treatment of the topic;*
· If you want to quote from the article, use indirect speech.	→ *the author claims/writes/believes that ...; as stated in the article, ...; in the author's opinion ...*
· Write a convincing concluding sentence.	→ *All in all, there can be no doubt that ...; In conclusion, the evidence given shows that ...; The question can longer be whether ..., but ...; May I suggest following up the article of ... with a further one, which this time includes ...*
· Sign the letter and give your hometown.	

Structure
· Use all aspects for writing a formal letter (sender's address, date, recipient's address, reference line, salutation, body, closing, signature). · Make your letter short and to the point. · Structure your arguments in a logical order and back them up with examples or facts.

Language
· Use indirect instead of direct speech. · Use formal language. · Be polite. · Use connectives.

How to write an argumentative essay

In an argumentative essay, you **discuss** a topic or statement by presenting different positions or points of view. After having read your essay the reader should be aware that there are different ways of looking at the given topic or statement and should be well informed about the various positions. In contrast to a comment, it is not your aim to try and convince the reader of your opinion throughout the essay. At the end of the essay you can, however, give your own opinion or simply appeal to the reader to draw his own conclusion.

The structure of your argumentative essay can vary, depending on the topic or statement that you write about. In some cases you need to divide the topic into different aspects and deal with the various positions on these aspects paragraph by paragraph. In other cases you can present one position first and then deal with the second position. This structure is often used when there are two opposing views. In any case, your argumentative essay should be made up of three parts: the introduction, the main part (body) and the conclusion. Use paragraphs for each part.

Before you start writing, read the task carefully, then brainstorm ideas on a sheet of paper. Collect arguments and corresponding examples for the different positions, then decide on the structure of your essay and the sequence of the arguments.

Introduction	
· Write a clear, thought-provoking introduction in which you present your issue / statement and show why it is important to discuss this issue. · Attract the reader's attention with the help of a recent event, a personal experience, a reference to a famous person.	→ *In this essay, I want to investigate ...; This essay will concentrate on ...; My discussion draws into focus ...; ... seems to be an inexhaustible source of controversy, ... is a hotly debated topic at the moment; The problem of ... has met with a lot of attention lately* → *It is interesting to weigh up the benefits and drawbacks of ...; Therefore one should discuss the issue .../wonder about/ask the question of whether ...*
Body	
· Use a sentence that connects the introduction and the main part.	→ *In the following I shall be concerned with .../I intend to present arguments in favour of ..., Some experts state that ..., many people believe/claim that ...*
· Present the different positions / points of view and the corresponding arguments. · Provide examples for each position / point of view / argument (facts, statistics, etc.). · Use one paragraph for each single position / point of view / argument. · Start each paragraph with a topic sentence which expresses what the whole paragraph is about. · Do not express your own position in the main part of your essay but only present the various positions / points of view / arguments.	→ *Firstly, ... secondly, ... another point, in addition, besides ..., furthermore ..., on top of that ...* → *for example, for instance, such as, e.g., to illustrate this idea, I would like to ...; This idea can best be demonstrated by an example.*

<table>
<tr><th colspan="2">Conclusion</th></tr>
<tr><td>· Briefly refer to the original question and wrap up the discussion.
· Make sure that you do not introduce any new ideas in your conclusion.</td><td>→ All in all, it can be said that …; In conclusion, I would like to say that …; I would like to conclude by saying that …; After weighing up the arguments carefully …; The conclusion I draw is as follows: …; As a consequence …; As a result of …; The most important aspect one has to keep in mind is …, after all</td></tr>
<tr><td>· Give your final position on the topic (this can be a compromise) without repeating your arguments or leave it to the reader to draw his own conclusion.

· You can also refer to the event or personal experience you have mentioned at the beginning or speculate about the significance of the topic / statement in the near future.</td><td>→ In my opinion …; Apparently …; obviously, therefore, to my mind …; I firmly believe that …; to a certain extent, I can accept …, but …; Although … we must admit that …; There can be no doubt as regards …; I am absolutely convinced of …</td></tr>
<tr><th colspan="2">Structure</th></tr>
<tr><td colspan="2">· Structure the text into introduction, main part and conclusion.
· Make sensible use of paragraphs within the main part.</td></tr>
<tr><th colspan="2">Language</th></tr>
<tr><td colspan="2">· Use connectives within the text, e.g. This means that …, Thus …, As a consequence …
· Avoid imprecise and overused adjectives/adverbs, i.e. not: good, bad, happy, sad, … but: convincing, positive, helpful, harmful, negative, …
· Avoid generalizations, be as precise as possible, the following words and phrases might be useful: … tends to be …, many, a considerable number of, almost, at least, particularly, rather, etc.
· Vary your sentence structure. For example, use participle constructions, subordinate clauses, etc.</td></tr>
</table>

Self-assessment sheet: How to write a comment

I have to ...	tick
1. Introduction	
... write a clear introduction in which I mention the topic / statement and explain what it means for me *The problem of ... has met with a lot of attention lately; As far as I understand/can see ...; There are many reasons for ...; There is no doubt that ...*	
... attract the reader's attention with the help of a recent event or a personal experience that illustrates the topic and / or shows its significance	
... mention my thesis in the introduction if I think this attracts the reader's attention *Mr. XY ... claims that ..., yet I strongly disagree with him/her. Mrs. XY ... claims that ..., I fully agree with him/her and in this comment I will show why ...*	
2. Main part	
... use a sentence that connects the introduction and the main part *In the following I shall be concerned with ..., I intend to present arguments in favour of ...*	
... give arguments in favour of my opinion *Firstly, ... secondly, ... another point, in addition, besides ..., furthermore ..., on top of that*	
... give evidence to explain/illustrate each of my arguments (numbers, statistics, events, etc.) *for example, for instance, such as, e.g., to illustrate this idea, I would like to ..., This idea can best be demonstrated by an example*	
... **I can** also mention arguments against my thesis / opinion in order to show to the reader that I'm not ignoring these arguments. If I do so, I should present a strong counterargument in the same paragraph *There are sceptics who say ..., but ..., I am fully aware that there are people who ..., but ..., You may have heard of people who claim ..., but ...*	
... use one paragraph for each single argument	
... start each paragraph with a topic sentence which expresses what the whole paragraph is about	
3. Conclusion	
... briefly refer to the original question and repeat my opinion *In conclusion, I would like to say that ..., After having read and assessed the arguments carefully I'm sure you agree that ..., The conclusion I draw is as follows: ..., I think it has become obvious that ...*	
... **I can** also refer to the event or personal experience I have mentioned in the beginning or speculate about the significance of the topic / statement in the near future	
... make sure that I do not introduce any new ideas in my conclusion	
4. Structure	
... structure the text: introduction, main part, conclusion	
5. Language	
... use connectives within the text, e.g. *This means that ..., Thus ..., As a consequence ...*	
... avoid imprecise and overused adjectives/adverbs, i.e. not: *good, bad, happy, sad, ...* but: *convincing, positive, helpful, harmful, negative, ...*	
... avoid generalizations and be as precise as possible. The following words and phrases might be useful: *... tends to be ..., many ..., a considerable number of..., almost..., at least..., particularly..., rather...,* etc.	
... vary my sentence structure. For example, use participle constructions and subordinate clauses, etc.	

These aspects of my comment are already good ☺	These aspects need improvement ☹

Words that I need to write a good comment

Self-assessment sheet: How to write a summary

In a summary you restate a text or a film in your own words. Since the summary has to be much shorter than the original, you only give the information a reader needs in order to understand the general idea of what the text is about. Therefore, it is essential that you read the text carefully and look for keywords before you start writing your summary. It also helps to state in one or two sentences what the text/film is about. Use the five W's (who? What? When? Where? Why?) to make further notes.

I have to ...	**tick**
1. Content	
... write an introduction that includes the author, title, type of text and year of publication *The text/article/film "..." deals with .../was published in .../was written by ... in ...*	
... state the topic of the text/film and the underlying problem *The text is about/shows/presents/depicts/alludes to/refers to/criticizes/comments on ... the fact that/the problem of ...*	
... focus on basic information (i.e. leave out examples/details)	
... write a text that is no longer than about one third of the original	
... refrain from using my own ideas	
... stay neutral (no personal opinion) and write from the point of view of the author *According to the author, ...; The author says ...; As stated in the text ...; As pointed out by the author ...; In the author's opinion ...*	
2. Structure	
... write short paragraphs summing up the central aspects	
... arrange the different aspects in a logical order	
3. Language	
... use present tense	
... use indirect instead of direct speech	
... use my own words (no quotes)	
... use connectives	
... use formal language	
... use subordinate clauses	

These aspects of my summary are already good ☺	These aspects need improvement ☹

Words that I need to write a good summary

Self-assessment sheet: How to analyze and interpret statistics

I have to ...	tick
1. Introduction	
... write an introduction in which I mention the origin/source, the author and the date *The survey at hand carried out by ... and published in ... on ... focuses on/deals with ...; This table shows/is about/provides information about ...; The pie chart/bar chart/line graph shows/represents the percentages of/numbers of/relationship between ... and how they have changed/altered/developed ...*	
... roughly (one sentence) outline what the statistic depicts in general *This table shows/is about/provides information about ...*	
2. Formal components	
... explain the formal components of the statistic (table, graph, chart): a. general structure *The chart consists of ...* b. period of time *It covers the years from ... to ...* c. axes labels *The horizontal axis represents ...* d. information on the units ... in percent/millimeters/kilograms/ absolute numbers	
3. Description	
... describe the contents and details: a. changes and developments over time: *Between ... and ... there is an increase in ... a significant increase in ...; In 2011, there were ...; There is a slight rise ...* b. peak and low points *to reach a peak/a low point in .../an all-time high* c. relationships and connections: *Compared to ...; the majority of ...; nearly half of ..., one in ten ..., In the first column, ...*	
... describe in a systematic way (i.e. mention the most important aspects first)	
... consider why the numbers are presented as, for example, a table or a chart	
... concentrate on the most remarkable data	
4. Interpretation/Conclusion	
... draw conclusions from the numbers *As you can see from the diagram, ...; This development clearly shows/indicates that ...; The path of the curve reveals ...; As a result of ...; ... suggests a relation between ... and ...; so it is difficult/easy to estimate/judge/make precise comments; All in all, the statistics for ... reveal/show that ...*	
... explain my conclusions with my background knowledge of the topic	
... be critical about the form of presentation: e.g. easily understandable form? Reliable source? Up-to-date numbers? *The data confirm/contradict/are not consistent with ...; The chart is more/less effective than ... because ...*	
... discuss how the figures are presented – in a positive, negative or neutral light?	
... make sure that the conclusions drawn are in line with what the numbers say	
... put my conclusions into a larger context *... can be expected/is likely to occur ...*	
5. Structure	
... structure the text: introduction, main part, conclusion; paragraph properly	
... main part: paragraph sensibly within the main part; use topic sentences	
6. Language	
... use connectives within the text, e.g. *first, on the one hand ..., additionally, to put it in a nutshell*	
... use phrases that are essential for this text type	
... use interesting words (no overused words)	
... use different sentence structures (e.g. participle constructions and subordinate clauses)	

These aspects of my statistic analysis are already good ☺	These aspects need improvement ☹
Words that I need to write a good analysis of statistics	

Self-assessment sheet: How to analyze and interpret pictures

I have to ...	tick
1. Introduction	
... mention the name of the photographer/artist and when/where the picture/photo/drawing was taken *The photo/picture/drawing by ... was published in ...; The photo was probably taken in/at/to ...*	
... roughly outline what the visual depicts in general *The picture/photo/drawing refers to .../deals with .../represents ...; The topic/subject of the picture is ...; The picture shows/illustrates ...*	
... state my first impression of the picture *When I first saw the picture, I thought ...; The picture gives the impression that ..., The picture reminds me of ...; I was deeply moved by the picture because ...; My first thought when I saw it was ...; The photo is shocking/disgusting/amazing/spectacular/special ...*	
2. Description	
... describe the visual clearly and concentrate on the relevant aspects only *In the center, there is/are ...; In the background, one can see ...; In the picture you can see ...; There is a contrast between ... and ...; ... is clearly visible; The field size is a close-up/medium shot/long shot; ... is seen from above/below/the front/the back*	
... describe in a systematic way – start with the dominant aspect and describe it in detail without forgetting the aspects in the background *The focus of attention is ...; What strikes the eye is ...*	
... if there are lots of different things or if there is no difference between foreground and background, I may start with the foreground and then turn to the background or work from the top down to the bottom or start at the left and then work across to the right *in the foreground, you can see ...; at the top/bottom ...; In the centre of the picture there is ...; in the top left-hand corner/bottom right-hand corner ...*	
... describe which techniques the photographer/painter has made use of (e.g. use of light and colour) *The artist used oils/water colours/light brush strokes ...; The photographer used colour/a soft focus/a sharp focus/showed the subject close up ...; The colours are bright/dark; The painter employs ...*	
... describe body language and facial expressions and speculate about who the people are and what their relationship is like *The figure on the left/in the foreground/in the top left-hand corner bears likeness to .../is supposed to be .../represents ...; .../shows X as a ...; From their looks, I can assume that ...; X seems to be sad/distracted/angry/embarrassed ... because ...*	
3. Analysis/Interpretation	
... state what the artist is trying to say and how he/she does it *The picture refers to/deals with/stands for/represents ...; It is meant to criticize/satirize ...; By employing ..., the artist ...; The artist intends to ...; The artist criticizes/wants to point out that ...; According to the artist/photographer, ...*	
... speculate about the possible addressee; I have to mention the source and if necessary, interpret with regard to it (the political leaning of the newspaper or the age of the picture may have an influence on the meaning) *Since it was published in ..., one might assume that ...*	
... state whether the photo was taken with a special intention (i.e. snap shot ↔ staged photograph) and assess the effect on the viewer *The photograph was staged to achieve a certain effect ...; It is a realistic picture of ...*	
... discuss how the characters are presented: in a positive, negative light or neutral light? How is this done? *... is represented as .../comes across as being ...; The characters come across in a positive/negative light; The light/colours/position of/expression of ... contribute to ...*	
... explain the (intended) effect on the viewer and the way it is achieved (e.g. mention pictorial elements that back up the message as 'evidence') *The photo comes across as ... This is achieved by ...; the colours support the impression that ...; This is due to their facial expressions/gestures/what they are saying ...; The picture arouses a feeling of ... by ...; The atmosphere in the picture seems ... since the artist uses ...*	

... wrap up my interpretation in a final statement *All in all/In general, the painter/photographer wants to make the reader aware of the fact that .../criticize/is trying to say that ...; The photographer wants to make fun of/ridicule/point out/show ...; The photo is meant to criticize ...*	
4. Evaluation	
... explain the effect the visual has on me *Personally, I like/do not like the photo, because ...; the photo/drawing touches me/leaves me cold because ...; My initial reaction to the photo/picture was ...; but on second glance I believe that ...*	
... evaluate the artist's presentation from my point of view and assess the success of the message: is it presented convincingly? *The picture is/is not effective in its presentation of ... because ...; In my opinion, the painter/photographer has successfully shown that ...; The picture does not reach its intended target group because ...; It could have been more effective if it had ...*	
5. Structure	
... structure the text: introduction, main part, conclusion; paragraph properly	
... main part: paragraph sensibly within the main part and use topic sentences	
6. Language	
... use connectives within the text (e.g. *first, on the one hand, ...*)	
... use phrases that are essential for this text type (e.g. *the painter shows ... By presenting ..., the photographer ...*)	
... vary my sentence structure by using subordinate clauses and participle constructions	

These aspects of my picture analysis are already good ☺	These aspects need improvement ☹
Words that I need to write a good analysis of pictures	

Self-assessment sheet: How to analyze and interpret cartoons

I have to ...	tick
1. Introduction	
... mention the name of the cartoonist, when/where the cartoon was published *The cartoon at hand by ... was published in ...*	
... roughly outline what the cartoon depicts in general *The cartoon refers to .../deals with .../represents ..., the topic/subject of the cartoon is ...; The situation reminds me/one/you of ...*	
... give my first response to the cartoon *My first thought when I saw the cartoon was ...; The cartoon reminds me of ...*	
... state possible reasons for the representation provided	
2. Description	
... describe the cartoon in detail but make sure that I concentrate on the relevant aspects only *In the centre, there is/are ...; In the background, one can see ...; In the cartoon you can see ...; There is a contrast between ... and ...; ... is clearly visible; The cartoonist employs ...*	
... describe in a systematic way and start with the most important elements without forgetting those in the background *The focus of attention is ...; What strikes the eye is ...; The cartoon depicts/shows ...*	
... identify the current events/people/institutions referred to *The figure on the left/in the foreground/in the top left-hand corner bears a likeness to .../is supposed to be .../represents ...; ... shows X as a ...*	
... link texts to the drawing *There is a caption at/on/in ... and speech bubbles containing/enclosing the following: ...; The caption says ...*	
... describe artistic techniques the cartoonist used *The cartoonist used color/showed the subject close up ...; The colors are bright/dark ...*	
3. Analysis/Interpretation	
... state what the cartoonist is trying to say. Use the context of the cartoon as well as a possible addressee. Think about the source it was taken from and base my interpretation on this *The cartoon refers to/deals with/stands for/represents ...; It is meant to criticize/satirize ...; The cartoonist intends to ...; According to the cartoonist, ...; The cartoonist criticizes ...; Since it was published in ..., one might assume that ...*	
... examine whether the characters or issues are presented in a positive or a negative light and say how this is done. Pay attention to the devices used – such as the use of exaggeration, irony, puns and symbols *... is represented as .../comes across as being ...; The characters come across in a positive/negative light. This is due to their gestures/what they are saying/...*	
... explain the (intended) effect on the viewer and the way it is achieved (e.g. mention pictorial elements that back up the message as 'evidence') *This is achieved by ...; the colours/the inconsistency between drawing and text contribute to ...; Although/Even though ..., the real point the cartoon seems to be making is ...*	
... wrap up my interpretation: what the cartoonist is trying to say/criticize *All in all/In general, the cartoonist wants to make the reader aware of the fact that ...; The cartoonist wants to make fun of/ridicule/point out/show ...*	
4. Evaluation	
... mention my personal opinion regarding the artist's representation and his/her message	
... outline the effect the cartoon has on me *The cartoon touches me/leaves me cold*	
... assess the success of the message *The cartoon is/is not effective in its presentation of ... because ...; In my opinion, the cartoonist has failed to ...*	

5. Structure	
... structure the text: introduction, main part, conclusion	
... main part: make sensible use of paragraphs within the main part	
6. Language	
... use connectives within the text (e.g. *first, on the one hand, ...*)	
... use phrases that are essential for this text type (e.g. *the cartoonist shows ... By presenting ..., the cartoonist ...*)	
... vary my sentence structure. Use participle constructions and subordinate clauses.	

These aspects of my cartoon analysis are already good ☺	These aspects need improvement ☹
Words that I need to write a good analysis of cartoons	

Self-assessment sheet: How to analyze a speech

I have to ...	tick
1. Introduction	
... write an introduction in which I mention the speaker, his role at that time, the relevant circumstances in which the speech was delivered *The speech ... delivered in ... on ... by ..., at that time ..., deals with ...; It is addressed to ...; It is an election speech/address/a state of the nation speech*	
... identify the type of speech	
... describe the topic as well as the speaker's supposed intention *The focus is on ...; The speaker wants to/is aiming to/is trying to ...; The speaker is canvassing for ...; The speaker wishes to stir/persuade his audience ...*	
2. Main part	
... summarize the structure of the speech *In his/her opening words, ...; In the first half of the speech ...; Halfway through the speech ...; Towards the end of his speech ...*	
... list different stylistic devices/strategies in order of importance *A recurrent rhetorical device ...; One device the speaker uses ...; A striking rhetorical device ...; At one point in his speech he/she makes use of ...; One of the most effective devices is ...*	
... use quotes to exemplify the devices/strategies employed *In line ..., the speaker argues/illustrates/claims that "..."; As the speaker observes in line ..., ...*	
... explain their intended effect a. in general (e.g. *to emphasize his/her message*) b. in the context of the speech *to establish a personal relationship with ...; to make the audience aware of ...; to make the audience feel understood; to trigger off emotions; to engage the listeners effectively; to create immediacy and urgency; to make a lasting impression by ...; to involve the difference between A and B; to deceive an audience; to avoid offense; to heighten the audience's attention; to make a speech more memorable; to make easily recognizable references; to emphasize sth; to make the listeners aware of the extent of the problem; to arouse interest; to simplify complicated matters by referring to everyday experiences; to launch into a polemic against ...; to appeal to the listeners' conscience; to leave no room for doubt; to impose one's opinion on ...; to increase intensity; to create the illusion of mutual understanding; to win over so.*	
3. Conclusion	
... briefly summarize my results *All in all, ...; To put it into a nutshell, ...*	
... evaluate the effect with reference to the speaker's supposed intention *The speaker displays a thorough/intimate/superficial knowledge of ...; The speaker twists/perverts the truth; The speech deeply moved me/left me cold/made me laugh ...; The speech made me think about ...; From my point of view, the speech is convincing because ...*	
4. Structure	
... structure the text: introduction, main part, conclusion	
... main part: use sensible paragraphs to structure the list of devices/strategies (one each) and write topic sentences	
5. Language	
... use connectives within the text (e.g. *additionally ...*)	
... use phrases that are essential for this text form (e.g. *the frequent use of ... establishes a personal relationship with the audience, to trigger off emotions*)	

These aspects of my speech analysis are already good ☺	These aspects need improvement ☹
Words that I need to write a good speech analysis	

Self-assessment sheet: How to write a speech

I have to ...	**tick**
1. Preparation	
... carefully read the assignment: what is the topic of my speech? Do I have to refer to other material (e.g. newspaper article, a certain event, another speaker)?	
... take into consideration a possible role I have to take. What is this person like (age, knowledge, position, relationship to others)?	
... think about the purpose of the speech – Do I want to inform, demonstrate, persuade or entertain?	
... think about the audience (background, age, knowledge, interests ...) What do they already know about the topic?	
... list aspects I could talk about after having researched the topic.	
... structure my ideas logically.	
2. Introduction	
... directly address the audience with a note of welcome *Ladies and gentlemen, fellow students, my friends, members of ..., my fellow countrymen ... It's an honour for me to be here today at ...; I really appreciate being here with you today ...; I feel greatly honoured by your invitation ...*	
... create an effective lead-in to grab the listeners' attention by using, for example, a provocative statement, a surprising fact, a new discovery, an anecdote, a rhetorical question or a quotation.	
... present the topic/problem *In the following I shall be concerned with/deal with the problem/subject/issue of ...; As some of you might know, ...; We are here today to ...; I intend to present arguments in favour of/against ...*	
3. Main part	
... develop my ideas step by step and organize my speech according to the structure of a comment *Undoubtedly, this is a time of ... but at the same time it is also a period of ...; It is generally believed that ...; At first sight this seems to be true but ...; In addition, ...; However, ...*	
... concentrate on the most important aspects (no more than five) and be specific and direct instead of giving too many ideas	
... start with the least important point and work up to the most important one. Alternatively, I can start with the most important one and then work progressively from my least important point up to the second most important one.	
... provide background information if necessary	
... support my point of view with examples/facts/statistics *Take for example ...; There is some evidence to suggest that ...*	
... Use stylistic devices to emphasize the main message (e.g. repetition, contrast, rhetorical questions, metaphors and similes)	
... link ideas and arguments *Let us now return to ...; This brings me to the next point; In addition to this point I want to stress that ...; Take for example ...; There seems to be a contradiction here ...; Hence, ...; the result of this is as follows ...; Having discussed ... it is now appropriate to mention ...*	
... repeat the most important ideas, emphasize phrases or passages	
... establish contact with the listeners by addressing them directly/flattering them/using the first-person plural/appealing to shared experiences *We all know that ...*	
... show my conviction *undoubtedly/certainly/definitely/indeed/surprisingly/strangely enough/first and foremost*	

4. Conclusion	
... briefly summarize my main points *All in all, I think it can be said that...; To put it into a nutshell, ...; In conclusion, I would like to say that ...; Let me conclude with the words of ...; Looking at all the facts and figures, I have to draw the conclusion that ...; What it all boils down to is the following: ...*	
... call for action, look into the future, use a relevant quotation or a promise *Let us all work together to ...; We have to ensure that ...; In the near future ...; In the long run ...; We are confident that ...; We should take on new roles.*	
... clearly finish my speech and thank the audience for their attention	
5. Structure	
... structure the text: introduction, main part, conclusion	
... use sensible paragraphs within the main part	
6. Language	
... incorporate connectives and transitions (e.g. *additionally ...; however, ... that is why ...; in short, ...*)	
... use a mixture of mostly short and only a few long sentences	
... use striking adjectives and adverbs.	
... use the appropriate register and tone (e.g. formal, informal, entertaining, serious, witty etc.)	
7. Presentation	
... rehearse my speech before delivering it.	
... speak clearly and neither too quick nor too slowly	
... modulate my voice (volume, speed)	
... stress important words to emphasize my key points	
... establish contact with the audience, maintain eye contact	
... use helpful body language (gestures, facial expression)	

These aspects of my speech are already good ☺	These aspects need improvement ☹

Words that I need to write a good speech

Self-assessment sheet: How to write a letter to the editor

I have to ...	tick
1. Content	
... write a reference line in which I state which article I am referring to e.g. *"Edward Snowden is no hero", June 16th, 2013*	
... start the letter with "Sir or Madam"	
... name the article/column/public statement I am referring to *In his article of 13th August 2013, "..." (title/headline) the author ... mentioned/said/wrote that ...; With reference to your article of 13th August 2012 ...; I would like to ...; I am writing in response to your article ...; Having read your article "...", I would like to*	
... give reasons for writing the letter in the opening sentence/paragraph *I would like to object to ...; I utterly agree with you that ...; I would like to point out that ...; I would like to congratulate you on ...; As a firm believer of ..., I ...; I think you are mistaken if you believe ...; After carefully studying your suggestions, I am sorry to say that ...; Please allow me to voice my criticism of ...; I would appreciate more objectivity when ...; I would like to express doubts about ...*	
... use indirect speech when quoting from an article *the author claimed/wrote/believed that ...; As stated in the article, ...; In the author's opinion ...*	
... write a convincing concluding sentence *All in all, the evidence given shows that ...; The question can no longer be whether ..., but ...; May I suggest following up the article of ... with a further one, which this time includes ...*	
... sign the letter and give my hometown (no "Yours sincerely" etc. at the end)	
2. Structure	
... use all aspects for writing a formal letter (sender's address, date, recipient's address, reference line, salutation, body, closing, signature)	
... make my letter short and to the point (no summary writing!)	
... structure my arguments and back up my points with examples or facts	
... structure my letter in a logical order	
3. Language/style	
... use indirect instead of direct speech	
... use formal language	
... be polite	
... use connectives	

These aspects of my letter to the editor are already good ☺	These aspects need improvement ☹

Words that I need to write a good letter to the editor

Self-assessment sheet: How to write an argumentative essay

I have to ...	tick
1. Introduction	
... write a clear, thought-provoking introduction in which I present the issue/statement and show why it is important to discuss it *In this essay, I want to investigate ...; This essay will concentrate on ...; ... seems to be an inexhaustible source of controversy, ... is a hotly debated topic at the moment; The problem of ... has met with a lot of attention lately* *It is interesting to weigh up the benefits and drawbacks of ..., Therefore one should discuss the issue .../ wonder about/ask the question of whether ...*	
... attract the reader's attention with the help of a recent event, a personal experience, a reference to a famous person	
2. Main part	
... use a sentence that connects the introduction and the main part *In the following I shall be concerned with .../I intend to present arguments in favour of ..., Some experts state that ..., many people believe/claim that ...*	
... present the different positions/points of view and the corresponding arguments *Firstly, ... secondly, ... another point, in addition, besides ..., furthermore ..., on top of that*	
... provide examples for each position/point of view/argument *for example, for instance, such as, e.g., to illustrate this idea, I would like to ..., This idea can best be demonstrated by an example*	
... start each paragraph with a topic sentence which expresses what the whole paragraph is about	
... make sure that I do not express my own opinion in the main part of my essay but only present the various positions/points of view/arguments	
3. Conclusion	
... briefly refer to the original question and wrap up the discussion *All in all, it can be said that ...; In conclusion, I would like to say that ...; I would like to conclude by saying that ...; After weighing up the arguments carefully ...; The conclusion I draw is as follows: ...; As a consequence ...; As a result of ...; The most important aspect one has to keep in mind is ...; After all ...*	
... make sure that you do not introduce any new ideas in your conclusion	
... give my final position on the topic (this can be a compromise) without repeating my arguments *In my opinion ...; Apparently ...; Obviously; Therefore; To my mind ...; I firmly believe that ...; To a certain extent, I can accept ..., but ...; Although ... we must admit that ...; There can be no doubt as regards ...; I am absolutely convinced of ...*	
... I can refer to the event or personal experience I have mentioned in the beginning or speculate about the significance of the topic/statement in the near future	
4. Structure	
... structure the text: introduction, main part, conclusion	
... main part: make sensible use of paragraphs within the main part	
5. Language	
... use connectives within the text, e.g. *This means that ...; Thus, ...; As a consequence, ...*	
... avoid imprecise and overused adjectives/adverbs, not: *good, bad, happy, sad, ...* but: *convincing, narrow-minded, selfish*	
... avoid generalizations and be as precise as possible. The following words might be useful: *tends to be ...; many, a considerable number of, almost, at least, completely, particularly, rarely, rather,* etc.)	
... vary my sentence structure. For example, use participle constructions and subordinate clauses, etc.	

<table>
<tr><td>These aspects of my argumentative essay are already good ☺</td><td>These aspects need improvement ☹</td></tr>
<tr><td></td><td></td></tr>
<tr><td colspan="2">Words that I need to write a good argumentative essay</td></tr>
<tr><td colspan="2"></td></tr>
</table>

Ready reference – challenges and choices in an insecure world

aspects	details / words in context	German translations	reference to *Half Broke horses* and *Crash* in this theme
challenges	Our lives are full of challenges. Each day we are *confronted with challenges*, some are minor and we don't even consider them to be challenges such as getting up in the morning or loading the dishwasher. Others are enormous and we only can only *meet them* with considerable *effort*. And because we are all part of highly complex societies and we live in a globalized world, most of the serious challenges we *face* cannot be solved on an individual level only. What's necessary is a *combined effort* by individuals and institutions such as governments and agencies. Unemployment or terrorism are challenges that can only be overcome on a global level. Some of these challenges have existed for hundreds or even thousands of years whereas other challenges have come into existence recently such as global warming or overpopulation. Some of these challenges appear so enormous that it seems difficult to imagine a solution. Yet we must bear in mind that in the past the world has also been confronted with serious challenges and mastered them. The Cold War with the omnipresent danger of a nuclear war was *a challenge that the world has overcome. Improvements have also been achieved* with respect to AIDS. Thus disillusionment or frustration are inappropriate reactions to the current challenges. If we *are determined to surmount the challenges* we face, we can be successful.	*challenges* = Herausforderungen *to be confronted with challenges* = sich Herausforderungen gegenübersehen *to meet a challenge* = eine Herausforderung meistern *effort* = Anstrengung *to face a challenge* = sich einer Herausforderung gegen-übersehen *a combined effort* = eine vereinte Anstrengung *to overcome a challenge* = eine Herausforderung meistern *to achieve improvements* = Verbesserungen erreichen *to be determined* = entschlossen sein *to surmount a challenge* = eine Herausforderung überwin-den	no explicit references in the introductory theme
choices	Our lives are also full of choices. People's choices are influenced by factors such as date of birth, place of birth and family background. Yet we are not *merely* the product of our environment. Of course *there's no denying that we are exposed to* a number of influences that *shape* our lives. Yet we are also individuals *capable of making up our minds* and capable of taking more or less reasonable decisions. This becomes obvious when we look at the field of education. Students usually don't choose between a dozen different schools. Most students attend a school that is close to their home. And they can't choose the teachers they get and have hardly any influence on the curriculum. But what they can *determine* for themselves is the effort they put into a subject. What they can do is *take the initiative* and suggest certain topics for lessons or complain about a grade that to them seems unfair. This shows that the number of choices that we have also depends on ourselves. If we accept everything the way it is, our choices are very *limited*. If we don't, *we have lots of choices available.* This is only true for some countries and some societies. In other countries as well as in the past in Western Europe, people's choices were very limited. Up to this day, many people have very *little influence* on their social position and can't *climb the social ladder*. If children don't have any *formal education* because their parents are so poor that *they can't afford* such an education and instead have to work *to make a living*, then for them there's hardly any chance of upward mobility. The same is true for family life. In many countries parents choose spouses for their children. Some children or young adults are grateful to their parents and *approve of this custom*. Others aren't, but because it's hard for children *not to meet their parents' expectations*, they usually accept their parents' choice.	*merely* = nur *there's no denying that* = man kann nicht abstreiten, dass *to be exposed to influences* = Einflüssen ausgesetzt sein *to shape* = formen *capable of making up our minds* = in der Lage, uns eine eigene Meinung zu bilden *to determine* = bestimmen *to take initiative* = die Initiative ergreifen *limited* = begrenzt *we have lots of choices available* = uns stehen viele Mög-lichkeiten zur Verfügung *to climb the social ladder* = gesellschaftlich aufsteigen *formal education* = reguläre Schulbildung *they can't afford* = sie können es sich nicht leisten *to make your own living* = dir deinen eigenen Lebens-unterhalt verdienen *to approve of this custom* = diesen Brauch gutheißen *to meet their parents' expectations* = den Erwartungen ihrer Eltern gerecht werden	no explicit references in the introductory theme
insecurities	Compared to our *ancestors* who lived hundreds of years ago we – in the Western world - live in a fairly *secure world*. Many countries have a functioning police force, a functioning judiciary system and offer some sort of *health care* to their citizens. Thus the chances of dying at an early age as a result of a disease or in a war are fairly low nowadays. In other areas of the world people *live under more difficult circumstances* and their lives *are threatened by* diseases, wars, civil wars and crime. The lives of Americans have certainly become more secure. The early immigrants and settlers were confronted with all sorts of insecurities. What's interesting about US history is that people have traditionally looked at insecurities and problems as challenges that needed to be tackled and overcome. Individualism has always been *a major trait* of American national identity and many Americans have regarded themselves as individuals who can perfectly *deal with the insecurities* and challenges themselves. They have not only *rejected* any kind of help from institutions such as governments, they have viewed government action as *an attempt to encroach on people's privacy*, as a way of limiting people's choices. If you look at the graphs in this book you may *get the impression* that this attitude has changed. The world has become so complex that most insecurities and challenges cannot be solved by individuals, no matter how determined and capable people are. The fact that many Americans *have a lot of confidence* in the health care system offered by the government might *serve as evidence* that people's attitudes have changed to some degree.	*ancestors* = Vorfahren *a secure world* = eine sichere Welt *health care* = Krankenversicherung *to live under difficult circumstances* = unter schwierigen Umständen leben *to be threatened by* = bedroht sein durch *a major trait* = ein wichtiges Merkmal *to deal with insecurities* = mit Unsicherheiten umgehen *to reject* = zurückweisen, ablehnen *attempt* = Versuch *to encroach on people's privacy* = sich in die Privatsphäre der Leute einmischen *to get the impression* = den Eindruck gewinnen *to have a lot of confidence in* = ein großes Vertrauen haben in *to serve as evidence for sth.* = als Beleg dienen für etwas	no explicit references in the introductory theme

Ready reference – race and ethnicity

aspects	details / words in context	German translations	reference to *Half Broke horses* and *Crash* in this theme
history of race relations	The institution of slavery has influenced the relationship between African Americans and whites up to this day. Slavery was introduced into the colonies in the 17th century because it was regarded by farmers and plantation owners as the best solution to the problem of *labor shortage*. Africans *proved suitable* for lifetime slavery because they were physically fit for the climate in the South. In order to *legitimize* slavery white farmers and planters claimed that Africans were *innately inferior* and therefore were not *entitled* to basic rights such as liberty. This view formed the basis of slave codes that defined the status of Africans giving white slave owners absolute power over their slaves. This was the time when black and white were established as racial categories and were *assigned* the *attributes* that we can find in the stereotypes of both blacks and whites (see below). It is important to note that these are not – in the first place – biological but cultural and ideological categories that have been used as legitimization of white dominance. The official end of slavery in 1865 changed the *legal status* of African Americans but had no *impact* on the relationship between whites and African-Americans. Racism was still *widespread* among whites and society was *segregated*. It wasn't until the Civil Rights Movement of the 1960s that race relations began to change: African Americans such as Rosa Parks, Martin Luther King and Jesse Jackson organized protests against racial injustice and soon thousands of African Americans as well as many whites took part in boycotts, sit-ins, demonstrations and *filed law suits*. This movement resulted in a number of laws known as Civil Rights Acts that are considered *milestones* on the way to racial equality. Affirmative Action is one of the measures that is called for in these Civil Rights Acts. The election of Barack Obama as US President can be interpreted as another milestone in African American history. Yet it doesn't mean that race as a category or racism has *disappeared*. His famous speech on race that he delivered in 2008 is clear evidence that racial categories still influence public life in the US. Another *piece of evidence* is Paul Haggis' *Crash*, a movie that deals with race and ethnic minorities and questions the very existence of these categories.	*labor shortage* = Mangel an Arbeitskräften *to prove suitable* = sich als geeignet erweisen *to legitimize* = legitimieren *innately inferior* = von Natur aus untergeordnet *to be entitled to* = einen Anspruch haben auf *to assign* = zuordnen, zuweisen *attribute* = Merkmal, Eigenschaft *legal status* = rechtliche Stellung *impact* = Einfluss *widespread* = verbreitet *segregation* = Rassentrennung *to file a law suit* = Klage einreichen *milestone* = Meilenstein *to disappear* = verschwinden *to deliver a speech* = eine Rede halten *piece of evidence* = Beweis	*Crash* extensively deals with the category of race including diverse characters within supposed monolithic groups (e.g. whites, blacks, Hispanics). The differences between Peter and Anthony, Cameron Thayer and Shaniqua Johnson are striking, yet characters like John Ryan ignore these differences and apply the racial category of "black" when dealing with them. When witnessing Officer Hansen's conversation with Peter we learn how persistent racial categories are: even though we have known him as an open-minded person who condemns John Ryan's racist behavior, he resorts to prejudices himself and ends up killing Peter thinking that he was about to produce a gun. The film is also occupied with the way African Americans see themselves. And again, the film offers a range of self-perceptions concerning race. While Anthony constantly talks about himself as a member of the black community, Christine Thayer calls herself a white woman and tells her husband that the "closest (he) ever came to being black was watching the Cosby Show."
stereotypes, prejudices and discrimination	Stereotypes are generalizations, are oversimplified ideas or images of people or things that *emphasize* certain traits or aspects in a way that *distorts reality*. *With respect to* African Americans there are a number of long held stereotypes three of which are the African American as Sambo, a *docile*, *simple-minded* black man, the African American as Savage, apelike in appearance and mentally and culturally inferior and the stereotype of the Mammy, a large woman with shining white teeth who knows white lifestyle and who is always there for her master's family. Stereotypes are not necessarily negative. A prejudice is a *preconceived* opinion or thought that is not based on *reason* or actual experience. A widespread racial prejudice is that black men are more aggressive than white men. Even though in everyday language many people don't *distinguish between* stereotype and prejudice, there is agreement among sociologists that a stereotype is an idea or an image *whereas* a prejudice is a thought or a feeling. Racism, for example, is considered a prejudice. Discrimination is positive or negative actions towards the objects of prejudice. Common forms of discrimination are racial discrimination or discrimination based on *gender*.	*to emphasize* = betonen *trait* = Charakterzug *to distort reality* = die Realität verzerren *with respect to* = mit Bezug auf *docile* = fügsam, unterwürfig *simple-minded* = einfältig *preconceived* = vorgefasst *reason* = Vernunft *to distinguish between* = unterscheiden *whereas* = wohingegen *gender* = Geschlecht	Anthony in *Crash* regards himself as a victim of racial discrimination because – that's his thesis – people think in stereotypes and he corresponds to a long held stereotype. What's interesting is that in several situations (e.g. in the restaurant) he in fact behaves stereotypically. This way the film discusses the effect of stereotypes on our behavior. There are many other situations in which the characters' behavior is guided by stereotypes. By and large one can argue that people in *Crash* resort to stereotypes when they are anxious and insecure, when they fear a loss of status or a loss of self-control.
affirmative action	Affirmative Action is one of the measures that is *laid down* in the Civil Rights Act of 1964. The term was first used by President John F. Kennedy in Executive Order 10925 which was *issued* in 1961. This order requires government contractors "to take affirmative action *to ensure* that *applicants* are employed and that *employees* are treated during employment *without regard to* their race, creed, color or national origin". Executive Order 10925 was aimed at ending racial discrimination as well as discrimination of other ethnicities or minority groups. The policy has since been applied especially in the fields of education and public administration. As a consequence the numbers of African Americans employed in these areas rose. Although being highly controversial and the subject of numerous law suits the policy *is still in place*. It's difficult to *assess* its effect on race relations since affirmative action did not only offer opportunities to African Americans and other minorities but also caused strong *sentiments* against those who profited from the policy. Some even argue that affirmative action has led to an increase in racism.	*to lay down* = festschreiben *to issue* = ausgeben *to ensure* = sicherstellen *applicant* = Bewerber *employee* = Angestellter, Mitarbeiter *without regard to* = ohne Rücksicht auf *to be in place* = bestehen *to assess* = beurteilen, abschätzen *sentiment* = Gefühl	Officer Ryan and Shaniqua Johnson have a conversation about affirmative action, in which Ryan at first attacks the policy by saying "I can't look at you without thinking of the five or six more qualified white men who didn't get your job," then he explains to her what effect affirmative action had on his father's life. Officer Ryan can be regarded as an example of someone who thinks affirmative action has led to reverse discrimination.

Ready reference – immigration

aspects	details / words in context	German translations	reference to *Half Broke horses* and *Crash* in this theme
history of immigration	colonial period (1607 – 1776): In 1607 104 British settlers *founded* the first permanent settlement in the New World and called it Jamestown (after King James I.). After serious setbacks the colony eventually *prospered* and the settlers started growing tobacco. Most members had joined this enterprise because they were looking for adventure and hoped to become rich. Only 13 years later, in 1620, a second colony was founded hundreds of kilometres north of Jamestown by British Puritans: Plymouth colony. These settlers, who came to be known as the Pilgrim Fathers, were looking for a place where they could *worship* without *interference* by society or the government. *It is a common belief that* they had their first harvest supper in the autumn of 1621 and invited their Indian friends and neighbors to celebrate the first Thanksgiving Day. Old Immigration (1790 – 1890): Most immigrants during this period came from Northern and Western Europe, *predominantly* from Britain, Ireland, Germany and Scandinavia. Up to the 1830s immigrants arrived in *comparatively* small numbers. In the following decades the numbers *rose constantly* until, in the 1880s, they *reached a peak* with more than 400,000 immigrants arriving in the US *annually*. Several factors *account for* this *influx* of immigrants: - economic conditions in Europe were difficult and social mobility there was very limited - the USA offered, even advertised cheap land and jobs in prospering industries - the introduction of steam-powered ships in the 1870s made the voyage cheaper and faster - the more immigrants from a certain country settled in certain areas, the easier it was for their *relatives* and friends to immigrate (chain or serial migration) New Immigration (1890 – 1930): While the number of immigrants from Northern and Western Europe *declined* due to economic *improvements* in these countries, immigrants from Southern and Eastern Europe arrived in great numbers until around 1930. Most of them settled in big cities, kept their language and traditions and worked in industry. Immigration during the Great Depression and World War II Due to *a lack of opportunities* in the USA and because of *legal restrictions* on immigration only a very few people *migrated to the USA* between the late 1920s and the early 1940s. Immigration after 1965: *In the wake of* a new immigration law known as the Hart-Celler Act people from Asia and Latin America entered the country in great numbers and permanently changed *the social fabric* of American society. This new wave of immigration *peaked* in the late 1980s with around 800,000 immigrants arriving annually, most of them from Latin America and Asia.	*to found* = gründen *to prosper* = sich gut entwickeln *a second colony was founded* = eine zweite Kolonie wurde gegründet *to worship* = den Glauben leben, Gott anbeten *interference* = Einmischung *it is common belief that* = nach allgemeiner Meinung *predominantly* = vorwiegend, überwiegend *comparatively* = vergleichsweise *to rise constantly* = stetig zunehmen *to reach a peak* = einen Höhepunkt / Gipfel erreichen *annually* = jährlich *to account for* = verantwortlich sein, erklären *influx* = Zustrom *to advertise* = bewerben *steam-powered ships* = Dampfschiffe *relatives* = Verwandte *to decline* = sinken *improvements* = Verbesserungen *a lack of opportunities* = ein Mangel an Möglichkeiten *legal restrictions* = gesetzliche Beschränkungen *to migrate to a country* = in ein Land einwandern *in the wake of* = als Folge von, im Zuge von *the social fabric* = die soziale Zusammensetzung *to peak* = den Höchststand erreichen	In chapter 1 of *Half Broke Horses* we learn that Lily's grandfather came over from Ireland and started a farm in New Mexico in 1868. Thus he was among the great number of settlers who were lured into the country by the promise of cheap land. Officer Hansen's ancestors probably also came from Northern Europe, possibly Scandinavia (Hansen is a Scandinavian name). Officer Ryan's ancestors very likely came from Britain or Ireland, Ryan being an English name. We can assume that the Asian woman who is involved in the accident at the beginning of *Crash* immigrated fairly recently, probably after 1965, and is a first generation immigrant, because she is not completely fluent in English. Farhad is also a first generation immigrant who came from Iran. Ria and Daniel are second generation immigrants. Ria explicitly says: "My father's from Puerto Rico and my mother's from El Salvador."
reasons and consequences	reasons: Historians and social scientists have often described immigration as a combination of "push-factors" and "pull-factors." Push-factors help explain why immigrants leave their home countries while pull-factors refer to the attractions of the country they choose as their new home. Important push-factors are political, ethnic or religious *oppression*. Immigrants often *flee from* war or civil war, from *poverty* or from a lack of educational and economic opportunities. By contrast, typical pull-factors are political and religious freedom, ethnic tolerance, better jobs and *prospects for higher social status*. One of the most important pull-factors in the 19th century – when the USA *expanded* westward – was cheap land. consequences: Typically, immigrants to the United States have become *thoroughly* Americanized while at the same time many, if not most of them have tried *to keep alive* some elements of their *respective* culture of origin, for instance in the areas of language and religion, rituals and festivities, foods and fashions. Most immigrants arriving in the period of old immigration have become easily integrated into American society. With immigrants from Southern and Eastern Europe arriving in great numbers after the 1880s, *fears grew* among some Americans that these immigrants might have a negative *effect* on American politics and culture, because they didn't integrate as easily as immigrants from Northern and Western Europe. As a consequence of the mass immigration of people from Asia and Latin America in the second half of the 20th century, the USA has become a multicultural society.	*oppression* = Unterdrückung *to flee from* = die Flucht ergreifen vor *poverty* = Armut *prospects for higher social status* = Aussichten auf einen höheren sozialen Status *thoroughly* = gänzlich *fears grow* = Ängste wachsen *to make fun of sth.* = sich über etwas lustig machen *to keep alive* = wachhalten *respective* = jeweilig(e) *effect* = Auswirkung	From what we learn about Lily's grandfather we must conclude that he came because of cheap land in the West. We don't have any reliable information why the characters from *Crash* or their ancestors entered the country. The characters in *Crash* are representatives of a multicultural society. They all live in the USA, speak English to some degree, yet most of them stay among people from the same ethnic background. Farhad, the Asian woman and Daniel are confronted with racial prejudices and their English is made fun of.
illegal immigration	*According to reliable estimates* there are around 11 million illegal immigrants in the USA. Most of these *undocumented workers* – a term that is preferred by many Americans, including members of the Hispanic community – come from Latin America and make a living as migrant workers in the fields of agriculture, construction and the service industry. After having debated for decades how American society could deal with undocumented workers, it seems that a *comprehensive solution* is at hand *that grants the majority of these workers amnesty* and gives them the chance to stay in the US legally.	*according to reliable estimates* = seriösen Schätzungen zu Folge *undocumented worker* = Arbeiter ohne Papiere *comprehensive solution* = umfassende Lösung *that grants the majority of these workers amnesty* = die der Mehrheit der Arbeiter Amnestie gewähren wird	Maria has possibly entered the country illegally, but has probably acquired citizenship (otherwise she wouldn't work in the house of the attorney general). Daniel is very likely a second generation immigrant whose parents may have entered the country illegally.

Ready reference – crime

aspects	details / words in context	German translations	reference to *Half Broke horses* and *Crash* in this theme
Crime	A crime is an action that *constitutes* an offense that may be *prosecuted* by the state and is *punishable* by law. A person who has committed a crime is called a *perpetrator*, *culprit* or offender. A person who has been attacked is called a *victim*. Among the most common crimes are *theft*, *burglary*, *robbery*, *murder*, *rape*, *assault* and *fraud*. Many crimes are prosecuted by law enforcement agencies such as the police. Offenders are usually *apprehended* by the police, then they face a *trial* at a court. Trials are conducted by judges, in most courts in the USA the *verdict* (guilty or not guilty) is handed down by a jury, then the judge passes the *sentence*. Both psychologists and criminologists provide theories of crime explaining why people commit crimes and become perpetrators.	*to constitute* = bilden, darstellen *to prosecute* = strafrechtlich verfolgen *punishable* = strafbar *perpetrator, culprit* = Täter *victim* = Opfer *theft, burglary, robbery, murder, rape, assault, fraud* = Diebstahl, Einbruch, Raub, Mord, Vergewaltigung, Angriff, Betrug *to apprehend* = festnehmen *trial* = Prozess *verdict* = Urteil *sentence* = Strafmaß	*Crash* is full of crimes. Peter and Anthony commit an act of robbery when they force Jean and Rick out of their car and drive away with it. They commit various other crimes in the course of the action, including hijacking. Officer Ryan abuses his power as a policeman when he frisks Christine Thayer. The undercover police officer possibly committed murder when he shot the driver of the Mercedes. The killing of Peter could be interpreted as an act of self-defense, which is not a crime, but the way Officer Hansen tries to cover up the killing is certainly a crime.
How the individual can meet the challenge	Crimes constitute a challenge both for the individual and for society. Many individuals try to protect themselves against crimes. Theft and burglary are among the most common crimes, that's why many people lock their houses and cars hoping to *prevent* property crimes. Another *attempt* of *reducing* or preventing property crimes are neighborhood watches. People watch their neighbors' houses and the streets they live in reporting *suspicious* activities and hoping that criminals are *deterred* by their presence. A similar type of protection are gated communities, *residential areas* or *housing estates* that are typically surrounded by walls or fences. Entrance into the community is restricted to *residents* and their friends and families and is controlled by security guards. Many Americans also own guns for self-protection.	*to prevent* = verhindern *attempt* = Versuch *to reduce* = verringern *suspicious* = verdächtig *to deter* = abschrecken *residential area* = Wohngebiet *housing estate* = Wohnsiedlung *resident* = Bewohner	At the very beginning of *Crash* Farhad buys a gun for self-protection. Yet later he uses the gun attempting to kill Daniel who – in his eyes – destroyed his existence, thus turning the tool that he bought for self-protection into a tool that he uses for an attack. The availability of a gun would almost have led to Daniel's or his daughter's death.
How society / governments can meet the challenge	In contrast to individuals, governments deal with crime in a systematic way. Parliaments pass laws, thereby establishing a system of rules which is equally *binding* for all citizens. The various governments in the USA (state governments and the federal government) all have *law enforcement* authorities that make sure that people *abide by the rules*. This system is supposed to create a high degree of security. *Violations* of laws are dealt with by law enforcement authorities and courts. When people seriously violate the law and have been arrested and successfully prosecuted, they receive prison sentences. *Juvenile delinquents* are often sent to *boot camps* or take part in other programs that aim to change *participants'* attitudes and behavior and get them back on the right track.	*binding* = verbindlich, bindend *law enforcement* = Gesetzesvollzug *to abide by the rules* = die Regeln einhalten *violation* = Verstoß *juvenile delinquents* = jugendliche Täter *boot camp* = Erziehungscamp für jugendl. Straftäter *participant* = Teilnehmer	The police play an ambivalent role in *Crash*. On the one hand the LAPD (Los Angeles Police Department) is shown as a racist organization which is barely capable of preventing crimes and protecting people. On the other hand there is Officer Ryan who risks his life when pulling Christine Thayer out of her car before it explodes.
Gun culture in the US	According to reliable *estimates* there are 270,000 to 310,000 privately owned firearms in the USA. Around 40% of Americans live in a household with a gun which means that many *gun-owners* own more than one gun. The USA are the country with the highest gun ownership rate in the world, followed by Yemen and Switzerland. Guns have played a major role in American history, especially in the settlement of the continent and in the various wars that have been fought by Americans. As a means of self-protection and as a tool for hunting guns were *vital* to American settlers. In American popular culture, guns have often been *depicted* in a positive light. Just think of Western movies or the characters played by Arnold Schwarzenegger. At the same time gun ownership has for a long time been a hotly debated topic, each school shooting serving as the trigger of another round of discussions. *Proponents* of gun ownership such as the National Rifle Association (NRA) point to the 2nd Amendment to the Constitution and consider every *attempt* of the government to *restrict* gun ownership as an *encroachment* on their personal freedom. *Claiming* that hundreds of people use guns each year for self-defense, they believe that privately owned guns reduce crime rather than causing it. *Opponents* of gun ownership, on the other hand, point to studies that show a *decline* in *homicides* and suicides by firearms after the introduction of stricter gun laws. In addition they maintain that guns in households can easily lead to accidents or an escalation that wouldn't have happened if a gun hadn't been involved.	*estimate* = Schätzung *gun owner* = Waffenbesitzer *vital* = unverzichtbar *to depict sth.* = darstellen, zeigen *proponent* = Befürworter *attempt* = Versuch *to restrict* = einschränken, begrenzen *encroachment* = Eingriff, Übergriff *to claim* = behaupten *opponent* = Gegner *decline* = Rückgang *homicide* = Mord	Lily's father owns a gun and wants to take the law into his own hands and shoot his neighbor Old Man Pucket, because he had killed his dogs. Again, the availability of a gun would almost have led to a killing, if the women in the household hadn't prevented it. Many conflicts in *Crash* involve the usage of firearms. In two cases people get killed, in the other cases killings seem almost inevitable and are only prevented at the last minute. If firearms had not been available to the people in the conflicts, the killings wouldn't have happened. One could thus argue that the film is a strong statement against the omnipresence of firearms in American society.

Ready reference – American myths and American realities

aspects	details / words in context	German translations	reference to *Half Broke horses* and *Crash* in this theme
myths	The term "myth" has various meanings. Sometimes people use the term to refer to "a traditional, typically *ancient* story dealing with *supernatural beings*, *ancestors*, or heroes that serves as a fundamental type in the worldview of a people, as by explaining aspects of the natural world or delineating the psychology, *customs*, or ideals of society." The story of Ulysses belongs in the category of mythical stories. *Colloquially* the term "myth" is often used to refer to "something that many people believe in but that does not exist or is false". The term "myth" can also be defined as "a popular belief or tradition that has grown up around something or someone; *especially*: one *embodying* the ideals and institutions of a society or segment of society". Martin Luther King and Woodstock have become myths in this sense.	*ancient* = uralt *supernatural beings* = übernatürliche Wesen *custom* = Brauch, Sitte *ancestor* = Vorfahre *colloquial* = umgangssprachlich *to embody* = verkörpern	Lily Casey is given mythical qualities by the author. She embodies lots of characteristics that are regarded as typically American (e.g. qualities of pioneers).
frontier	The term "frontier" has various meanings: in a general sense it means the line separating two countries. The term is also used to refer to areas that are close to a *boundary*. In the context of American history it means the area between civilization in the East and the "Wild West", a place that has been given a *mythical quality*. An American historian named Frederick Jackson Turner has *been influential in popularizing* and mythologizing the term frontier by arguing that the frontier has *shaped* American democracy and the American character. This argument came to be known as the frontier-thesis. The validity of his thesis has been *doubted* by other historians. Turner was only one among many who *contributed* to the creation of the frontier myth. Other contributions came from artists who belonged to the Hudson River School and who are known for their romanticized *depiction* of the frontier and the West. Famous members were Albert Bierstadt, Frederic Edwin Church and Thomas Cole.	*boundary* = Grenze, Rand *mythical quality* = mythische Bedeutung *be influential in doing s.th.* = einen entscheidenden Beitrag dazu leisten, dass … *to popularize* = bekannt machen *to shape* = prägen, formen *to doubt* = anzweifeln *to contribute to* = etwas beitragen zu *depiction* = Darstellung	In 1901, when Lily Casey Smith was born, the frontier had been history: the construction of a coast-to-coast railway was finished, the West was effectively settled and the Western states were admitted to the Union. Yet there are references to the frontier in HBH, for example when Lily talks about her grandfather, who had been a homesteader in Hondo Valley (p. 18).
American Dream	The term "American Dream" was first used by the American historian John Truslow Adams in his book "The Epic of America" (1931). The concept, however, had existed long before Adams and *stood in stark contrast* to the European concept of social hierarchy at that time (Ständegesellschaft). Adams defined the American Dream as "the dream of a land in which life should be better, richer and fuller." The idea that everybody should be *granted* the opportunity to *prosper* and succeed in life had already been laid down in the Declaration of Independence which *proclaimed* "life, liberty and pursuit of happiness" as *unalienable* rights. *Popularized* by *countless* movies, songs and novels – including "Ragged Dick" – the idea of the American Dream has *lured* thousands of immigrants to the USA. Whether the Dream can actually be *attained* or not has always been debated and – like the other great American myths – the American Dream has been the subject of criticism and deconstruction not only in numerous essays but also in such famous works of art as Arthur Miller's "Death of a Salesman".	*to stand in stark contrast* = in deutlichem Gegensatz stehen zu *to grant* = gewähren, zugestehen *to prosper* = gedeihen, wachsen *to proclaim* = ausrufen, verkünden *unalienable* = unveräußerlich *to popularize* = popularisieren *countless* = unzählige *lure* = locken *to attain* = erreichen	Lily's optimistic outlook on life, her conviction that you can do anything as long as you have the will to do it can be interpreted as manifestations of the American Dream. Her success as a woman caring for herself and her family in difficult and male-dominated times can also be regarded as an American success story.
success stories	The phrase "From *Rags* to riches" refers to any situation in which a person rises from poverty to wealth, and in some cases from *obscurity* to *fame*. According to this myth becoming wealthy does not depend on your social background, but depends *solely* on qualities such as *perseverance*, punctuality and courage. Arnold Schwarzenegger und Ragged Dick serve as examples that rising from rags to riches is actually possible in the USA. The idea that anyone can make the American Dream come true and write his own success story has been *called into question* on a massive scale after the financial crisis of 2011 that increased the gap between the rich and the poor and put millions of American *on the brink* of financial ruin. The Occupy movement has not only protested against the *greed* of corporations and against their influence on governments, they have also deconstructed the myth that anyone can make it by working hard and being honest.	*rags* = Lumpen *obscurity* = Bedeutungslosigkeit, Unklarheit *solely* = ausschließlich *perseverance* = Durchhaltevermögen, Ausdauer *to call into question* = in Frage stellen *gap* = Kluft *on the brink of* = am Rande von *greed* = Habgier	Lily can not be interpreted as a typical personification of an American success story, yet she is the protagonist of many small success stories. Time and again she begins anew and achieves considerable success. There are only few references to the American Dream in *Crash*. One could assume that the Asians in the white van had learned about American success stories and as a result emigrated to the US.
combining myths and realities	Traditionally Republicans have *emphasized* the choices and responsibilities of the individual and have aimed to reduce the influence of what they call *big government* on people's lives. The Democrats, on the other hand, have stressed the importance of society and the responsibilities of the government. Both Bill Clinton and Barack Obama in their speeches call for more equality and *encourage* people *to be committed to* each other. Their *approach* can be interpreted as a reaction to current realities, especially to the growing gap between the poor and the rich without *rejecting* American traditions and myths. When Obama says "It is now our generation's task to carry on what those pioneers began", he *makes an explicit reference* to American history trying to put his aims in a historical context, something that all American presidents do.	*to emphasize* = betonen *to encourage* = ermutigen *to be committed* = sich engagieren, sich verpflichtet fühlen *approach* = Ansatz, Zugang *to reject* = ablehnen, zurückweisen *to make a reference* = einen Bezug herstellen	

Ready reference – freedom versus security

aspects	details / words in context	German translations	reference to *Half Broke horses* and *Crash* in this theme
The individual and society	Since man is a social creature, the relation between the individual and society is inescapable. But what is the ideal relationship between man and society that will guarantee that everyone's needs can be met? There are different theories as to what is essential to human needs. One of them is Maslow's theory about human motivation which outlines five basic needs to be met in order to find personal fulfillment. These needs can be divided into two groups: deficiency needs which *stem from* a lack of something and growth needs which *enable you to* grow as a person. Lower level needs like biological and physiological needs have to be satisfied before moving to a higher level but humans will not always *live up to their expectations* of personal fulfillment. Various documents have considered aspects such as happiness and the chance *to fulfil one's potential* which are of fundamental importance to the human condition and motivation. *The Declaration of Independence*, for instance, guarantees "life, liberty and the pursuit of happiness" as a right for all men created equals, a moral standard to which the United States should *strive* continuously. The role of society/government outlined in these documents is based on people's needs and accordingly, American politicians have always emphasized the idea of individual freedom and *self-reliance* while at the same time underlining the importance of a limited influence of government. As a Republican, Ron Paul has always been a *fervent advocate* of a *strict adherence* to the principle of individual liberty. He criticizes that recent governments have *abused their power* and neglected these principles in favor of the demands of a few. The war on terror, drone warfare and the right to arrest American citizens without any charges or trial are examples of the *erosion of rights* as guaranteed by the Constitution.	*to stem from sth.* = auf etwas zurückzuführen sein *to enable sb. to do sth.* = jemanden befähigen, etwas zu tun *to live up to one's expectations* = seinen Erwartungen gerecht werden *to fulfil one's potential* = sein Potential ausschöpfen *to strive for sth* = etwas anstreben, für etwas kämpfen *self-reliance* = Eigenverantwortlichkeit *fervent advocate of* = leidenschaftlicher Verfechter von *strict adherence to* = strikte/genaue Einhaltung von *abuse of power* = Machtmissbrauch *erosion of rights* = Aushöhlung/Erosion der Rechte	Lily Casey embodies both – the craving for individual liberty and the trust in her individual abilities to be relied on if need be as well as the pragmatic belief in the importance of society.
9/11 and its aftermath	The four coordinated *attacks launched* by the Islamic terrorist group al-Qaeda upon the US which *targeted* the World Trade Center, the Pentagon and Washington D.C. on September 11, 2001, were part of Osama bin Laden's declaration of a holy war in which he called for the killing of American citizens in *retaliation* for what he regarded as the *humiliation* of and lack of respect towards the international Muslim community. In the attacks almost 3000 people were killed and a huge area of New York City was destroyed. The attacks had *a profound impact* on the economy and *shattered* people's sense of security. Until then the mainland of the USA had never been attacked and Americans had developed a sense of invulnerability. Some Americans responded to the attacks with fear and anger as well as a growing intolerance against people from the Middle East after they learned that the hijackers were born in this region. In the days immediately following the attacks, Muslim Americans, more than any other immigrant group, were the *victims* of *harassment*, hate crimes and other *hostile behavior*.	*to launch an attack* = angreifen *to target sth.* = etwas ins Visier nehmen *retaliation* = Vergeltung *humiliation* = Demütigung *a profound impact on sth.*= ein tiefgreifender Einfluss auf etwas *to shatter* = zerstören *victim* = Opfer *harassment* = Belästigung *hostile behavior* = feindseliges Verhalten	Dirk, the owner of the gun shop, tells Farhad to "plan the jihad on (his) own time," when he talks to his daughter Dorri in Persian about ammunition. This is an example of hostile behavior towards people from the Middle East after 9/11.
policies following 9/11	On September 14th, 2001, as a reaction to the terrorist attacks, the House of Representatives and the Senate passed a resolution authorizing the United States Armed Forces to use military force against those responsible for the attacks. The military operation that has followed is known as the war on terror. Usually referred to as AUMF (Authorization for Use of Military Force), this joint resolution has formed the legal basis for the war on terror up to this day. According to President Bush the *purpose* of the war is to *ensure liberty and security*, *eliminate* al-Qaeda and *remove* regimes that support militant Islamists. Many countries *came to America's aid*, among them GB and other NATO and non-NATO nations. As part of the war on terror, the Bush administration established a *detention camp* in Cuba on Guantanamo Bay Naval Base, where they *detained* people who were suspected of being terrorists or of supporting terrorism. Because the camp was located outside the USA, detainees *were not entitled* to a regular trial, something which is guaranteed by the Sixth Amendment to the Constitution. Some detainees have spent years in the camp without a trial. After being released many former terror suspects *gave detailed accounts* of torture and abuse. Another measure following 9/11 is the USA PATRIOT Act that was signed into law by President Bush on October 26th. Comprising 10 titles on over 340 pages the law generally *broadens* the power of law enforcement agencies. The creation of the United States Department of Homeland Security was another consequence of the attacks of September 11th. It comprises 22 agencies such as the U.S. Secret Service, the Transportation Security Administration (TSA) and the U.S. customs service. Many of these agencies *exercise powers* given to them by the USA PATRIOT Act.	*purpose* = Zweck *ensure liberty and security* = Freiheit und Sicherheit garantieren *eliminate* = vernichten *remove* = beseitigen *to come to someone's aid* = jemandem zu Hilfe kommen *detention camp* = Internierungslager *to detain* = internieren, gefangen halten *to be entitled to sth.* = Anspruch haben auf etwas *to give a detailed account* = einen detaillierten Bericht liefern *to broaden* = ausweiten *to exercise power* = Macht ausüben	
surveillance	The NSA and other intelligence agencies were originally responsible for *monitoring*, collecting, decoding and interpreting foreign data in order to learn more about the political and military aims of foreign nations. After 9/11 the agency was given the right to order Internet service providers to *disclose* IP addresses and login times of anyone suspected of involvement in terrorism. From then on it also operated within the US, collecting data on US citizens. Like other *intelligence agencies*, the NSA carries out its missions by *clandestine* means. When the public learned that the NSA has collected the data of millions of internet and phone users worldwide, its director defended the measures by pointing out that thanks to the NSA's surveillance activities dozens of terrorist plots had been *thwarted*. Critics such as Ron Paul, on the other hand, claim that the collected data could easily be misused and that the NSA's activities are just one *piece of evidence* that shows that US governments have abused their power and *violated* basic principles laid down in the US constitution.	*to monitor* = überwachen *to disclose* = offenlegen, enthüllen *intelligence agency* = Geheimdienst *clandestine* = heimlich, verborgen *to thwart* = stören, zerschlagen (Pläne) *piece of evidence* = Beweisstück *to violate* = verletzen, missachten	

Bildquellen

10 l.: alamy images, Abingdon/Oxfordshire (© Gabe Palmer); **10 m.:** INTERFOTO, München (imagebroker); **10 r.:** Picture-Alliance GmbH, Frankfurt/M. (© dpa/Hugo Burnand/Clarence House); **12:** plainpicture, Hamburg (Gallery Stock); **21/1:** Corbis, Düsseldorf (© Bettmann); **21/2:** Getty Images, München (Time & Life Pictures); **21/3:** Picture-Alliance GmbH, Frankfurt/M.; **21/4:** Picture-Alliance GmbH, Frankfurt/M. (AP); **21/5:** ullstein bild, Berlin; **22/10:** Getty Images, München (Life Images/Francis Miller); **22/6:** Getty Images, München (Archive Photos/Robert Abbott Sengstacke); **22/7:** akg-images GmbH, Berlin; **22/8:** Picture-Alliance GmbH, Frankfurt/M. (dpa/Michael Reynolds); **22/9:** Focus Photo- u. Presseagentur GmbH, Hamburg (© Elliott Erwitt/Magnum Photos); **24 o. l.:** Picture-Alliance GmbH, Frankfurt/M. (fStop); **24 o. r.:** Getty Images, München (Ralf Hiemisch); **24 andere, 26 Asian:** Apolloscreen GmbH, Neubiberg; **29 o. l.:** Black Film Center/Archive, Bloomington; **29 r.:** Picture-Alliance GmbH, Frankfurt/M. (The Advertising Archives); **29 u. l.:** Life Magazine, New York (Ferris State University Jim Crow Museum); **30:** Apolloscreen GmbH, Neubiberg; **33:** laif, Köln (The New York Times Cartoons); **34:** BJR Productions, Anthem AZ; **35:** Hennig, Benjamin D./Worldmapper Project (http://www.viewsoftheworld.net/); **37:** ApolloProScreen GmbH + Co. Filmproduktion KG, Neubiberg; **39:** Bridgeman Art Library Ltd. Berlin (© Collection of the New-York Historical Society, USA); **40:** Picture-Alliance GmbH, Frankfurt/M. (newscom/Picture History); **42:** Apollo ProScreen GmbH + Co. Filmproduktion KG, Neubiberg; **43 melting pot:** Glow Images GmbH, München (ImageBroker/Heinz-Dieter Falkenstein); **43 pizza:** fotolia.com, New York (© Svenja98); **43 quilt:** iStockphoto, Calgary (© Emilia Kun); **43 salad:** iStockphoto, Calgary (© akdemirhk); **46/1:** Georgia State University Library, GA 30303-3202; **46/3:** The Ohio State University, Billy Ireland Cartoon Library & Museum, OH 43210-1393; **46/4:** ullstein bild, Berlin (The Granger Collection); **46/5:** William L. Clements Library (Vincent Gillam); **46/6:** wikimedia.commons; **54:** Apolloscreen GmbH, Neubiberg; **55 o.:** Corbis, Düsseldorf (© Lucas Jackson/Reuters); **55 u. l.:** Getty Images, München (Mario Tama); **55 u. r.:** fotolia.com, New York (© dinostock); **56:** Shutterstock, New York (Mark Winfrey); **58/1:** Picture-Alliance GmbH, Frankfurt/M. (ed1/ZUMAPRESS.com); **58/3:** alamy images, Abingdon/Oxfordshire (© dov makabaw); **58/4:** Picture-Alliance GmbH, Frankfurt/M. (dpa/Keystone mark Allen Johnson); **61 m. l.:** Picture-Alliance GmbH, Frankfurt/M. (landov/George Frey); **61 m. r.:** Picture-Alliance GmbH, Frankfurt/M.; **61 o.:** Picture-Alliance GmbH, Frankfurt/M. (dpa/Pete Souza); **61 u.:** laif, Köln (Fabio Cuttica); **63:** laif, ~~Köln (Scott~~ Houston/Polaris); **66 o.:** wikimedia.commons (© 1899, Courier Litho. Co., Buffalo, N.Y.); **66 r.:** Picture-Alliance GmbH, Frankfurt/M. (The Advertising Archives); **66 u.:** mauritius images GmbH, Mittenwald (John Warburton-Lee); **68 l.:** Bridgeman Art Library Ltd. Berlin; **68 r.:** wikimedia.commons; **69 o.:** University of Oklahomy Libraries, Norman, Oklahoma (Western History Collections/Cunningham-Prettyman 90); **69 u.:** Avenue Images GmbH, Hamburg (DANITA DELIMONT STOCK/agefotostock); **71:** Bridgeman Art Library Ltd. Berlin (Private Collection); **72 o.:** Bridgeman Art Library Ltd. Berlin; **72 u.:** Picture-Alliance GmbH, Frankfurt/M.; **73 m. l.:** Picture-Alliance GmbH, Frankfurt/M. (abaca); **73 m. r.:** Picture-Alliance GmbH, Frankfurt/M. (Newscom/Monika Graff); **73 o. l., o. r.:** Picture-Alliance GmbH, Frankfurt/M. (landov); **73 u.:** mauritius images GmbH, Mittenwald (ib/Jim West); **78:** ullstein bild, Berlin; **80:** wikimedia.commons; **84:** Simon & Schuster UK Ltd; **85 l.:** Picture-Alliance GmbH, Frankfurt/M. (dpa); **85 m.:** Focus Photo- u. Presseagentur GmbH, Hamburg (Susan Meiselas/Magnum); **85 r.:** Corbis, Düsseldorf (Elder); **86:** Picture-Alliance GmbH, Frankfurt/M. (Abaca 39646); **87:** Thiel/images.de, Berlin (Thiel); **91:** Picture-Alliance GmbH, Frankfurt/M. (dpa); **94 o.:** INTERFOTO, München (Mary Evans Picture Library); **94 u.:** INTERFOTO, München (SuperStock); **95:** The Washington Post Writers Group, Washington, D.C. (Nick Anderson/© 2013); **96 l.:** Blickwinkel, Witten (McPHOTO); **96 r.:** Picture-Alliance GmbH, Frankfurt/M. (dpa); **99:** Verlagsarchiv, Braunschweig; **101 o.:** Narelle, Brian, Rohnert Park (© 2009 / http://www.narellecartoons.com); **101 u.:** Picture-Alliance GmbH, Frankfurt/M. (Glenn Greenwald/Laura Poitras © dpa); **105:** mauritius images GmbH, Mittenwald (Cultura); **106 l.:** KCS, Buchholz; **106 r.:** Fox News Insider Blog, New York.

Textquellen

12-13: "Ragged Dick: Street Life in New York with the Boot-Blacks" by Horatio Alger, The Floating Press Ltd 2009; **13-14:** "My Two Lives" by Jhumpa Lahiri, from Newsweek, 6 March 2006. Copyright © 2006 IBT Media. All rights reserved; **47-48:** Eliseo Medina: on "Our national interests require a path to citizenship for the 12 million legal immigrants presently here", part of the 'National Discussion and Debate Series: Immigration'. Copyright © 2008 Eliseo Medina. Used by permission of the University of Virginia, Miller Center; **48-49:** Mark Krikorian: on "Our national interests require a path to citizenship for the 12 million legal immigrants presently here", part of the 'National Discussion and Debate Series: Immigration'. Copyright © 2008 Mark Krikorian. Used by permission of the University of Virginia, Miller Center; **76:** Bill Clinton: Speech at the Democratic National Convention, 5 September 2012. Copyright © 2012 Bill Clinton; **76:** Barack Obama: Second Inaugural Address, 21 January 2013. Copyright © 2013 Barack Obama; **80-81:** Ron Paul: Farewell Address to Congress, 14 November 2011. Copyright © 2011 Ron Paul; **84-85:** "Falling Man" excerpt by Don DeLillo, Simon & Schribner Ltd: Schribner 2007. Copyright © 2007 Don DeLillo, used by permission of Wallace Literary Agency, Inc.; **88-89:** George Bush: Speech to Congress, 20 September 2001. Copyright © 2001 George Bush; **97-98:** "NSA collecting phone records of millions of Verizon customers daily", by Glenn Greenwald, in The Guardian. Copyright © Guardian News & Media Ltd 2013; **98:** "USA Prism program taps into user data of Apple, Google and others" by Glenn Greenwald, in The Guardian. Copyright © Guardian News & Media Ltd 2013; **98-99:** "NSA director: Surveillance foiled 50 terror plots" by Kevin Johnson, in USA Today, 19 June 2013. Copyright © USA Today; **101-102:** "Edward Snowden: the whistleblower behind the NSA surveillance revelations" by Glenn Greenwald, Ewen MacAskill and Lauren Poitras, in The Guardian. Copyright © Guardian News & Media Ltd 2013; **103:** "Edward Snowden is no hero" by Philip Lohaus, in The Daily Caller, 16 June 2013. Copyright © The Daily Caller; **106:** "The 'Fear Industrial Complex'" by John Stossel and Natalie D. Jaquez, on ABC News.com, 23 February 2007. Copyright © 2007 ABC News